HITLER'S
SPY PRINCESS

HITLER'S
SPY PRINCESS

THE EXTRAORDINARY LIFE OF
STEPHANIE VON HOHENLOHE

MARTHA SCHAD

Translated and annotated by Angus McGeoch

SUTTON PUBLISHING

First published in 2002 by Wilhelm Heyne Verlag GmbH & Co. KG,
Munich, under the title *Hitlers Spionin*.
This English translation first published in 2004 by Sutton Publishing
Limited • Phoenix Mill • Thrupp • Stroud • Gloucestershire • GL5 2BU

Translation and annotation: Angus McGeoch

British Library Cataloguing in Publication Data
A catalogue record for this book is available from the British Library.

ISBN 0-7509-3514-6

Typeset in 11.5/15pt Photina.
Typesetting and origination by
Sutton Publishing Limited.
Printed and bound in England by
J.H. Haynes & Co. Ltd, Sparkford.

Contents

CHAPTER ONE

The Girl from Vienna

'"A woman's will is God's will" was a saying I often heard as a little girl in Vienna.' It is with this sentence that Stephanie Richter, later to become Princess von Hohenlohe-Waldenburg-Schillingsfürst, begins the autobiography that she never completed. It was the motto she believed had governed her extraordinary life, a life which spanned the years from 1891 to 1972, and thus saw the decline and fall of the Austro-Hungarian Empire, the First and Second World Wars and the postwar period in Germany and the United States.[1]

Stephanie Maria Veronika Juliana Richter was born in a Viennese town house, Am Kärnterring 1, directly opposite what was then the Hotel Bristol, on 16 September 1891. She was given the first of her names in honour of Crown Princess Stephanie, the consort of Crown Prince Rudolf of Austria, who had committed suicide at Mayerling in 1889.

Stephanie described her father, Dr Johann Sebastian Richter, as a successful lawyer. He had really wanted to become a priest, but then fell in love with Ludmilla Kuranda and married her. Stephanie saw her parents – neither of them Jewish, she was at pains to point out – as people who should never have married one another, yet she and her sister Milla (christened Ludmilla, and five years her senior) nonetheless had a happy childhood. And in a 'morning monologue', a kind of one-sided conversation with her maid Anna, Stephanie von Hohenlohe later wrote: 'I grew up in Vienna. . . I loved Vienna. . . I was a Viennese girl. And like all the others, I sang: *Wien, Wien nur Du allein. . .*'[2]

Her father, as she remembered him, was incredibly kind and full of tender affection for her, but her mother was excessively anxious and seemed to nag constantly. Thus she grew up a somewhat spoiled, but also rather subdued child.

When her nursemaid pushed her through the park in her pram, the little girl with the big, radiant blue eyes was always the object of admiration. Later, when she began to walk, '"Steffi's little calves" (were) famous amongst all child-lovers in Vienna'.

Her mother Ludmilla came from an old Jewish family, the Kurandas of Prague. Her father, Johann (known as Hans) Richter, was a Catholic, and a few days before their wedding Ludmilla also adopted the Catholic faith. With a good income from his law practice, Hans Richter could give his family a comfortable life. Yet he was often very generous to his clients as well and even took on cases free of charge, a fact that did not please his wife, who was something of a spendthrift. On one occasion Richter was imprisoned for embezzling funds entrusted to him on behalf of a minor. Towards the end of his life he became increasingly pious. And when his health began to deteriorate, he withdrew mentally, and in the end physically as well, from all worldly things, and joined the Order of Hospitallers. He was accepted as a lay brother, which meant that his family could visit him whenever they wanted.

From Stephanie's half-sister, the writer Gina Kaus,[3] we get a more authentic account of Stephanie's parentage: her natural father was *not* Hans Richter, the Viennese lawyer born on a farm in northern Moravia, but a Jewish money-lender named Max Wiener. While Richter was serving a seven-month prison sentence for the aforementioned embezzlement, his wife had a relationship with Wiener, then a bachelor, which went beyond the mere arrangement of a loan. Not long afterwards, Wiener married another woman and had a daughter, Gina. Notwithstanding, on 16 September 1891 the Richters became the proud parents of a baby girl they christened Stephanie. When Gina Kaus was very old, she was again asked about her half-sister. 'Princess Hohenlohe was my half-sister – though maybe she never knew it', Gina replied. 'My father – a very unsophisticated man – occasionally mentioned that before he married my mother he had an affair with a Frau Richter, while her husband

Hans was in prison. However, Richter acknowledged the child, who was Steffi, and perhaps a sum of money changed hands . . .'[4]

Gina Kaus followed her half-sister's hare-brained ploys with mixed feelings. Steffi repeatedly hit the headlines in Nazi Germany, and again years later in the United States.

Stephanie had a sheltered upbringing. She was very reluctant to go to day-school and was a poor pupil there. At the end of her years at school she was sent for four months to a college in Eastbourne, on the south coast of England. This was followed by piano lessons at the Vienna Conservatoire. She remembered ruefully that her teacher rapped her knuckles with a small stick whenever she played a wrong note. Stephanie's mother wanted her to become a pianist, but her hands were so small and narrow that she could not span an octave properly, so a professional career was out of the question.

Stephanie never read a book and took no interest in such 'feminine' accomplishments as sewing, embroidery and crochet. Nor could she cook; she could not even boil a saucepan of water without getting someone to light the stove for her. But she adored animals. And she enjoyed sport of every kind: she played tennis, swam, sailed, hunted, cycled and rowed. She was particularly good at skating, performing waltzes on the ice, and met all her boyfriends at the Vienna Skating Club. She did not have any special friends of her own sex. At the age of fourteen she was rolling her own cigarettes in the school lavatories. With her innate intelligence, she had no great difficulty in mastering foreign languages.

During a summer holiday at the lovely lakeside resort of Gmunden, in the Salzkammergut, the fourteen-year-old Steffi went in for the annual beauty contest, even though, as she herself writes, she was still a rather podgy teenager. Nonetheless, she won. From then on she attracted attention; other girls began to copy the hairstyle and clothes worn by 'Steffi from Vienna'.

One of the grandest clients of her father's law practice was the childless Princess Franziska (Fanny) von Metternich (1837–1918). She had been born the Countess Mittrowsky von Mittrowitz and was the widow of Prince von Metternich-Winneburg und Beilstein. The *Grande Dame*, as Stephanie later called her, liked Dr Richter's teenage daughter and asked him if she might take her out from time to time. Richter was happy to agree to this. In this way the young Stephanie came into contact with Vienna's exclusive aristocratic society. She quickly learned how to behave and move in those circles, and avidly acquired the lifestyle of the *beau monde*. People were enchanted by her smile and her charm; and her skill as a horsewoman soon won her an admirer in the person of a Polish nobleman, Count Gisycki. The Count took her to the Schloss that he owned, near Vienna. However, she rejected his proposal of marriage, since the good-looking playboy was old enough to be her grandfather, let alone her father.

Count Joseph Gisycki was divorced from an American heiress, Eleanor Medill Patterson, who had returned to the United States with their daughter Felicia. At that time no-one could have guessed that Felicia Patterson would marry a man who was to play an important part in launching Stephanie von Hohenlohe's postwar career as a journalist; he was the influential and highly respected American columnist, Drew Pearson.

At the age of fifteen, Steffi had set herself an ambitious goal in life: she would marry a prince – although he would not show up until 1914, when she was twenty-three. She claims in her memoirs, however, that she was seventeen when she got married. When she was still only fifteen, Steffi received her next proposal of marriage, from Count Rudolf Colloredo-Mannsfeld. But she turned the nobleman down because he was such a skinflint.

With the death of Hans Richter in 1909, Stephanie's family fell into dire financial straits. Who would lend money now to the widow and her daughters? The answer to all their problems was provided by Ludmilla's brother. As a young hothead, Robert Kuranda had run away from home and had never been heard of again. Yet now he was standing at the door, having returned from South Africa a rich man. Kuranda made lavish financial provision for his sister Ludmilla and his nieces. While Ludmilla was apparently incapable of handling money, Stephanie invested her share well and made an excellent return. At that time her mother had another 'informal relationship' with a businessman. The family now had enough money to go on summer holidays abroad, and did so very frequently.

On these trips Stephanie, Milla and their mother were accompanied by Aunt Clothilde, their mother's sister, who had been briefly married to the Vienna correspondent of the London *Times*, Herbert Arthur White. Clothilde owned a handsome town house in Kensington as well as a beautiful mansion on the shore of Wannsee, a lake near Berlin. She was famous for her parties. She had style and could afford to invite the most famous ballerina of the day, Anna Pavlova. There were expeditions to the spas of Marienbad and Karlsbad, to Venice, Berlin, Paris and Biarritz, to Kiel for the regatta, to the Dalmatian coast, to Corsica and to Prague.

Stephanie tells us that, at a hunt dinner given by Princess Metternich, she was asked to play something on the piano. A young man joined her at the keyboard and that is how she first met her future husband – Prince Friedrich Franz von Hohenlohe-Waldenburg-Schillingsfürst (1879–1958). The next day, Stephanie wrote, the two met again and he offered to drive her home. It was then that he noticed that Stephanie was being chaperoned by a governess. But even this obstacle was overcome, and Stephanie managed to arrange three secret trysts with the prince. 'And within two weeks he asked me to marry him.'

When her mother found out about these clandestine walks in the park, she was furious. And Prince Friedrich Franz found relations with his future mother-in-law difficult. Stephanie was not present at the serious discussion that took place between the prince and her mother, but in the end the prince won Ludmilla over completely. 'My future husband had, at one time, served as military attaché in St Petersburg and had a brilliant war record. . . And so at seventeen I got married. Half the royal houses of Europe now called me "cousin".' That is how Stephanie, in her autobiographical sketches, describes her path from happy-go-lucky Viennese teenager to Princess von Hohenlohe. However, she was putting this period of her life in a thoroughly idealised light as well as being dishonest about the dates.

The memoirs written by her son tell a different story. He claims that, through her rejected suitor Count Colloredo-Mannsfeld, she got to know another member of the house of Hohenlohe, Prince

Nikolaus von Hohenlohe-Waldenburg-Schillingsfürst (1877–1948). However, Stephanie found him excessively arrogant and turned him down in favour of his younger brother, Prince Friedrich Franz, whom she had met while riding to hounds. The prince was searching desperately for his pince-nez, which he had lost while jumping a fence. Steffi helped him look for the spectacles and he fell in love with her. Steffi was actually about to reject *his* marriage-proposal as well, but her mother took charge of the situation and threatened to put Steffi into a convent if she turned Friedrich Franz down. She accepted his suit.

The prince, whose full names were Friedrich Franz Augustin Maria, was the offspring of the marriage between Prince Chlodwig Karl Joseph von Hohenlohe-Waldenburg-Schillingsfürst (1848–1929) and Countess Franziska Esterházy von Galántha (1856–84). At the time when Friedrich Franz and Stephanie planned to marry, he was military attaché at the Austro-Hungarian embassy in St Petersburg, then the Russian capital. The ambassador now had to be informed of the betrothal, as did the Ministry of Foreign Affairs in Vienna. The approval of the Emperor himself had to be obtained, as well as that of the head of the house of Hohenlohe, Prince August Karl Christian Kraft von Hohenlohe (1848–1926).

Putting up the marriage banns necessitated so many formalities that in the end the prince suggested they should marry, not in Vienna, but in London. One might think that for foreigners to get married in London would have been just as difficult. However, it seems that speed was of the essence, for 'Steffi from Vienna' was expecting a baby – and her bridegroom was not the father! The willingness of Prince Friedrich Franz to marry Steffi may well be explained by the fact that his bride was wealthy enough to settle his not inconsiderable gambling debts – 'debts of honour' as he would have called them.

The actual father of the child was another man: among the many aristocratic admirers of the middle-class Steffi Richter there had been one of particularly high rank, Franz Salvator of Austria-Tuscany (1866–1939). He was the son of Archduke Karl Salvator of Austria-Tuscany and of Maria Immaculata of the house of Bourbon-Sicily.

More importantly he was a son-in-law of Emperor Franz Joseph I of Austria and Empress Elisabeth ('Sissi').

The imperial couple had four children: the Archduchesses Sophie and Gisela, the Crown Prince Rudolf and the Archduchess Marie Valerie. Sophie died young, Gisela married Prince Leopold of Bavaria, and the Crown Prince, heir to the throne, committed suicide at Mayerling as the result of a scandalous love affair. The youngest daughter Marie Valerie, who was particularly close to her mother, married the Archduke Franz Salvator on 29 July 1890 at the church in Ischl. The marriage resulted in no fewer than ten children. The Archduchess was forty-two years old when, in 1911, she gave birth to her last child, Agnes, at the imperial mansion in Ischl. The baby lived for only a few hours. Marie Valerie, a very pious woman with a tendency to melancholia, spent a great deal of time alone with her children at Schloss Wallsee. Her fun-loving husband seems to have neglected her for much of the time.

The liaison between Archduke Franz Salvator and Stephanie Richter dated from 1911. And, as already mentioned, was not without consequence. When Stephanie was expecting the Archduke's child, Emperor Franz Joseph obligingly arranged her betrothal to the aforementioned Prince Friedrich Franz von Hohenlohe-Waldenburg-Schillingsfürst. Yet the manner in which the wedding took place does not exactly suggest a marriage of true love. It was held very quietly on 12 May 1914, in London's Roman Catholic cathedral in Westminster. Only Stephanie's mother was present. The witnesses were hired at short notice, and the couple did not even stay at the same hotel. Stephanie appraised her new husband coolly: 'Not tall – and I like tall men – but certainly very well-proportioned.'

Thus Stephanie Richter returned to Vienna from London as Princess von Hohenlohe-Waldenburg-Schillingsfürst. She was a citizen of the Austro-Hungarian Empire. However, at the end of the First World War in 1918, when the empire and its dual monarchy collapsed, her husband opted to take up not Austrian, but Hungarian citizenship, to which he was entitled through his Esterházy mother. Stephanie likewise held a Hungarian passport for the rest of her life.

As no mention had been made of the wedding in any Austrian newspapers, and not even announcement cards had been sent out, the young wife's social standing in Vienna was problematic.

Seven months after the wedding, on 5 December 1914, Stephanie gave birth in a private clinic to her (illegitimate) son, Prince Franz Joseph Rudolf Hans Weriand Max Stefan Anton von Hohenlohe-Waldenburg-Schillingsfürst, always to be known as 'Franzi'. [*Note that the Christian names include those of the Austrian emperor, Stephanie's benefactor, as well as that of her natural father, Max, and adoptive father, Hans*. Tr.] At a solemn baptism in St Stephen's Cathedral in Vienna, the duties of godfather were assumed by Stephanie's former admirer, Count Colloredo-Mannsfeld.

Franzi later described his childhood as a happy one. He spent the greater part of his early years in the elegantly furnished apartment owned by his mother and grandmother, at Kärnterring 1. Whenever the political situation seemed to be getting particularly tense, he was sent away from the city with his nursemaid. It was then that he usually went to a house near the Danube, belonging to Count Gisycki. The little boy enjoyed that very much, as he was allowed to romp around the garden with the dogs.

He began his schooling in Vienna, then followed several years in Paris. At the age of ten Franzi went to a private boarding-school in Switzerland, Le Rosey, near Lausanne, where wealthy parents sent their hopeful offspring to be educated. (The present Prince Rainier of Monaco was a pupil there some years later.) The young Prince Franz then went on to the Collège de Normandie, near Rouen, and finally to university at Magdalen College, Oxford.

When the First World War broke out, Stephanie's husband had to join his regiment. Touchingly, Franzi's natural father, Archduke Franz Salvator, took care of the boy and his mother. As Stephanie herself writes, the Archduke had secured an audience for her with the Emperor in Vienna. We may suppose that this audience took place *before* her marriage to Friedrich von Hohenlohe, which the Emperor had commanded. Even before her liaison with Franz Salvator, Stephanie had had a brief fling with another scion of the

Habsburg dynasty: Archduke Maximilian Eugen Ludwig (1895–1952), the younger brother of Emperor Karl, who in 1916 briefly succeeded Franz Joseph to the Austro-Hungarian throne. In 1917 Maximilian married Franziska Maria Anna, Princess von Hohenlohe-Waldenburg-Schillingsfürst (1897–1989).

Archduke Franz Salvator even took Stephanie with him to the Emperor's hunting estate near Ischl, where she shot her first stag. She was entranced by the beauty of the mountain landscape, and learned that it was there that the old emperor spent the happiest hours of his life, surrounded only by a few huntsmen. Stephanie also wrote enthusiastically about the imperial mansion in Ischl, a charming little town in the Salzkammergut lakeland. In her unpublished memoir she described in detail the spartan furnishing of the Emperor's rooms. She noticed the prayer-stool and the desk with the photograph of his consort, Elisabeth, who in 1898 had been tragically stabbed to death in Geneva by a deranged anarchist. In front of it lay a few dried flowers and a little framed poem, which the Empress had given him on the day of their engagement.

Stephanie must have been to Ischl quite often. Yet whenever she stepped inside the imperial mansion she was unable to shake off an oppressive feeling; she could not forget the many blows that Fate had dealt to the Habsburg dynasty: the terrible death of the Empress, the tragic suicide of Crown Prince Rudolf after he had murdered the young Baroness Vetsera; the assassination in Sarajevo in 1914 of the heir to the throne, Franz Ferdinand and his consort, Countess Sophie. Stephanie only ever went to Ischl when the imperial family were absent.

During the First World War Archduke Franz Salvator, a general in the cavalry, served as Inspector-General of Medical Volunteers, in which capacity he ran an aid operation for prisoners-of-war in Russia. In 1916 he received an honorary doctorate from the faculty of medicine at Innsbruck University, and became Patron of the Austrian Red Cross and of the Union of Red Cross Societies in the lands under the Hungarian crown. It was not long before the Princess also took an interest in nursing work.

Soon after the birth of her son, Stephanie volunteered as a nurse and received her basic training in Vienna. After that she worked for three months as 'Sister Michaela' under the direction of the 'melancholy beauty', Archduchess Maria Theresa, who was a very popular member of the Austrian royal family. Stephanie claims that it was through the Archduchess that she first met Franz Salvator, the old Emperor's son-in-law, and that this happened in the hospital in Vienna's Hegelgasse. However, this account does not correspond with the known facts.

Working as a Red Cross nurse in Vienna became too tedious for Stephanie. She wanted to go to the Front, and Archduke Franz Salvator made arrangements for her to be posted there. She gives a vivid account of her experiences. She went first to the Russian Front, to a field hospital in Lvov, which then bore the German name of Lemberg. Stephanie's sister Milla had also decided to work there as a Red Cross nurse. Stephanie travelled with her butler and her chambermaid, Louise Mainz. As if this was not enough to raise eyebrows, the rubber bath-tub she brought with her struck people as especially odd. For a nurse, admittedly, hygiene was very important. And in order to protect herself from the stench of ether and gangrenous flesh, Stephanie almost continuously smoked the Havana cigars that she had, with considerable foresight, brought in large quantities from Vienna. She did not last very long at the Front. The medical officer in charge of the field hospital, Dr Zuckerkandl, showed no great enthusiasm for his 'nurse'. Stephanie described him as very nervous and irritable, though a brilliant physician.

In the middle of the First World War, on 21 November 1916, Emperor Franz Joseph died. Princess Stephanie drove to Vienna and wanted to mingle with the mourners at the Hofburg palace. However, she was not permitted to do so. Ironically, the new Emperor's High Chamberlain, who denied her access to the palace, was also a Hohenlohe, Prince Konrad Maria Eusebius (1863–1918). So she had to content herself with the role of a spectator outside St Stephen's Cathedral.

Stephanie was very moved by the sight of the young Emperor Karl and the Empress Zita, as they left St Stephen's Cathedral, together with the Crown Prince, the little Archduke Otto, to the sound of a

41-gun salute and a carillon of bells. She was convinced that 'each individual would have willingly given his heart, his blood, all he had, and laid it at the feet of the three young people, to help them carry their new, heavy burden and make a success of it'.

In Vienna Stephanie and Archduke Franz Salvator spent hours together in the park and zoo at Schönbrunn palace. Since at that time the park was not yet open to the public, the two could stroll there completely unobserved. But on one occasion there was a mishap: when Stephanie tried to feed a bear and stretched her hand through the bars, it bit one of her fingers. She was afraid she might develop blood-poisoning and wanted to have an anti-tetanus injection immediately. But who could drive them to a doctor? The Archduke's hands were tied, since he had picked up Stephanie from her apartment in Hofgartenstrasse in a coach with gilded wheels, which was reserved exclusively for members of the royal family. There would have been a scandal if the public had found out that, while the court was in mourning, the Archduke has been strolling with his mistress in the royal zoological park. He therefore took her to the nearest tram-stop, so that she could go to the doctor on her own.

Her friendship with the Archduke continued to mean a great deal to Stephanie. It was 'genuine and heartfelt, a friendship that could only be ended by death', as Stephanie summed it up in 1940, a year after Franz Salvator died.

Her next assignment as a Red Cross nurse was with the Austrian army, on its way to fight the Italians at the battle of the Isonzo river, in 1917. As the Austrian troops were advancing exceptionally fast, many comic situations arose. The ditches were filled with large cheeses, wine barrels and other things that the soldiers had looted, intending to send them home, but which were now being thrown away.

Stephanie recounted that, after the capture of Udine, soldiers had shot holes in the wine casks, got very drunk and nearly drowned. Most of them had poured vast amounts of wine into empty stomachs, often fell senseless and then lay in the wine flowing from the bullet-riddled barrels. She felt that many soldiers behaved quite atrociously in the occupied territories. But it was not just the common soldiery who went on these rampages; officers also helped themselves generously. Stephanie believed she might have done the same herself and was only restrained by her timidity, not by any high ideals. 'All our officers took whatever they wanted.' Count Karl Wurmbrandt-Stupach, one of her Red Cross friends, apparently despatched wagon-loads of fine glassware and antiques from Italy back to Vienna. She herself became the owner of the bed in which Napoleon slept at Campo Formio, after signing the peace treaty there a century earlier. However, she had not stolen the bed, but bought it from a starving farmer.

In the region around Tolmezzo, where Stephanie was working in the hospital, the local inhabitants were very short of food. People often came to the hospital and offered beautiful hand-woven linen in exchange for sugar, salt and bread, and so the doctors and nurses later returned home laden with valuable items.

Stephanie was in the town of Görz (now Gorízia in Italy) shortly after it was captured. All the houses had been destroyed and the surrounding forest completely burned down. The townspeople had fled and were living in little huts in the mountains or huddling in the abandoned trenches.

In all her spells of duty in the different field-hospitals Stephanie got on best with patients from the Tirol, from Hungary and Russia. They could stand pain and were very courteous. She thought that the Czechs and the Viennese were the worst – always moaning, always complaining, never satisfied – at least that was her experience of them.

Stephanie spent some time in Friuli, the Italian region bordering what is now Slovenia. She witnessed Austria's defeat on the River Piave, in a battle that raged from 15 to 24 June 1918, when the Italians took their revenge for their humiliation at Caporetto. The princess had long ago become convinced that this war could not be won. 'But when she tried to talk to her friends about her disillusionment, she was accused of defeatism', her son Franz writes.

The situation at the Front had deteriorated seriously. There was nothing to eat, either in the hospitals or for the fighting troops.

Morale was far from good. Then one day Stephanie received an urgent order to leave the war-zone. All the wounded able to travel were sent back to their home countries, and there was less for the nurses to do. Stephanie set off from Trieste back to Vienna. The journey of about 250 miles took her three days and nights.

In midsummer 1918 the princess moved with her son for a time to Grado, a resort on the Adriatic that was then still in Austrian territory and which, in the final months of the war, was a pleasanter place to be than Vienna. The armistice on 11 November 1918, which had rapidly followed the abdication of the German Kaiser, also meant the break-up of the Austro-Hungarian Empire.

The socially unequal marriage between Stephanie and Prince Friedrich Franz von Hohenlohe came to an end in 1920. On 29 July of that year their divorce was formalised in Budapest. Friedrich Franz made it very clear that he wished a separation from his wife. What greatly annoyed Stephanie was the fact that only six months later he remarried, although he had sworn to her that there was no question of him marrying again. It was on 6 December 1920 that the Countess Emanuela Batthány (1883–1964), who had left her husband and three children, became Prince Friedrich Franz's second wife.

One of the chapters in Stephanie's memoir is entitled 'Europe between the Wars'. She makes no secret of having greatly enjoyed the 1920s. She was now free to do or not do whatever she chose. As she explains, in Austria under its first republic, just as in Germany's Weimar Republic, there was a great pursuit of pleasure, especially among the rich. And yet Stephanie was well aware of the political difficulties in Germany which, having lost the war that it started, was saddled with massive reparations and – as she put it – 'robbed Peter to pay Paul' by printing money and devaluing its currency in order to make these payments. She also observed with great anxiety the chaos into which the Balkan states, in particular, were descending.

In Vienna she sensed serious social unrest and thought to herself: 'What could we, and what especially can I, as a woman, do about all this?' She gave her own answer: 'Nothing, except entertain the tired diplomats and ministers, in whose overburdened laps these responsibilities lie. They always like to chat with a woman after a hard day signing treaties.' In Vienna Stephanie was among the chosen circle around Frau Sacher, the proprietress of the Hotel Sacher, which still exists today. She spent much of her time there making new friendships and cultivating them in discreet private dining-rooms. But it was also on the golf-course and in hunting-parties that she got to know rich and usually aristocratic men.

At the time the princess was certainly not aware that the contacts she made in those turbulent and pleasure-seeking days would one day be of incalculable value to her. But in retrospect she confirmed that 'they provided me with a "passport" that could open any door for me, and later that is just what happened'.

The stories that Stephanie planned to write about the international high society in which she moved would, as she herself admitted, have been extremely amusing but also pretty revealing about a number of personalities in the public eye. Her anecdotes would to a degree reflect what people in those high positions said and thought.

Stephanie then produces a list of people who, in those 'peacetime years' and later on, played a part in her life: the Duke and Duchess of Windsor, the Aga Khan, Lloyd George, Clemenceau, Popes Pius XI and Pius XII, Arturo Toscanini, Lady Cunard, Sir Thomas Beecham, King Gustav of Sweden, King Manuel of Portugal, Sir Malcolm Sargent, Lord Rothschild, Leopold Stokowski, Admiral Horthy (the Regent of Hungary), Neville Chamberlain, Geoffrey Dawson (editor of *The Times*), the journalist Wickham Steed, Fritz Kreisler, Lady Londonderry, the Maharaja of Baroda, Margot Asquith, Lord Brocket and Lord Carisbrooke.

The princess's drawing room in Vienna was frequented by many friends and admirers. As her son repeatedly assures us, she received a steady series of marriage proposals, but she wanted to go on living a life without attachments. One of her many admirers was George de Woré, the Greek Consul-General in Vienna. He came from an extremely wealthy Athenian family and his real name was

Anastasios Damianos Vorres. He offered her the kind of life she liked. All year round they travelled together from one end of Europe to the other, and at no time did Stephanie have to worry about money.

Then along came a rich American, John Murton Gundy, followed in turn by a married millionaire named Bernstiehl, her 'devoted slave', who lavished gifts on her.

Yet Stephanie began to realise more and more that the war had robbed Vienna of its sparkle, that the end of the monarchy had brought many changes, and that now, when she went with some rich, influential *galant* to her much-loved Hotel Sacher, she felt she was being watched.

The threat of inflation was very much in the air. And being the clever woman she was, she decided in 1922 to leave Austria. She managed quite quickly to find a buyer for her apartment, along with all her furniture, porcelain, and cars. Her son describes the sum she received for them as 'astronomical'. However, she did not pay the money into a bank account. Instead, she stuffed the notes into several suitcases and headed for Paris. But then, at the last minute, probably because of the cold winter weather – it was just before Christmas – she decided to take a train to Nice. Needless to say, she did not travel alone. With her were her son Franzi and his nanny, a maid, a butler, her sister Milla, and her friends Ferdinand Wurmbrandt, Karl Habig, and Count and Countess Nyári.

When they arrived in Nice, the party poured out from the *wagon-lit*, quickly followed by several dogs and any number of trunks and suitcases. After she had rented a villa at 123 promenade des Anglais, she acquired a motor-car, with one object in mind – to make a splash: it was a yellow Chenard & Walker tourer with a shiny silver bonnet and a second windscreen for the rear seats.

Stephanie lived life to the full. She was a frequent visitor to the casino – once, as her son tells us, 'with no brassière under her transparent muslin dress'.

Among her friends were many Russians who had fled from the Revolution and were now living in the south of France. Many of them were grand dukes, and Stephanie had an intense flirtation with Grand Duke Dimitri. His name was also romantically linked with that of Coco Chanel, founder of the famous fashion house. Both she and Stephanie were also on close terms with the Duke of Westminster, who invited Stephanie to go fishing with him in Scotland. There she was attended by a Scots ghillie and had to spend hours practising her casts. She did not see the Duke until the evening, and after a week's rather solitary stay in the wilds of the Highlands she graciously declined his proposal of marriage. She passed him on to Coco Chanel, who did not marry him either.[5]

A very long and 'rewarding', in other words lucrative, relationship then developed with John Warden, an American from Philadelphia. He initiated her into the financial mysteries of the stock market, where she became very successful. For more than ten years Warden worshipped her; then he married a young Polish woman, who soon afterwards became an extremely rich widow.

In autumn 1925 the princess set herself up in a Paris apartment at 45 avenue Georges V, in the exclusive 8th *arrondissement*. At that time the household employed a staff of nine. Living in the same building was a British insurance tycoon, Sir William Garthwaite. Sir William and the lady from Vienna became close, and he frequently helped her out when she was financially embarrassed. On one occasion, when she claimed to have been robbed of everything in broad daylight, Garthwaite took up the case on her behalf and after several years of dispute her insurers made good the 'loss'.

The following episode is also worth mentioning. Stephanie loved dogs; her favourite was a Skye terrier, whose sire had been a present from her early admirer Rudolf Colloredo-Mannsfeld. When Stephanie's butler was taking her terrier for a walk in the park, a man came up to them and said he was interested in just such an animal. He was Michel Clemenceau, son of the indomitable former prime minister of France, Georges 'Tiger' Clemenceau (1841–1929). Michel was looking for a pet for his old father and immediately went to introduce himself to Stephanie; he was bowled over by her and wanted to marry her. She preferred to keep the relationship on an informal level, but it lasted for several years nevertheless.

From time to time Stephanie von Hohenlohe lived in Monte Carlo, but the city soon seemed to her 'as dreary as stale water'. She preferred Cannes. There she met François André, who had risen from being an undertaker's assistant to a leading owner of luxury hotels. He also owned the casino in Cannes, where Stephanie won and lost large sums.

She also liked to spend the summer season in Deauville, the fashionable resort on the Channel coast of Normandy. There she met the multi-millionaire Solly Joel, principal shareholder of the South African diamond company, De Beers Consolidated Mines.

The summer of 1928 was taken up with a tour of Europe in the pleasant company of Kathleen Vanderbilt and her husband, Harry Cushing Sr, as well as Robert Strauss-Huppé, later the US ambassador in Colombo, Brussels and Stockholm, and a number of other upper-crust Americans.

For a variety of reasons, the year 1932 saw a major change of direction in Stephanie's life. For one thing she had a road accident while being driven to Trieste by her chauffeur, Mostny. The car was a write-off. So the princess made her own way to Trieste and took the next fast train back to Paris. It was on that journey that she met a good-looking American banker, Captain Donald Malcolm, and for a time the two were inseparable. The greatest change, however, was that the princess found a highly paid political job working for the London newspaper publisher Lord Rothermere, whom she had known since 1925.

CHAPTER TWO

A Mission for Lord Rothermere

'A number of people have written that from the outset I was
determined to play an influential part in international politics.
Nothing is further from the truth.' We find this clarification at the
beginning of the notes Stephanie jotted down in the form of short
headings for the benefit of her ghost writer Rudolf Kommer. Her
political activity did not start until she was retained by the British
press baron, Harold Sydney Harmsworth (1868–1940) who, in
1913, was elevated to the peerage as Lord Rothermere. The first
time Stephanie met him was in Monte Carlo in 1925. He was a
very well known figure on the Côte d'Azur; his power, wealth and
influence were common knowledge. He was a passionate gambler
and it was in the Monte Carlo Sporting Club that she came across
him, surrounded as always by toadies and hangers-on. He invited
her to a drink and from that developed a relationship that would
last thirteen years.

However, there is another version: that the introduction came
about through James Kruze, an employee of his company, whose
wife Annabel was a former mistress of Rothermere. However, it is not
impossible that the sixty-year-old Englishman and the 34-year-old
Viennese princess could have got to know each other at the gaming-
tables in Monte Carlo. Lord Rothermere was having a run of bad
luck and Stephanie, who was playing next to him, helped him out

with 40,000 francs. It appears that in return she was given some shares in his newspaper concern.

At any rate, after their first drink together, Lord Rothermere invited Princess Stephanie to his villa, La Dragonière, in Cap Martin. Though the princess may have hoped for another conquest, for the moment Rothermere only wanted to talk business.

Harold Rothermere was married, but his wife Mary had left him soon after the end of the First World War, preferring a life of freedom in France where she mixed with literati like André Gide.

Rothermere himself lived very modestly but had one weakness – attractive young women. Since he was a friend of the Russian ballet director, Sergei Diaghilev, until the latter's death in 1929, he often romped around with ballerinas or put on evening performances at one of his magnificent residences, featuring the leading dancers of the day.

Rothermere was the younger brother of Alfred Harmsworth who, as Lord Northcliffe, became famous as the owner of the *Daily Mail* before and during the First World War. In the years of Germany's postwar Weimar Republic, Northcliffe became one of Germany's harshest adversaries and a strong supporter of France's position. After Northcliffe's death in 1922, his brother took over full responsibility for the press empire that included the *Daily Mail*, *Daily Mirror*, *Evening News*, *Sunday Pictorial* and *Sunday Dispatch*.

In the summer of 1927 Stephanie was staying with Lord Rothermere in Monte Carlo. She ran into a journalist who was desperate for a story for his paper. Stephanie mentioned in an offhand way that it might be a good idea if he wrote about the situation in Hungary. Rothermere, who was present, was very intrigued and asked Stephanie to 'enlighten' him on the subject. First of all a large map of Central Europe was purchased, on which Stephanie showed him Hungary, within its diminished post-1918 frontiers. In her memoirs the princess asks herself the question whether her heart would have beaten so strongly for Hungary, had she not, by marriage, become a member of the Hungarian branch of an aristocratic Austro-German family. 'Would I have acted for Czechoslovakia, if I had married a Prince Lobkowitz instead of a Prince Hohenlohe?' In the end, she explained her interest in Hungary by her love of its people and stressed that at the time she had no political motives whatsoever.

Stephanie suggested that the Hungarian ambassador in London, Baron Rubido-Zichy, should be invited to Paris to hold talks about the restoration of the monarchy in Hungary. But the ambassador declined. Lord Rothermere now launched a campaign in his papers in favour of revising the terms that had been imposed on Hungary in the Treaty of Trianon, which was signed in parallel with the Treaty of Versailles. In his *Daily Mail* on 21 June 1927 he published an article under the headline, 'Hungary's place in the sun'. Not just the title, but the whole article, had been written by the princess, and proved an incredible success; the editorial offices received 2,000 readers' letters in one day.

Prominent Hungarians got in touch with Rothermere, and an extravagant programme for the restoration of the Hungarian monarchy was launched. A group of active monarchists even offered the crown of Hungary to Lord Rothermere himself, an idea that for a moment he took seriously. He soon had second thoughts, however, and put forward his son Esmond in his place, as a candidate for the vacant throne. All this greatly annoyed the princess, since she had been wondering whether her own son, though his Esterházy connections, might not be able to become King of Hungary.

In 1928 the Hungarian parliament passed a resolution officially expressing the thanks of the Hungarian people to the British peer. The University of Szeged offered him an honorary doctorate 'for his selfless efforts in the Hungarian cause'. However, Princess Stephanie advised him rather to send his son Esmond to Hungary, so that the people there might get to know him. Esmond was duly welcomed with great enthusiasm and even received a solemn blessing from the Primate of Hungary, Cardinal Serédi. On his father's behalf he accepted a hand-built motor-car, whose chassis was made from reinforced silver and the radiator covered in pure beaten gold.

However, it is important to note that neither the prime minister of the day, Count Bethlen – who still championed a Habsburg succession to the throne – nor the Regent of Hungary, Admiral Horthy, who was nurturing secret plans for a dynasty of his own, paid any attention to the Ruritanian events surrounding the young Englishman. Even the British government warned the Hungarians against dealing with Lord Rothermere.

In 1932, Stephanie's position in France was becoming increasingly uncomfortable. The French government did not want anyone 'messing around with the Little Entente'.[1] There were rumours that the princess was the driving force behind the Hungarian campaign which was filling the newspapers. The *Review of Reviews* demonstrated clearly how she had set the entire operation in motion. She was put under official pressure to give up her activities with Rothermere. The press baron himself made no comment. Stephanie was even being accused of espionage, so she promptly quit Paris and moved with her mother and her dogs to London.

If we read the unpublished memoirs of the former Berlin journalist, Bella Fromm, they shed new light on Princess Stephanie's time in Paris.[2] Fromm insists that in 1932 Stephanie was expelled from France because of her espionage activities. For quite some time she had been in touch with Otto Abetz,[3] a German who was in France working for better understanding between the two nations. At that time Abetz was not yet a member of the Nazi Party and had no inkling that one day he would be Hitler's ambassador to Vichy France. A memorandum concerning Princess Stephanie circulated by the US government on 28 October 1941 also mentions her expulsion from France on the grounds of espionage.

Even before she left Paris in 1932, Stephanie was seriously short of money, since not even the occasional gifts of money or jewellery from Lord Rothermere were enough to maintain her extravagant lifestyle. So at the beginning of 1932 she had to ask Rothermere for a loan of £1,000. He did not give it to her.

However, Captain Donald Malcolm, who had lost part of his fortune in the Wall Street Crash of 1929, had moved to London, near the princess, and offered his services as her financial adviser. He advised Stephanie to negotiate a contract with Rothermere under which she would be employed as a society columnist. Malcolm drew up the contract himself, and Rothermere signed it on 27 July 1932. It was to run initially for three years, but he later renewed it for a further three. Her annual income was to be the not inconsiderable sum of £5,000 (about £125,000 in today's terms). But that was just her retainer. For every assignment completed she would receive a further £2,000 (£50,000). This contract remained in force until early 1938, by which time the princess had collected well over £1 million in today's money.

In London, the exclusive Dorchester hotel was being managed by the former director of the Hôtel du Palais in Biarritz. He offered the princess accommodation at the Dorchester at a reduced rent, because he thought her aristocratic credentials would further enhance the hotel's reputation. However, after a short stay there, she decided to move into a private apartment of her own.

Now that Stephanie von Hohenlohe was on the payroll of an influential newspaper publisher, a completely new life opened up for her. Her first assignment, in August 1932, took her to the country estate of Steenokkerzeel in Belgium, where the ex-empress Zita, widow of Karl, the last Austro-Hungarian emperor, was living with her children. For the journey she was about to undertake, Stephanie asked Rothermere to have a Rolls-Royce painted for her in black and yellow, the colours of the Habsburg coat of arms. The princess's task was to give the former empress more details about Lord Rothermere's plans in the cause of Hungary and at the same time to offer her an annual pension.

According to the memoirs of Stephanie's son Franz, published in 1976, the princess was received at Steenokkerzeel by a brother of the empress Zita, Prince Sixtus. Stephanie informed him of Rothermere's great interest in Hungary and of his offer to provide an annual allowance for the empress, who had now been living in exile for fourteen years. The prince viewed the whole matter with obvious distrust, and demanded that the 'offer' be made in writing.

However, a very different account is given by Gordon Brook-Shepherd in his 1991 biography of the empress Zita, based on research in the Habsburg archives in Vienna.[4] According to Brook-Shepherd, the princess first telephoned Steenokkerzeel and asked to speak to the empress. But Zita was away in France at the time, and Stephanie was only able to meet a lady-in-waiting, Countess Viktoria

Mensdorff, one afternoon at a hotel in Brussels. She presented her letter of introduction from Lord Rothermere, as well as another letter in the same handwriting, addressed to the empress personally. Stephanie knew the huge annual provision that was being offered to the empress: £30,000, equivalent to about £750,000 today.

The lady-in-waiting gave her the empress's address and telephone number in the French spa town of Vichy, and the princess made her way there. To this day, it is not clear whether the offer of £30,000 a year was accepted. Countess Mensdorff supposed that the money was intended for use in winning the European press over to the monarchist cause. Of the princess, she wrote: 'I thought she might be a flirt of L[ord] R[othermere], and that she had picked a good moment to ask for the money from him, because she mentioned how Lord Rothermere took such a great interest in His Majesty.'[5]

'His Majesty' was in fact the pretender to the throne, Otto von Habsburg who, many years later, put the whole matter in a clearer light: 'The Rothermere affair rose up like a soufflé in the summer of 1932. We never got fully to the bottom of it but our feeling was that it was really somehow linked to Archduke Albrecht and his ambitions to secure the Hungarian throne for himself. If, as we suspected, this was an attempt to get Rothermere, with his great wealth and influence, on his side, then it was a grave matter, because Albrecht had always been the main challenger from within my family – backed by his mother, of course, who hated my parents. Indeed this went on into the Second World War, when we were in America, and the future of the Hungarian constitution again became critical.'[6] Archduke Albrecht (1897–1955) was the only son, born after eight daughters, of Archduke Friedrich and Princess Isabella von Croy-Dülmen. After 1918, these two supported efforts to make their son Albrecht king of Hungary.

At Rothermere's request, Princess Stephanie's next trip took her to Budapest to meet another of her close friends, the Regent of Hungary, Admiral Horthy. Her task was to sound out the attitude of leading members of the government there to the question of restoring the Habsburg monarchy. It was quite apparent that – apart from a few hundred royalists – no-one in Hungary wanted to see a Habsburg on the throne. Nonetheless, Rothermere held the view that the only possible successor to the throne of Hungary was Otto von Habsburg.

On 29 October 1932 the princess was sent to Hungary for the last time on Rothermere's orders. This time she was to arrange a meeting with the Hungarian prime minister, General Gyula Gömbös (1886–1936). Gömbös was on the conservative right wing, and her task was to warn him of the 'red menace' that was spreading throughout Europe. Rothermere wanted to convey to Gömbös as urgently as possible the idea that a monarchic constitution represented the mightiest bulwark against Bolshevism, and advocated that Hungary should closely emulate Mussolini's Italy, though his grasp of Italian politics was weak. Gömbös gave the princess a letter to take back to Rothermere, thanking him for everything he had done for Hungary.

Budapest, 4 November 1932

Dear Lord Rothermere,

I very much appreciate the message that you have asked Princess Hohenlohe to pass on to me. Please accept my grateful thanks; everything else I have to say on that subject, the Princess will report to you by word of mouth. In this letter I would like to thank you for everything you have done for our country up to now, and to express the hope that you will continue to do so in the future.

Your most obedient servant
Gömbös

While Lord Rothermere maintained his interest in a restoration of the monarchy in Hungary, he was now also putting out feelers towards the dynasty that had ruled Prussia since the seventeenth century and the German Empire from 1871 to 1918 – the house of Hohenzollern. Thus another of Stephanie's missions in the summer of 1932 was to Schloss Doorn in the Netherlands, now the home of the exiled German Kaiser, Wilhelm II, who had abdicated in 1918. It was not difficult for Stephanie to be admitted to his presence since she was already a friend of the Kaiser's son, Crown Prince Wilhelm, with whom she had flirted outrageously.

Of her visit to Doorn she wrote: 'The Kaiser receives me himself. He is friendly, but not enthusiastic about the scheme. Rothermere's brother, Lord Northcliffe, had [during the First World War] coined the phrase "Hang the Kaiser!" The Kaiser was naturally suspicious about entangling himself with a member of Northcliffe's family.' In a further conversation the former monarch told her: 'My dear princess, it is very kind of Lord Rothermere to show this concern for me. But my answer today is, as it has always been, that whatever happens I need weapons and soldiers. Is his lordship prepared to support me to that extent?'

Stephanie was of course unable to give the ex-Kaiser the reply he wanted. 'Another polite refusal', was how Stephanie described this failure. She went on: 'I am convinced that my connection with the Hungarian campaign has cooled both the [former German] Kaiser and the Empress [of Austria] towards me.'

There is no doubt that there was a time when Hitler himself considered the restoration of the monarchy in Germany a desirable aim. At a dinner in early February 1933, a few days after the Nazis seized power, Hitler told his foreign affairs adviser, Joachim von Ribbentrop, that he was considering the Kaiser's other son, Prince August Wilhelm, as a new German Kaiser. Three years later, when Rothermere met Hitler at the Reich Chancellery, he expressed some surprise that all the leading figures in the new government were from southern Germany. Hitler retorted: 'The Hohenzollerns were South Germans too!'

However, with Hitler as Chancellor, the re-establishment of the imperial throne would have pointed too clearly to a consolidation of Germany's strategic position in Europe and would thus be an apparent threat to the British notion of the 'balance of power' on the continent. That is why Hitler abandoned that possibility at an early stage.

Although the reaction of the ex-Kaiser could not have been clearer, Rothermere still wanted the princess to get in touch with the Kaiser's eldest son in Berlin. Initially 'Crown Prince' Wilhelm's attitude to Nazism had been favourable, though unlike his younger brother August Wilhelm, known as 'Brownshirt Au-Wi', he was never an enthusiastic supporter of Hitler. Nonetheless, Wilhelm had been a member of the Nazi Party since 1930, and in 1933 had joined the party's paramilitary wing, the SA.

Stephanie was received by the crown prince at his palace on the Unter den Linden avenue. Wilhelm seemed very impressed by Rothermere's proposals and his offer of assistance. Since Stephanie was still concerned about the failure of her earlier mission, she now asked the crown prince to telephone Rothermere immediately.

On her next visit she met the crown prince at the Cecilienhof palace in Potsdam, the Hohenzollern seat near Berlin. She found it hard to believe that Wilhelm commuted daily to his Berlin office, driving a racing-car along the autobahn.

There then began a lively exchange of letters between Rothermere and the crown prince, who invited the press baron and his emissary several times to his palace in Potsdam. In the course of these visits the crown prince had to convince Lord Rothermere that is was not he who had been chosen as the saviour of Germany, but Adolf Hitler. Crown prince Wilhelm knew very well that he would never achieve anything on his own, but believed he very well might with a man like Hitler at his side.

At the end of one of her visits, Stephanie was handed a lengthy letter for her British patron. It is certainly surprising that the crown prince should set out his views on the political situation in the German Reich in such detail, for the eyes of a British newspaper owner. If certain passages in the letter had been published, it would have put him in an extremely difficult position. (This letter, a historical document of the highest importance, is reproduced in full in Appendix III.)

At the time when Crown Prince Wilhelm wrote this letter, he had already turned his back on Hitler in fury. One reason for this was that the Führer had cancelled all public celebrations of his father the Kaiser's seventy-fifth birthday, on 27 January 1934. Even the ambitious press baron rapidly lost interest in the Hohenzollern 'operation'. He decided to plunge into a new adventure; he would no longer give his support to the scions of monarchic dynasties, but instead to a German who was a man of the people: Adolf Hitler.

CHAPTER THREE

Hitler's 'Dear Princess'

In the notes for her planned memoirs Princess Stephanie dealt very exhaustively with Anglo-German relations in the interwar period. She writes that many influential people in Britain, like Lord Rothermere, were very well disposed towards Germany. They were convinced that the Treaty of Versailles had been excessively harsh on the Germans, whose side they often took at the expense of the French. The princess seeks to explain that people like Rothermere were gripped by an obsessive fear of communism. They saw Germany as the most important bulwark against communism and the might of Russia.

Thus it is no surprise that, even after 1933, many Britons were willing to take a very benevolent attitude towards the 'new Germany' of Adolf Hitler. Stephanie recalls that 'it is certainly very rare for a nation to show as much good will to a former enemy as the British did in the 1930s – what is more, towards a dangerous dictator.'

After Hitler's seizure of power in 1933, Lord Rothermere wanted to become personally acquainted with this 'new man', who had set the world back on its heels. Enthusiasm for the 'Führer' spread far beyond the borders of the German Reich. 'All political camps and classes donned the brown shirt; even the *Stahlhelm* [the army veterans' organisation] went over to the Nazis', complained Bella Fromm, the Berlin journalist who worked for the liberal Ullstein newspapers.[1] And she got extremely angry with people like Lord

Rothermere, who complained in his own newspaper on 10 July 1933 about 'old women of both sexes' in Britain, mounting 'a clamorous campaign of denunciation against what they call "Nazi atrocities" which, as anyone who visits Germany quickly discovers for himself, consist merely of a few isolated acts of violence . . . but have been multiplied and exaggerated to give the impression that Nazi rule is a bloodthirsty tyranny.' He went on to add that Germany had been 'liberated' by Nazism from 'the rule of the frowsty, down-at-heel German republic . . . where fraud and corruption had begun to spread on a large scale'. Bella Fromm could only retort: 'What a pity that the noble Lord has not had the opportunity to experience [this liberation] in a concentration camp!'[2]

On the other hand, Stephanie wrote of her own role in this: 'Rothermere was mad keen to find out Hitler's real political intentions. He chose me as his "adviser", and for a time, from 1934 to 1938, I was an important witness to world events. There was a moment when I stood at the very centre of things.'

Lord Rothermere knew very well that it could also be of interest to Hitler to be on terms with Britain's biggest newspaper owner. In the *Daily Mail*, a mass-circulation paper then as it is today, he frequently published articles aimed at convincing his readers of the virtues of Nazi Germany. In Rothermere's mind, Nazism and fascism were the answer to all the political problems of the age, and he was a supporter of Oswald Mosley, the leader of the British Union of Fascists, though even at its height in 1934 that organisation never had more than about 40,000 members.

Rothermere gave the princess the task of establishing personal contact with the German Chancellor. Once again it was the crown prince, 'Little Willie', who set up the appointment for Stephanie by making a telephone call to the Reich Chancellery.

As always, the princess checked in at Berlin's top hotel, the Adlon, where she found a note to say that the Reich Chancellor was expecting her; and in half an hour a car came to pick her up. This was in fact quite unnecessary, as the Reich Chancellery was only a few yards from the hotel. The exact date of this meeting is not known. Stephanie only tells us that it was early in December 1933.

It was extremely unusual in itself for the Führer to receive a woman sent on a political mission. Hitler had frequently spoken very scathingly about women in politics, and pointed out that history provides many examples to prove that a woman, however intelligent, is incapable in politics of separating emotion from reason.[3] On the same theme Hitler once declared: 'In my view, a female who gets involved in politics is an abomination. In military matters, it's completely intolerable! No woman should have even the smallest position in any local Party branch. In 1924 some political women turned up at my door . . . they wanted to become members of the Reichstag . . . I told them, 99 per cent of the matters debated are men's business, which they can have no opinion on!'[4]

In view of all this, Stephanie von Hohenlohe, as the political emissary of a British press baron to Hitler, was very much the exception. But to Hitler, of course, her only importance was that she had been sent by a man who, as a powerful publisher, could be helpful to the cause of National Socialism in Britain.

The petite princess now made her grand entrance in the Reich Chancellery. Adolf Hitler greeted her with a charming kiss on the hand; beside him stood Dr Hans-Heinrich Lammers who, since the Nazis took power in January, had been the administrative head of the Chancellery. Hitler invited her to take a seat and tea was immediately served. The princess handed Hitler the letter from Lord Rothermere, which he passed on to Lammers without opening it.

Stephanie von Hohenlohe had arrived wearing her most elegant outfit. The Führer wore his usual fawn military-style jacket, a white shirt, brown tie fastened with a swastika tie-pin, and black uniform trousers. Stephanie thought his black socks and black patent leather gloves most inappropriate. Once she was beside him, the Führer did not take his eyes off her for a moment. Yet, for her part, she was struck by his totally insignificant appearance. He seemed to her like a minor clerk, albeit a very neat and tidy one, and just an ordinary and sincere man.

There are very few personal records by women who came to know Hitler personally and who described his appearance and the effect he had on them. One was the American journalist Dorothy Thompson, who interviewed him in 1931, before he had achieved supreme power. What she wrote resulted in her being expelled from Germany. Thompson and Stephanie met in London around that time, and again later in the USA. Women, and especially those who had studied Hitler's racial theories, were astonished at how poorly he matched his own ideals. Stephanie later made notes on her observations of Hitler's appearance:

The most surprising thing about his appearance was the colour of his hair. I had imagined his hair to be dark, almost black. In fact it isn't. It's light brown. The often caricatured forelock that seems to fall over his face with every movement is in reality much less pronounced than in photos. He combs it diagonally across his forehead . . .

The ugliest things about him are his nose, his moustache, his mouth and his feet. His nose is too large. Not at the bridge, but from nostril to nostril. The bit between the nostrils is a very ugly shape, so that one is forced to stare at it and wonder what it is. His moustache really does look like Chaplin's and is narrower than his mouth, which is small anyway. It is very much narrower than the base of his nose, and draws attention to the whole thing even more . . .

When Hitler talks, you hardly see his teeth, but when you do, neither their colour nor their shape are at all attractive, and his front teeth are edged with a thin gold strip. His mouth is small, far too small for a man, and when he opens it, especially when he gets worked up, it is extremely unappetising. It becomes distorted into an ugly little hole . . .

His eyes, which are a pleasant pale blue, could be called beautiful if they were not slightly protruding. This, combined with his very fine, almost translucent, skin, and the fact that he is always very pale, or else has little pink spots on his cheeks, gave me the impression that he is not very healthy . . .

The nicest thing about him are his hands. They are not only a beautiful shape, but are genuinely the hands of an artist. The contrast between those exquisite hands and his coarse feet could not be greater. Apart from that, he constantly scratches nervously with his thumbnail on the skin of his index finger so that he always has a sore there.

One very unpleasant thing that stuck in her memory was the fact that, even in 1933, when he had lived in Germany for about twenty years, Hitler still spoke with an Austrian accent 'of the lowest class. Like someone who is trying to express himself in a language that he is not born to. Frightfully stiff and bombastic.'

Hitler took his leave of the princess with an almost ceremonial solemnity. She returned to London with a letter written by Adolf Hitler to Lord Rothermere. He in turn was so delighted that he paid his envoy a bonus of £2,000. He now launched an uncompromisingly pro-Hitler campaign in his newspapers.

Hitler's letter to Rothermere, dated 7 December 1933, is reproduced in full in Appendix II and sets out what amounts to a basic political programme, with particular attention paid to Franco German relations. The letter begins:

Dear Lord Rothermere,
You were kind enough to convey to me through Princess Hohenlohe a series of proposals, for which I wish to express my sincere thanks.

In addition, I would like to voice the feelings of countless Germans, who regard me as their spokesman, with regard to the shrewd and well-directed journalistic support of the policy which we all hope will lead to the ultimate liberation of Europe. Princess Hohenlohe gave me a translation of the splendid article that Your Lordship has written; I have already taken the liberty recently of referring to the article. What I particularly welcome in the article is that it points out the value of an Anglo-French defence alliance. I am convinced that Anglo-French friendship can be very helpful in maintaining a genuine peace. Germany itself has no aggressive intentions whatever towards France; determined as we may be to defend ourselves against attack, we certainly do not harbour the slightest intention of provoking a war. As veterans of the Great

War – I myself was at the Front for four-and-a-half years, facing British and French troops – we all have a very personal experience of the horror of European war. While having no sympathy with cowards and deserters, we frankly accept our duty towards God and our country to prevent with all the means at our disposal the repetition of such a catastrophe. However, this can only be achieved for Europe if the treatment of that critical problem, whose existence cannot be denied, can be removed from the climate of hatred in which victor and vanquished confront each other, and placed on a basis where nations and states can negotiate with each other on an equal footing.

Granting such equality of status to Germany implies no threat to the security of France [. . .]

It should not be overlooked that I am offering the friendship of a nation of 66 million, which has much of value in other respects too. And just as I see no reason for a war in the west, no more do I see any for a war in the east.

Our efforts to bring about an understanding between Germany and Poland spring from the same desire to eschew the use of force and to approach the tasks we face pragmatically and without emotion [. . .]

If I have been frank in presenting these thoughts to Your Lordship, I have done so in order to express my appreciation of the high journalistic position held by Your Lordship in the British press.

I thank you once again for the support that you have shown for a genuine policy for peace in Europe.

Yours sincerely,
Adolf Hitler

At the end of December 1933 the princess travelled once more to Berlin, this time to present Hitler with a gift from her patron, worth about £50,000 in today's terms. It was a portrait photograph of Rothermere in a solid gold frame made by Cartier in Paris. Proudly displayed on the reverse was a reprint of the page from the *Daily Mail* of 24 September 1930 containing the article on the 'New

Germany'. Under a series of headlines: 'GERMANY AND INEVITABILITY
– A NATION REBORN – YOUTH ASSERTING ITS POWER – NEW CHAPTER IN
EUROPEAN HISTORY', the article begins:

> These last ten days have seen another milestone raised beside the
> march of European history. One of those immensely significant
> events has occurred which from time to time open up a new
> chapter in international affairs.
>
> The sweeping success of the German National Socialist Party –
> in other words, the Fascist Party, at the general election of
> September 14 will, it is my strong conviction, prove to be an
> enduring landmark of this time. It will stand out as the beginning
> of a new epoch in the relations between the German nation and
> the rest of the world.

Rothermere goes on to praise the vitality and ambition of the young
generation of Germans who 'retain only vague recollections of the
old Imperial Germany'. 'Under the leadership of Adolf Hitler, who
himself is only 41, [the Nazi Party] has already become the second
largest party in the state. I confidently believe the future of Germany
lies in its hands. [. . .] We can do nothing to check this movement,
and I believe it would be a blunder for the British people to take up
an attitude of hostility towards it.'

'If we do', Rothermere went on, referring back to the First World
War, 'sooner or later another and more terrible awakening is in store
for Europe.' Rothermere concluded that, as an ally, Nazi Germany
would be a valuable bulwark against Russian communism. He calls
for removal of the Versailles terms restricting Germany's army to
100,000 men, pointing out that her neighbours, Poland and
Czechoslovakia, have been steadily building up their armaments. He
ends: 'I confidently predict that within the next few years [the
inevitable force of history] will have altered not a few of the features
of the map of Europe, which the politicians assembled in Paris in
1919 complacently believed they had fixed for ever.'

Since neither the German Chancellor nor his head of
administration knew any English, the princess was obliged, at

Rothermere's behest, to translate the article word for word. Hitler was meant to be impressed by Rothermere's 'clairvoyant genius'. It was extremely uncomfortable for the princess to provide the translation, sunk deep in the soft armchair with the heavy photo-frame on her lap. What is more, her skirt had slid up over her knees, and this appeared to shock Dr Lammers. Yet Hitler liked the article: 'He glanced up at Lammers as if to say: "You see what a great man I really am. Even a lord has been quick to recognise my genius." But the civil servant showed absolutely no reaction. He sat there as stiff as a board. A fishy eye stared from his monocle, expressionless. The scars on his cheek did not even twitch once. The expression of pride and satisfaction on Hitler's face could have been quite moving, had he not at the same time been so ordinary and comical.'

Stephanie found the whole situation little short of ridiculous. 'So there I sat, flattering and acting up to a man who never seemed more gauche and plebeian to me than at that moment.'

At the end of the audience Hitler bade Stephanie von Hohenlohe convey his warmest thanks to Lord Rothermere for the gift. She was also to tell his Lordship that Hitler was sure his publications would convince the British that a strong and contented Germany was the best guarantee for the maintenance of a lasting peace.

Hitler's expectations were quickly fulfilled. In all his papers, Rothermere promoted the notion that, as regards his foreign policy, the German Reich Chancellor had only peaceful intentions and that he was the saviour of a defeated Germany.

However, it was not only Rothermere's *Daily Mail* that was singing the praises of the great Führer; so was the *Times* – which in those days was probably the most influential newspaper in the world. Not to be left out, a few years later the *Saturday Review* in London (on 7 March 1936) ran the headline 'Heil Hitler!' on its front page.

As a result of her activity on behalf of the British press baron, Stephanie also made some enemies in the Reich Chancellery. Hitler's foreign press spokesman, Dr Ernst 'Putzi' von Hanfstaengl, did not share his boss's obvious liking for the princess. He particularly resented the way Hitler showed favour to Stephanie von Hohenlohe. He had been watching her for a long time and warned Hitler against 'this professional blackmailer and full-blooded Jewess'. However, Hitler was so taken with her that he absolutely refused to pay any attention to these warnings. Hanfstaengl did everything he could to put an end to the relationship, since he feared that Princess Stephanie would beguile Hitler, just as she had other men, and would thus ruin his career.

It was not even any use pointing out to Hitler that such a close relationship with a 'full Jewess' could have a serious impact on German public opinion. In order to keep Hanfstaengl quiet, Hitler promised to have her family history checked out against the 'Aryan Laws'. The next time Hanfstaengl warned him to be cautious, Hitler retorted that the Gestapo had investigated the family tree of the allegedly Jewish woman and found it to be in order and unexceptionable.

On 3 March 1934 Hitler handed the princess a letter inviting his 'kindred spirit', Lord Rothermere, to visit him in Germany. He was unable, he said, to travel to England himself: '. . . partly due to my position today, and partly due to other difficulties, it is impossible for me to leave the borders of the Reich. However, I have already told the good lady who brought Your Lordship's letter and memento, how delighted I would be, on your possible visit to Germany, to describe in detail my views on the European questions that interest you.'

On this occasion, too, Hitler's farewell to the princess was remarkably friendly; he kissed her hand, then held it for a long time in his.

It was not until December 1934 that Lord Rothermere was able to accept Hitler's invitation. The German Chancellor greeted the British press baron, who arrived accompanied by his son Esmond Harmsworth, and Princess Stephanie. To cover the event for the press, Ward Price, the *Daily Mail*'s Europe correspondent, had also been brought along. Rothermere was absolutely delighted with his 'royal' reception and promised Stephanie that, in return for her good offices in arranging the meeting, he would ask Hitler to make her a duchess!

The return invitation took place on 19 December 1934, when Lord Rothermere asked the Reich Chancellor to join him at the Adlon hotel. This time the peer was accompanied not only by his son, and by Princess Stephanie and Ward Price, but also by the British banker, E.W.C. Tennant, who had good contacts in German industry. The invitation to Tennant, who was a well-known member of the Anglo-German Fellowship, was also connected with the fact that he was on friendly terms with Joachim von Ribbentrop, Hitler's foreign policy adviser, who in 1936 would be appointed German ambassador to Britain. On a recent visit to England Ribbentrop had claimed that he and not Rothermere had planned the invitation for Hitler in Berlin.

The other guests – there were twenty-five in all – included Germany's Foreign Minister, Baron Constantin von Neurath, and his wife, Joseph and Magda Goebbels, Ribbentrop and his wife Annelies, and Hermann Göring, accompanied by the actress Emmy Sonnemann, whom he later married, as well as other members of the government and their ladies, and several German opera singers.

At Rothermere's behest, Princess Stephanie had taken great trouble over protocol. At table, the *placement* followed 'French' rules: the host sat at the centre, with his guest of honour, Hitler, on his right. Stephanie acted as hostess and sat opposite Rothermere. Beside her sat Ribbentrop. His wife Annelies, who was just as 'anti-British' as her husband, sat next to Rothermere's son Esmond. Except for the journalist Ward Price, no other British were invited.

What Stephanie had not of course remembered, if she ever knew, was that exactly ten years earlier, on 20 December 1924, Hitler had been released from imprisonment in Landsberg Castle. Hitler began to talk at length about his far from displeasing sojourn in Landsberg. The British were unable to follow his monologue. No interpreter had been invited, so Stephanie von Hohenlohe undertook the task herself. But interpreting for Hitler was exceptionally difficult, since he never drew breath.

When the main course was served – roast chicken for everyone except Hitler, who had a vegetarian dish – the Führer plunged into the topic of Anglo-German friendship and its importance. Throughout the dinner no-one else was able to get a word in. Hitler did not touch his food at all. Rothermere could not even propose a toast, because the Führer went on talking and talking.

Finally the peer stood up to make his speech. But at that moment someone carelessly knocked over a vase of flowers, which fell to the floor with a crash. Immediately, men from Hitler's SS bodyguard burst into the room with pistols cocked, to protect their leader from what they took to be an attempted assassination. The Reich Chancellor left the hotel instantly, followed by Ribbentrop and his wife. Thus the meal ended without a dessert and with no warm speeches on the part of the guests.

Yet Rothermere remained as keen as ever about Hitler and continued to make his papers into a mouthpiece for the Reich Chancellery.

On 29 April 1935 Stephanie von Hohenlohe was once again the bearer of a letter from Rothermere, which she was to hand over personally to the Führer in Berlin. A mere four days later Hitler replied in an unusually detailed document which, because of its importance, is reproduced verbatim in Appendix IV.

In this letter Hitler sketched out his vision of the future, an edifice of world peace that was supported by two central pillars, Germany and Britain – the two great Germanic races which together were to be masters of the world.

When, on 2 October 1935, Italian troops invaded Abyssinia (now Ethiopia), the ancient east African country ruled by Haile Selassie, a storm of protest swept through Britain.[5] The Italian dictator Mussolini wanted to seize the whole vast country and colonise it. Lord Rothermere was at a loss as to how the spreading conflict might be halted. He wanted to hear Hitler's opinion on this, so that he could publicise it in his newspapers and also pass it on to the government of Prime Minister Stanley Baldwin. However, for the moment Hitler had no time to answer his questions, although the peer wrote to him: 'Princess Hohenlohe can provide you by word of mouth with further information about what I have in mind.' This shows us once again that Stephanie von Hohenlohe was more than just a female courier; she was extremely well acquainted with the contents of these politically important letters.

On 19 December 1935, at the end of a very troubled year, the Reich Chancellor expressed his views on the political situation in a detailed letter that he entrusted to the princess. This letter, in its translation by Hitler's interpreter, Paul Schmidt, is also reproduced in full in Appendix V. Hitler thanks Lord Rothermere for the letter conveyed to him by Princess Hohenlohe and goes on: 'In replying to you now, I must ask you, dear Lord Rothermere, not to make any public use of my reply, because it contains opinions, which I would otherwise express in a different wording or probably not express at all. This letter contains only opinions, and I have not the slightest doubt that they are entirely unsuited to influence public opinion or to make it change its own views in a world and at a time in which public opinion is not always identical with the innermost insight or wisdom. . .'

Shortly before Christmas 1936 Lord Rothermere once again asked Princess Stephanie to take a gift and an accompanying letter to Hitler in Berlin. The present was a beautiful tapestry worth £2,200 (£55,000). Lord Rothermere's letter reads:

My dear Reich Chancellor,
It gave me great pleasure to hear from Princess Hohenlohe that in spite of your tremendous work and the burden of your responsibilities, you are in high spirits and excellent health.
I have long intended to give Your Excellency a present as a token of my sincere friendship, and have therefore asked Princess Hohenlohe to go to Berlin and take, with my best Christmas wishes, a tapestry. In selecting my present I was guided by the thought of Adolf Hitler the artist and not the great leader, whose complete indifference to worldly possessions is common knowledge.
I hope that 1937 will bring prosperity to Germany and peace to the world.
In sincere admiration and respect,

Yours
Rothermere

This time too Lord Rothermere had given the princess a whole list of questions to put to Hitler verbally. But the Führer was unwilling to answer these in writing. The peer, who preferred the fine sunny weather of the Riviera to England's winter cold, was holidaying there when he received a letter of thanks from Hitler, which ended with the words: 'To answer the numerous and varied questions which Princess Hohenlohe has submitted to me is not terribly simple. Besides, I am very busy at the present time. Would you, dear Lord Rothermere, make [sic] me the pleasure of being my guest on the Obersalzberg between the 5th and 8th of January? We would then be able to discuss verbally and without haste all these problems.'

Lord Rothermere and his lady adviser were delighted with the idea of visiting the Berghof, Hitler's mountain retreat on the Obersalzberg, south of Munich. Hitler sent his special train to meet them at the Austrian border, and they travelled in it to Berchtesgaden. The saloon carriage greatly impressed the guests. Its interior was wood panelled and there was hot and cold running water. The floors were covered in velvet carpeting and a small wall-mounted telephone enabled them to communicate with the other carriages. They arrived at Berchtesgaden late in the evening and were allowed to spend the night at the Berghof – something that up till then no guest had been allowed to do. Also staying on the Obersalzberg were Magda and Joseph Goebbels, 'the almighty propaganda chief', as Stephanie called him. She took a strong dislike to him from the start; his wife, on the other hand, she found very pleasant.

Hitler's adjutants often complained about the lack of structure in his daily routine, especially when he was staying at the Berghof. Normally, he would not appear until about 2 in the afternoon. But at least while his British guests were there, he was up by 10 a.m. Stephanie noticed how puffy Hitler's face was. She presumed he was taking drugs.[6]

At 11 o'clock they all sat down to breakfast in the intimate surroundings of a small sitting-room with an old-fashioned tiled stove. The princess was allowed to sit on the Führer's right, with Lord Rothermere on his left. Stephanie observed Hitler very closely. He filled his teacup to the brim with sugar-lumps before having the tea poured on to them, and devoured three slices of cake.

The princess translated the exchanges between Hitler and Lord Rothermere, but if required, Hitler's personal interpreter, Dr Paul Schmidt, was on hand. Sadly, his memoirs contain no reference to this visit to the Berghof.

In the afternoon, Hitler took Rothermere for a walk. These walks were always downhill, to a place where a car would be waiting to drive the Führer and his companions back up again. Hitler was not athletic and disliked physical exertion of any kind. During his walks the whole area was sealed off.

As later records reveal, the two men chiefly discussed the possibility of a German alliance with Britain. Lord Rothermere was of the same opinion as his fellow press tycoon, Lord Beaverbrook, owner of the *Daily Express* among other papers. Both believed that there must never be another war between Britain and Germany. Hitler pretended to be satisfied with existing conditions but went on rearming. The second topic was the threat of international communism. And the third subject they broached was the 'Jewish Question'. Once again Rothermere found himself in the role of a silent listener. Hitler's monologue ended with the claim that the anti-Nazi campaign in Britain 'is being backed by Winston Churchill, on behalf of his Jewish paymasters. Just as they did in Germany before we took power, it is the Jews who control the press in Britain too.'

Much is revealed in Goebbels' diary entry for 7 January 1937:

Lord Rothermere and Princess Hohenlohe are here. Very small party for lunch. Rothermere pays me great compliments. Enquires in detail about German press policy. Strongly anti-Jewish. The Princess is very pushy. After lunch we retire for a chat. Question of Spain comes up. Führer won't tolerate a hotbed of communism in Europe any longer. Is ready to prevent any more [pro-Republican] volunteers from going there. His proposal on controls seems to astonish Rothermere. German prestige is thus restored. Franco will win anyway . . . Rothermere believes Brit[ish] government also pro-Franco.

After the evening meal the film '*Stosstrupp* [Shock-Troops] *1917*' was shown. Everyone was deeply moved, especially Lord Rothermere, who had lost two of his sons, Harold and Vere, in the First World War. The princess wept.

At that time Stephanie felt very happy in Hitler's company, since he declared himself fascinated by her and permitted himself to show little gestures of tenderness. As she never tired of relating subsequently, Hitler stroked her hair and once even gave her an intimate pinch on the cheek. To someone who believed she was a connoisseur of men, this was proof that Hitler did not have homosexual tendencies, as was rumoured, but in fact was 'utterly normal'.

In her private jottings we find the remark: 'Eva Braun in the house'. She knew about Hitler's mistress. Once again, Eva Braun had to suffer the humiliation of not being invited to join these guests for meals. Stephanie was sorry for Eva who, as she herself had experienced, was only allowed to enter the Reich Chancellery in Berlin by the tradesmen's entrance.

After the 'chat', Goebbels had another conversation with Hitler. They agreed that in certain circumstances Rothermere could be of very valuable service to the German Reich. He must therefore be well treated, not least in the eyes of the 7 million readers of his newspapers. The Propaganda Minister later confessed his expectations: 'Rothermere writes good and useful articles in favour of an Anglo-German alliance. He is a strong supporter of the Führer. Refers to the days he spent on the Obersalzberg. So they did do some good. But how far we still are from his goal!'

Very little about the two-day visit by the illustrious guests to the Obersalzberg was allowed to filter through to the general public. After consulting Hitler, Goebbels had issued express instructions to the Permanent Secretary at the Ministry of Propaganda and National Enlightenment that no written reports were to be released, only photographs.

Later, Stephanie was delighted to receive from Hitler a signed photograph in a silver frame and with the dedication: 'In memory of a visit to Berchtesgaden'. The photo is the only one that shows the princess in the company of the Führer, unusually wearing a lounge suit, and the other guests at the Berghof.

Before her return to London, while she was still staying at Munich's Vier Jahreszeiten hotel, Adolf Hitler also sent her a further token of his special friendship – a large bunch of roses as well as a sheepdog puppy, which she immediately christened Wolf, after Hitler's favourite Alsatian.

Back in London, Stephanie wrote him an extravagant four-page letter of thanks:

> 14, Bryanston Square
> London
> 12.1.37
>
> My very dear Reich Chancellor,
> Our goodbyes were so hurried and surrounded by so many people, that I hardly had time to thank you properly for your hospitality.
>
> You are a charming host – not to mention your beautiful and excellently run home in that magnificent setting – which all leave me with a wonderful and lasting impression. It is no empty phrase when I say, Herr Reich Chancellor, that I enjoyed every minute of my stay with you.
>
> 'My' dog visited me in Munich; he is very – very handsome. The man who brought him felt it would not be a good idea to take him with me straight away, without letting him first get used to me. As I am very selfish and want him to be really 'my' dog – I immediately agreed to this and would now like to ask if it might be possible to keep the dog where he is – and then take him over later when I go to Austria?
>
> Your gift of the dog has given me great pleasure, not only because I love dogs – but also because, to me, dogs symbolise loyalty and friendship – which in this instance pleases me all the more.
>
> What a shame that you are no ordinary mortal, to whom one can say – I hope we meet again soon. . . !
> Once again, many thanks for the two wonderful days.
> In sincere friendship
>
> Stephanie Hohenlohe

Hitler asked his adjutant, Fritz Wiedemann, to reply to Stephanie, now at the Igls Golf Hotel near Innsbruck, to say that the dog could stay in Munich for the time being. The princess never did pick up the animal. Wiedemann went on to thank her personally, and very warmly, for the two gifts sent to him from Paris labelled 'Samples: no commercial value' and signed off with a *'Heil Hitler'*. We have no clue as to what handsome gift the princess had sent to the adjutant. Wiedemann and 'Her Highness' had known each other at least since the Reich Party Rally of 1935.

Princess Stephanie's son, Prince Franz, writes in his biography of his mother that it was during her 1937 visit to the Obersalzberg that she made friends with Hitler's adjutant, a 'very cultivated, well brought-up man with considerable charm'.

However, we may suppose that on her frequent visits to the Reich Chancellery as a courier, she saw Wiedemann time and again. What is more, in November 1936, Fritz Wiedemann turned up at the Hotel Adlon in Berlin to see Princess Stephanie, on the pretext that he wanted to hand over in person a photograph and a letter from Hitler for Lord Rothermere.

Wiedemann asked 'Your Highness' – initially he wrote to the Princess in English – whether she could personally take the letter to Lord Rothermere; he also asked her to let him know where she could be reached. He went on to convey the Führer's warmest good wishes and ended: 'I kiss your hand as your very devoted Wiedemann.'

It was on this occasion at the Adlon that the two became closer. When Stephanie von Hohenlohe and Fritz Wiedemann fell in love with each other, both were forty-five years old. Wiedemann had been married for eighteen years to the kind and good-natured Anna-Luise, known as 'Gueggi', the daughter of a wealthy Zürich silk manufacturer, and they had three children.

The Führer's adjutant simply oozed charm and missed no opportunity to pay court to a beautiful woman. The daughter of the American ambassador in Berlin at that time, Martha Dodd, who attended many parties given by the top Nazis, gushed about the 'eroticism' exuded by this 'strong-man' in Hitler's closest circle. The young American woman saw him as: 'Tall, dark, muscular, he certainly had great physical brawn and the appearance of bravery . . . Wiedemann's heavy face, with beetling eyebrows, friendly eyes and an extremely low forehead, was rather attractive . . . But I got the impression of an uncultivated, primitive mind, with the shrewdness and cunning of an animal, and completely without delicacy or subtlety.'[7]

She went on: 'Certainly Wiedemann was a dangerous man to cross, for despite his social naiveté and beguiling clumsiness, he was as ruthless a fighter and schemer as some of his compatriots.'[8] Sadly, the princess has not left any record of her impression of Fritz Wiedemann, except to comment on his unattractive 'Prussian haircut'.

The six-foot tall Friedrich Wiedemann was born in Augsburg on 16 August 1891, took his school-leaving examination there and immediately embarked on a military career. Wiedemann and Adolf Hitler had known each other since the First World War, when they served together in the 16th Reserve Infantry Regiment, Wiedemann as a staff adjutant, Hitler as a messenger. In fact Wiedemann was Hitler's immediate superior. On 20 December 1918, a few weeks after the German surrender, Wiedemann was transferred to the 3rd Bavarian Infantry Regiment in Augsburg. On 19 June 1919 he was discharged from the army as a redundant officer, with the rank of 'acting captain'; on 18 December of that year he was retrospectively promoted to full captain, backdated to 18 October 1918.

Starting in July 1919 he became a small farmer with 20 acres in the Allgäu region of south-western Bavaria; then in 1921 he moved to Fuchsgrub in Lower Bavaria. It was there, in 1932, that he and some others set up the 'Pfarrkirchen Central Dairy', though the business soon ran into trouble with the Nazi authorities for giving short measure on its butter deliveries.

In 1933, when things were going badly for Wiedemann financially, he asked two old army friends, Bruno Horn and Max Amann, now a Nazi newspaper owner, to put in a word for him with Hitler and see whether he could be made an officer in the Reichswehr, the regular army of the Weimar Republic.

Before Christmas that year he had a meeting with Hitler at the Brown House in Munich, where the Führer offered him a post as his personal adjutant. So it was that on 1 February 1934 Wiedemann started work, initially for an induction period, on the staff of Rudolf Hess, the Deputy Führer. A month later, Hess' secretary, Martin Bormann, summoned Wiedemann, who was not then a member of the Nazi Party; Bormann offered him a starting salary of 400 Reichsmarks per month and accepted him as a party member, with a membership number somewhere above 3,600,000.

From the Brown House, the headquarters of the Nazi Party, Wiedemann went, on 2 January 1935, to the Reich Chancellery in Berlin, as Personal Adjutant to Adolf Hitler. Hitler continued to address Wiedemann by his military rank, as 'Captain', though there could be no doubt about which of them was the senior now. And Wiedemann recalled that this was the same man he had once ordered to give the canteen a coat of paint in France. In his memoirs he commented: 'It was certainly not the first time in world history that a man of humble and obscure origins . . . was driven to achieve things of which no-one would have thought him capable.' However, the welcome Wiedemann received in Berlin was less than cordial, especially from those who saw their own influence threatened by his closeness to Hitler.

It was known that Wiedemann was 'downright alarming in his youthful zeal for the Party' and that Hitler had a particularly soft spot for him. As Wiedemann recalled wryly: 'So as to appal my Party colleagues even more, I actually wore a monocle.'

In 1937 Hitler employed four personal adjutants: SA *Gruppenführer* Wilhelm Brückner; Julius Schaub, former head of his bodyguard, who had once been imprisoned with Hitler in Landsberg Castle, and rose to become his private secretary, general factotum and 'note book'; Fritz Wiedemann, and finally Albert Bormann, brother of the 'grey eminence', Martin Bormann, who in 1941 became chief of the Nazi Party Central Office, with the rank of minister.

Wiedemann made no secret of the fact that Hitler frequently gave him expensive presents, one of which was a six-seat Mercedes-Benz saloon. In 1934, through the publisher Max Amann, and very probably on Hitler's instructions, Wiedemann received a loan of 10,000 Reichsmarks, which he urgently needed for the dairy business in Fuchsgrub. Even while serving as an adjutant Wiedemann had retained his financial interest in the dairy. The good people of Fuchsgrub must surely have been amazed when Princess Stephanie went to visit him there in her luxurious drophead coupé. She asked to be given a guided tour of the dairy and met the entire Wiedemann family. Clearly, there was no question of the Wiedemanns separating.

At the start of his friendship with the princess, Wiedemann was given an important personal instruction by Hitler. He was authorised to disburse up to 20,000 Reichsmarks as a maintenance allowance. 'In money matters Hitler was very generous, because he had no feel for the value of money', Wiedemann said. He made extravagant use of his financial privilege, for the princess had her hotel and restaurant bills, telephone expenses, taxi and air fares and sometimes the clothes she bought, all charged to her friend Wiedemann's account.

Stephanie von Hohenlohe enjoyed Munich very much. In the summer of 1937, as she was strolling around the city, she ran into a man whom she had got to know well during her days and nights spent in Deauville: King Alfonso XIII of Spain. The monarch, who continued to cling to the Divine Right of his royal house of Bourbón y Austria to rule Spain, had left that country in 1931 but had not renounced his claim to the throne. In 1935, on the eve of the Spanish Civil War, Stephanie had, at the request of the king, who was staying in London at the time, asked Rothermere if he might support Alfonso in his efforts to return to the throne of Spain. However the press baron had emphatically dismissed the idea.

When they met in Munich, King Alfonso invited the art-loving princess to join him in a visit to the exhibition of 'Decadent Art', which the Nazis were currently showing in the city, in an attempt to discredit leading modern artists, especially if they happened to be Jewish. The king said he needed 'moral support'. There were no posters advertising the 'Decadent Art' show, only a slip printed in red, inserted in the catalogue of the 'Great Exhibition of German Art', which mockingly drew attention to the other exhibition a short distance away, in the Museum of Castings of Classical Sculptures.

King Alfonso XIII of Spain and Stephanie von Hohenlohe were among more than two million visitors who went to look at the paintings of Paul Klee, Max Beckmann, Otto Dix, Vasily Kandinsky, Jean Cocteau, Max Ernst, Giorgio de Chirico, Salvador Dalí and others – works which were described by the Nazis as 'the outpourings of lunacy'.

The paintings were deliberately hung badly in small rooms. Yet Stephanie and the Spanish king were thrilled by them, and felt none of the 'moral outrage' so earnestly desired by the National Socialists. We do not know whether the princess also visited the 'Great Art Exhibition' in the 'House of German Art', in order to be enthralled by the pure and noble creations of 'Aryan' artists.

The year 1937 also brought special recognition for Stephanie. For her tireless activities on behalf of the German Reich she was awarded, with Adolf Hitler's express approval, the Honorary Cross of the German Red Cross by its president, the Duke of Saxe-Coburg-Gotha. As the princess was staying at the Ritz in Paris at the time, her friend, Captain Fritz Wiedemann, travelled there and personally decorated her with the medal. He also handed her a document from Hitler authorising the award.

The year ended with a very friendly letter from the Reich Chancellor to his 'dear princess'. In it he thanked her at length for her work and for the sympathy she had shown for the German people.

In the following year, 1938, the princess received surprising, not to say sensational, news. On 8 June Fritz Wiedemann cabled her in Paris: 'Recommend you come Berlin urgently as Chief wants speak you this week.' Not even Wiedemann himself was yet privy to the fact that his mistress was to be formally honoured by the Führer.

On 10 June 1938 the princess spent many hours with Hitler in the Reich Chancellery, where a remarkable and solemn ceremony took place: Stephanie, Princess von Hohenlohe-Waldenburg-

Schillingsfürst, born plain Steffi Richter, both of whose parents were Jewish, became 'a bride of the National Socialist Workers' Party' as the Führer pinned the Nazi Party's Gold Medal of Honour to her bosom. The medal bore his signature on its reverse.

This award was reserved for a tiny handful of individuals. It was presented by Hitler exclusively to long-standing party members, whose membership number was lower than 100,000, as well as to 'those who have rendered outstanding service to the National Socialist movement and to the achievement of its goals'. Stephanie was now a *de facto* party member and of German blood, in other words an 'honorary Aryan'.[9]

Quite apart from the award of the party's Gold Medal, the fact that Stephanie had a four-hour audience with the Führer caused great surprise and considerable annoyance among his inner circle. One man who was particularly incensed was Herbert von Dirksen, who had been German ambassador to the Soviet Union from 1928 to 1933. He recalled that on his return from Moscow he had tried several times without success to have a personal interview with Hitler. Casting an eye towards Stephanie von Hohenlohe, he could not resist writing: '[Hitler] had received *her* for a conversation lasting several hours, a distinction that he notoriously denied the official representatives of the Reich abroad.'[10]

Even someone as senior as Göring expressed amazement that the Führer should spend four hours in conversation with the princess. He told Stephanie that he was fully informed about it: 'I know everything. It's my job to know everything.' To which Stephanie retorted: 'But do you actually know everything we talked about in all that time, *Herr Feldmarschall?*' Naturally, he was forced to admit he did not. But he was pleased when Stephanie, in order to quell his curiosity a little, told him that Hitler had also talked about *him*.

Stephanie was convinced that 'every one of their clique yearned to have the Führer or at least his ear, exclusively to himself. Every visit of mine to the Reich Chancellery seemed to them an impudent encroachment on their sacred privileges, and every hour that Adolf wasted upon me was an hour which he might have spent to so much greater advantage in their devoted company.'

It is striking that Stephanie von Hohenlohe here refers to Hitler by his first name. This could indicate that she was on such close terms with the Reich Chancellor that she addressed him with the intimate *Du*, something that would have to be scrupulously avoided in official company. One of the few other women who were on such close terms with Adolf Hitler was the English-born Winifred Wagner, daughter-in-law of the great composer and châtelaine of Bayreuth.

CHAPTER FOUR

Stephanie's Adversary: Joachim von Ribbentrop

We do not know when Princess Stephanie and Joachim von Ribbentrop first met. But we do know that when Lord Rothermere invited the Reich Chancellor and his party to dinner at the Adlon Hotel in Berlin in 1934, Stephanie von Hohenlohe was placed next to Ribbentrop. In her draft memoir, the Princess goes into considerable detail about Hitler's foreign policy adviser. She saw him as the man 'who considered himself the one and only political authority on England in the Third Reich, and anyone who did not agree with him that the English were hopelessly decadent, that they would never stand up to fight against the Germans, and that their world empire has reached its zero hour, was a personal enemy of his'.

Stephanie had made a fairly close study of the leading Nazis, including Hitler, Göring, Hess, Goebbels, Himmler and Julius Streicher. None of them had ever been to Britain. None could speak or write a word of English; most of them came from the lower middle class and had had very variable upbringing and education. Joachim von Ribbentrop, the one-time champagne salesman, was the only one of them with international experience. Before marrying into a wealthy German family he had spent much of his early life in England and Canada; he spoke exceptionally good English, dressed impeccably and always took care to behave like an English gentleman.

Ribbentrop, Stephanie wrote, 'was fairly justified in seeing himself as the only man of the world in the upper hierarchy of the Party'. However, she also saw how Ribbentrop overestimated himself when he posed as the great expert on Britain. She found his notions of Britain 'puerile, ignorant of all deeper issues and often tragically misleading', yet she did admit he was superficially well informed. By contrast, she felt that neither Hitler, Göring nor Hess had the first idea about Britain.

In November 1934, as Hitler's foreign policy adviser, Ribbentrop spent three weeks in London. He was deluged with invitations, which he gladly accepted. There he met not only Lord Rothermere and Princess Stephanie, but many others including Sir Austen Chamberlain (the former Foreign Secretary), George Bernard Shaw and the Archbishop of Canterbury. As Ribbentrop's biographer writes: 'It was the kind of world he liked, the world in which he wanted to move – rich, influential men, members of the best clubs, who were accustomed to the lower classes looking up to them with deference.'[1]

Naturally, Ribbentrop was interested to know more about this princess who was featuring so prominently in Hitler's orbit. So he began to look into her past, always hoping he would find some dark corner that would give him a reason to advise the Führer to be more sceptical towards her. 'Thus, in his eyes, I became an arch-fiend, a subversive meddler, a pestilential intruder.'

The British journalist Ward Price, whom Hitler held in high regard, shared the princess's opinion of Ribbentrop: 'His career was much more cosmopolitan' than those of the Chancellor's closest colleagues.

Ribbentrop was born in 1892, in the Rhineland town of Wesel, the son of an army officer. He spent his youth in various countries, where he quickly learned English and French. From the age of fifteen to seventeen he lived in Switzerland and England, and when he was eighteen he and his younger brother Lothar went to Canada. He went into business there, and moved in high society, but when the First World War broke out he returned to Germany. Rumour had it that he was deported for suspected espionage activities. He joined the German army, was awarded the Iron Cross 1st Class and promoted to *Oberleutnant*.

In 1920 he married Annelies Henkel, daughter of the enormously rich producer of Germany's most famous *Sekt*, the champagne of the Rhine. Ribbentrop was an excellent violinist, owned racehorses, hunted chamois in the mountains, and played golf well. But his subsequent career was truly astonishing. In the words of the German historian Joachim Fest, Ribbentrop rose rapidly to the top despite 'a downright dangerous lack of competence'.

At his very first encounter with Hitler, Ribbentrop was so impressed by him that he was convinced this was the only man who, with his party, could save Germany from communism.

The relationship between Ribbentrop and the princess became more complicated when he realised that she was the mistress of a man who had an extraordinarily powerful influence over Hitler – Fritz Wiedemann. Ribbentrop saw his own standing with Hitler now under threat from Wiedemann. And Wiedemann himself had a very low opinion of Ribbentrop.

Ribbentrop then found out that the princess was keen to see Hitler's adjutant made a minister, preferably Reich Foreign Minister. On this subject Stephanie's maid, Wally Oeler, commented: 'She always sleeps with Captain Wiedemann now, that's why I don't trust him. She wants to make a minister of him, come hell or high water . . . If he's to be a minister, he'll have to have done something special. So Milady is fixing it for him.'[2]

Ribbentrop's stubbornly anti-British attitude and Wiedemann's anglophile tendencies collided. At all events Ribbentrop 'made his personal contribution to the growing aversion to the Third Reich, which could be sensed in Britain'.[3] As Stephanie assures us in her memoir, Ribbentrop's motto was: 'War with Britain at any time, at any cost and under all circumstances.' Indeed, after Hitler, Ribbentrop was the greatest warmonger of all the Nazis.

In 1936 Ribbentrop was appointed German ambassador to Britain. Despite his protestations to the contrary, Ribbentrop apparently felt this posting to be a setback in his career planning. As a typical courtier, he presumably feared that once he was away from the capital his position would be undermined by cabals and political in-fighters. The elegant London building that housed the German embassy had been remodelled during the winter of 1936–7. Its location above the Mall, the processional avenue between Buckingham Palace and Admiralty Arch, could scarcely be more advantageous. At Hitler's request, his personal architect, Albert Speer, was summoned to London to oversee the conversion of the embassy premises. It was to be ready in time for the coronation of King George VI and was to make a special impression during the social events that would follow. The furniture was based on designs by Speer's mentor, Professor Troost, and shipped from Germany to save on foreign currency. Even the workmen on site were German. However, Speer tells us that Annelies von Ribbentrop chose the lavish décor herself, and he felt rather superfluous.[4]

The inauguration of the building duly took place in time for the coronation festivities in May 1937. Ribbentrop had invited Hitler's adjutant, Fritz Wiedemann, to a coronation party, as a member of the official German delegation, along with 1,400 other guests. But the princess's name was not on the invitation list.

However, Princess Stephanie was not going to accept this snub without a fight. She had to defend her quasi-official status in the German delegation. Lord Rothermere gave her the job of looking after the German guests and especially the head of the delegation, Werner von Blomberg, the Reich Minister of War, whom she was to interview for Rothermere. Blomberg had been sent as the representative of the German Chancellor and was staying at the ambassador's private residence.

The princess told Wiedemann to ask the Führer to have a word with Ribbentrop. When she had apprised Wiedemann of the situation in London, he broached the matter with Hitler, who ordered that the princess be invited immediately. Even so, it needed a second command from 'on high' before Ribbentrop decided to ask the princess to the party. Hitler even gave Ribbentrop an ultimatum, and forced him to apologise to Princess von Hohenlohe.

So it was that the first official appearance of the ill-matched couple, the personal adjutant of the German Reich Chancellor in the company of the divorced princess, thus took place in May 1937 at the German embassy in London, on the occasion of the coronation of George VI. The reason Ribbentrop had given for failing to invite the princess – of whom even in England it was whispered that she was a Jewess – was that the British aristocracy would refuse even to meet 'the Hohenlohe woman', let alone spend an evening with her. However, Ribbentrop's fears were unfounded.

Wiedemann was also thoroughly pleased with the outcome: 'When I escorted the princess to the reception, and she set foot inside the German embassy, I could observe how very warmly she was greeted on all sides, and everywhere accepted as a member of high society. Under the eyes of all the guests, she cleverly approached the Duke of Kent, the new king's younger brother, who courteously got up from his chair and engaged her in animated conversation for several minutes.'

Although Ribbentrop had predicted that as soon as the princess appeared, several guests, and notably the Duke of Kent, would immediately leave the party, on that night of 13 May nothing of the kind occurred. The guests included the brother of the Japanese emperor, the chief of the French General Staff, General Gamelin, and senior members of the British government. Only two weeks after the reception, Neville Chamberlain would succeed the retiring prime minister, Stanley Baldwin, but that evening Chamberlain was attending as Chancellor of the Exchequer, together with the Foreign Secretary, Anthony Eden. The following year, Eden would resign over the appeasement of Germany and be replaced by Lord Halifax, who was also at the coronation party. Another, perhaps more surprising guest was Winston Churchill MP, now sixty-three years old and out of office, but constantly warning Parliament of the Nazi threat. Also present were Lord and Lady Redesdale, parents of the egregious Mitford sisters, one of whom, Unity, was to become Stephanie's rival for the favour of Adolf Hitler.

Musical interludes were provided by Frieda Leider, of the Chicago Civic Opera who, from 1942, was a Nazi-approved soloist at the

Berlin State Opera, and Rudolf Bockelmann, another 'official' Nazi singer. Dancing went on until the early hours of the morning, to the legendary Barnabas von Géczy Orchestra, which was known as 'Hitler's house band'.

The evening turned into a social triumph for the princess, and she relished it to the full. On this occasion she had beaten Ribbentrop on his own turf. Even so, Wiedemann observed that after this successful performance by his mistress, relations between her and Ribbentrop were not quite so strained. In Ribbentrop's own memoirs, *Between London and Moscow*, we find not a word about his problems with 'the Führer's dear princess'.

A year later, Stephanie von Hohenlohe could scarcely believe it when Ribbentrop invited her to meet him for a discussion at the Kaiserhof hotel in Berlin. Ribbentrop, who by now had been promoted to Reich Foreign Minister, ran his office from a luxury suite at the hotel. The discussion that followed lasted an hour, but Ribbentrop did most of the talking. The chief point he wanted to convey to his guest was that the Führer was all too often misrepresented in the British and American press. In fact there had been no concrete reason for von Ribbentrop to summon Stephanie. Yet he knew that it was important for him to be on the best of terms with Hitler's 'ambassadress' – as she referred to herself.

Stephanie left the Kaiserhof with a great sense of relief. The reason for this was that, prior to the meeting, she had not been altogether sure whether Ribbentrop's invitation might not have some connection with a conversation she had had with Göring earlier the same day, of which more will be said.

CHAPTER FIVE

Lady Astor and the Cliveden Set

An article in the Home News section of the London *Daily Herald* of 1 July 1938, was headlined: 'Hitler's "dear princess" must pay £46 laundry bill', and ran as follows:

> Sued for a £46 laundry-bill at Brentford (Middlesex) County Court, Princess Stephanie von Hohenlohe-Waldenburg-Schillingsfuerst, in whose luxury Mayfair home stands a signed portrait of Hitler dedicated to his 'dear friend, the Princess', did not appear and was not represented . . .
>
> Judge Drucquer gave judgement by default to the laundry . . .
>
> Described on the [court] list as 'Her Serene Highness', the princess is one of the most powerful leaders of the Nazi colony here. She it is who provides a social platform for Hitler's envoys – not only in this country, but in the United States, too.
>
> In her house in Brook St, London W., there is a huge display of photographs of many of the most prominent figures in recent political history. Hitler is among them. . . . Her wholehearted admiration of Hitler has led to a close friendship between the two, and the Fuehrer has given her one of the highest decorations of Nazi Germany.

In the same year a journalist named William Hillman wrote an item for the *International News Service* under the headline: 'Princess Hohenlohe bewilders Europe as Hitler's "Madame de Staël"'. In it he named the princess 'Europe's Number One secret diplomat, Hitler's mysterious courier', and 'a modern Madame de Staël'. Hillman believed she had a very great influence on Hitler, and also that Hitler needed her.

Even the American press was taking an interest in this woman, who so clearly enjoyed the Führer's favour. Thus, the US journalist Hugo George Robosz told readers of the *New York Mirror* this about the princess's political influence: 'Her apartment in Mayfair has become the focus for those British aristocrats who have a friendly stance towards Nazi Germany. Her soirées are the talk of the town. Prominently displayed in her drawing-room is a huge portrait of Hitler. So it was only natural that her efforts on the Führer's behalf would also bring her into contact with the "Cliveden Set", whose members include some of the most important statesmen of the British Empire.'

The Cliveden Set was a group of people sympathetic to Germany, who advocated a policy of appeasement towards the Nazi regime. It existed alongside two other informal pro-German associations in London: the Link, and the Anglo-German Fellowship. Together they formed the basis for National Socialist infiltration of Britain, both on the political and the propaganda level. The Link received financial support from Berlin; it and the Anglo-German Fellowship were also backed by Lord Rothermere and his son Esmond. So it is no surprise that Princess Stephanie was made an honorary member of the Anglo-German Fellowship. Her most important and influential friends in this association were Lord Elibank[1] and Lord Sempill.[2] It was through these two members of the House of Lords that the princess was kept constantly informed about shifts in policy and sentiment within the British government.

But Stephanie also belonged to the exclusive Cliveden Set. This informal grouping took its name from the Thames-side country house, Cliveden, near Maidenhead, owned by Lord and Lady Astor. Lady Astor (1879–1964) was born Nancy Witcher Langhorne and brought up in Virginia, one of the five exceptionally good-looking Langhorne sisters. After an unhappy marriage to Robert Gould Shaw she was on her way to Europe in 1905 when she met William

Waldorf Astor (1879–1952), who in 1919 succeeded his father to become Viscount Astor of Hever. Before that, from 1910 to 1919, Astor had been the MP for Plymouth and, in the Lords, he continued his political career as a junior minister in the Foreign Office. In 1931 he was Britain's delegate to the League of Nations. Since 1911, Astor had also owned the London Sunday newspaper, *The Observer*,[3] and the *Pall Mall Gazette*, and was said to be one of the richest men in the world.[4] Nancy and William rushed headlong into marriage. At their wedding in May 1906 the bride's father made Nancy a present of Cliveden, as well as a London town house in St James's Square. Cliveden had been owned by the Astor family since 1893. Modelled on the Villa Albano in Rome, it was designed and built for the Duke of Sutherland by Sir Charles Barry, the architect of the Houses of Parliament, and stands on a wooded hill overlooking a bend in the Thames, upstream from Maidenhead.[5]

In the 1920s and 1930s Nancy Astor invited a long list of important figures to Cliveden, including the Queen of Rumania, George Bernard Shaw, Charlie Chaplin, the Irish playright Sean O'Casey, King George V and Queen Mary, Henry Ford, King Gustav of Sweden, and the Prince of Wales, later King Edward VIII. Nancy occasionally played golf with the prince and paid him the dubious compliment that it required a great deal of skill to lose a match against him.

Apart from this, Nancy, like her husband, devoted her life to social and political causes. In 1919, when Astor became a peer, Nancy took over his parliamentary seat and was the first woman to be elected to the House of Commons (as a Conservative), even before women were given the vote. She held her seat continuously until 1945, concerning herself with women's rights, state education and employment legislation, and campaigned for social reform. Her doughty duels of words inside and outside the House of Commons are genuine high points of this period. Her son David describes her as highly intelligent, and as an intuitive woman with great warmth of heart. Yet her kindness and affection for people were marred by intolerance. This trait in her character became more pronounced when she joined the Christian Science Church in 1914. She became even less tolerant towards her political and religious opponents – especially against the Roman Catholic Church, the Jews, and other minorities.

Nancy Astor admired not only Hitler's political leadership, but also his lifestyle. He neither drank nor smoked and this was very important to someone who had advocated Prohibition in the United States. Among the British Labour Party, Lady Astor was seen as trying to impose a pro-Hitler policy on the country. She was considered as a woman who was 'fighting bravely for Hitler and Mussolini'.

In London there were other hostesses who played a high-profile role in the three pro-German circles already mentioned. One was Lady Londonderry, wife of the Marquess of Londonderry, holder since 1935 the office of Lord Privy Seal, and another was Lady (Emerald) Cunard, another American-born Englishwoman. Lady Cunard, the widow of Sir Bache Cunard, maintained a literary and musical salon and was known as 'the Queen of Covent Garden'. In 1935 she was full of enthusiasm not only for Hitler but also for Ambassador Ribbentrop, and it was said that she, through Wallis Simpson, influenced the Prince of Wales to favour Germany. It was at the instigation of Lady Cunard that the conductor, Sir Thomas Beecham, gave a concert in the Berlin Philharmonic Hall, which Hitler himself attended.

In 1936 Lord and Lady Londonderry visited Hitler together; in February 1937 she described Hitler as the symbol of the new Germany, as its creator and a born leader, a captivating personality and a man who possessed the greatness 'to act in a perfectly normal way'. She was convinced that he was a guarantor of peace and of friendship with the British. He had preserved Germany from communism and he alone 'could be relied upon to save Europe'.

Through Nancy Astor, Stephanie made the acquaintance of yet another influential hostess: Margot Asquith[6] (Countess of Oxford and Asquith), the widow of a former prime minister, H.H. Asquith.[7] Her political dinner-parties were famous for their sophisticated, intelligent conversation. It was a genuine honour to be invited to her political salon. Stephanie was so fascinated by this Englishwoman that she intended to devote a whole chapter to her in the memoirs which, alas, were never written.

Lady Oxford had become a fervent admirer of the conductor Arturo Toscanini. As she often spent the summer months in Schloss Fuschl, a castle near Salzburg that Stephanie von Hohenlohe used to rent, Lady Oxford would attend every concert she could get to in the area, if it was conducted by Toscanini.

A frequent guest of Lady Astor at Cliveden was Joachim von Ribbentrop, whom she had known since the early 1930s. Once she asked him to lunch at a restaurant in St James's Square, not far from her London house. 'When someone in the restaurant came up to speak to him, his right arm shot into the air and he shouted "*Heil Hitler!*" I said: "None of that nonsense in here, thank you." I thought it was supposed to be a joke, but he was quite serious.' After a dinner with Ribbentrop, the hostess wrote that Ribbentrop had talked of a very uneasy Hitler, who thought that 'Britain would always treat him with condescension'.

At Cliveden Ribbentrop and Nancy Astor would often engage in fairly mild battles of words. Reinhard Spitzy, Ribbentrop's embassy secretary, recalled how the 'intelligent' Lady Astor was one of the people who tried again and again to pacify Ribbentrop in his tirades against Britain.

In February 1938 a bombshell was dropped. The highly respected London journalist, Claud Cockburn, published an article in *The Week*, a magazine he edited, exposing the Cliveden Set. He wrote: 'An informal but powerful pro-German group constitutes a second British Foreign Office', and claimed that high-ranking politicians foregathered at Cliveden every weekend. British foreign policy, he said, was no longer really being made in the Foreign Office but at Cliveden. His article unleashed a storm of speculation, but no-one was able to contradict him.

Looking back on this period, Stephanie wrote that after 1933 many people were indeed convinced that Adolf Hitler's new Germany should be given stronger support. All the same, she considered it 'ridiculous and futile to seek a political conspiracy behind these tendencies. The term "Cliveden Set", which was later bandied about by influential journalists, was an exaggeration. The Cliveden Set simply consisted of a number of leading British figures, who enjoyed Nancy Astor's hospitality over long and interesting weekends. It is correct to say that at Cliveden people frequently gathered, who had an emollient attitude towards conditions in the new Germany – but in those days "appeasement" was hardly a dirty word.'

It goes without saying that, from the outset, both the policy of 'appeasement' and genuine sympathy with Nazi Germany provoked determined and influential opposition. And the one politician who showed such great foresight in his warnings and in the political line he pursued was also a welcome guest of Lady Astor at Cliveden: it was there that Stephanie von Hohenlohe met Winston Churchill.

CHAPTER SIX

Stephanie, Wiedemann and the Windsors

Admirers of Adolf Hitler were not only to be found in the British Houses of Parliament; but on the very throne itself, in the person of King Edward VIII.

On 10 December 1936, after having succeeded to the throne only a few months earlier, the king abdicated, saying that he could not live without his great love, Mrs Wallis Simpson, but was not permitted to rule with her as his consort.[1]

In Hitler's view, the departure of the King of England from his throne was a disaster for Anglo-German relations. As early as January 1936, shortly after succeeding to the throne, the king had sent word to Hitler via a German kinsman, Carl Eduard, Duke of Saxe-Coburg-Gotha, to say that he believed an alliance between Great Britain and Germany was politically necessary and that it could even lead to a military pact including France. It was therefore his wish, King Edward said, to speak personally to the Reich Chancellor as soon as possible, either in Britain or Germany.

Hitler saw Edward's abdication as a victory for those forces in Britain that were hostile to Germany. Joachim von Ribbentrop, the German ambassador in London, confirmed Hitler's view that 'the King had a pro-German and anti-Jewish attitude, and had been deposed as the result of an anti-German conspiracy in which Jews, freemasons and powerful political interests had made common cause'.[2] Joseph Goebbels' comment on the king's abdication was less than friendly: 'He has made a complete fool of himself. What's more it was lacking in dignity and taste. It was not the way to do it. Especially if one is king.'[3]

When King Edward VIII saw that he was being forced to abandon the throne, rumours circulated not only in Germany, but also in Britain and the USA, about a 'plot behind the scenes' to remove the 'pro-Nazi' monarch. The fact that, in December 1936, the German press received instructions from the very highest level to be particularly reticent in its coverage of the Abdication Crisis, shows what far-reaching consequences these events were seen to have.

In London, Wallis Simpson found in her immediate vicinity someone to defend her love for the king. By pure coincidence, Mrs Simpson was living in Bryanston Court, near Marble Arch – the same building in which Stephanie had her apartment. And Stephanie was very favourably disposed towards the royal love affair. Edward, as Prince of Wales, had also known the princess for quite some time, having met her at various golf-clubs in England and the South of France.

Consequently, the press barons Lord Beaverbrook and Lord Rothermere, together with Princess Stephanie, stood up as champions of the king's cause. Stephanie had floated the idea of a morganatic marriage. As the best example of this, Stephanie reminded them of the marriage between the Heir Apparent to the Austrian throne, Crown Prince Franz Ferdinand, and the Countess Sophie Chotek who, though well-born, was by no means of royal blood. Had the couple not been so fatefully assassinated in Sarajevo in 1914, Franz Ferdinand would have duly become Emperor, but Sophie would only have been his consort, without the title of Empress; nor would children of that marriage have had any rights of succession.

Lord Rothermere's son, Esmond Harmsworth, invited Wallis Simpson to dinner and drew her attention to this possible form of marriage, for which she was most grateful. Yet what was feasible in other European dynasties failed in Britain. Since there is no tradition of morganatic marriage in English law, a special Act of

Parliament would be necessary. On 25 November, the prime minister, Stanley Baldwin, had a private meeting with the king, who asked him if such a measure might be possible. Baldwin said he would consult his cabinet and the prime ministers of the dominions on this question. On 2 December the two men met again, and Baldwin told the king that 'neither in the dominions nor here would there be any prospect of such legislation being accepted'. Baldwin reported this to the House of Commons on 10 December 1936, and added that, as far as His Majesty was concerned, 'the matter was closed. I never heard another word about it from him.'[4]

Nancy Astor, Edward's golf-partner of many years, had pleaded tearfully with him to give up Mrs Simpson once and for all. The reason was not that she was American, but that she had already been divorced twice and without the dispensation of the Church. The Archbishop of Canterbury therefore asserted that the king had no choice but to abdicate if he wanted to wed Mrs Simpson.

Finally, on 10 December 1936 King Edward VIII ordered his Abdication Statement to be read out to both Houses of Parliament in London. In the gallery of the House of Lords the statement was heard by a woman who, as the daughter of a peer, was entitled to be there. She was the fascist, Unity Mitford,[5] who had just returned from Germany. 'Oh dear, Hitler will be dreadfully upset about this', she wailed. 'He wanted Edward to stay on the throne.'

Joachim von Ribbentrop was certainly one of many who tried to use Wallis Simpson as a way of gaining access to Edward. His admiration for Mrs Simpson was also demonstrated by the fact that during his frequent stays in London he would have a bouquet of seventeen roses delivered every morning to her flat in Bryanston Court. Those roses were a popular topic of conversation, not only in London, but in Berlin's diplomatic circles. Even Adolf Hitler teasingly questioned his ambassador as to the secret of the seventeen roses. There was also talk of Ribbentrop sending baskets of orchids to Wallis Simpson. In Berlin's Wilhelmstrasse, headquarters of the Foreign Ministry, animosity towards Ribbentrop inspired numerous jibes about the 'pushy Nazi' and the 'travelling wine-salesman'.

There was even speculation about a sexual relationship between Wallis and Ribbentrop. The constant gossip about this 'love affair' annoyed Mrs Simpson so much that in May 1937 she gave an interview to an American journalist, Helena Normanton, in which she stated categorically that she had only met Ribbentrop on two occasions (although they frequently ran into each other at receptions). She vehemently denied being in any way whatsoever a tool of the Nazis in London.

But there was no denying the fact that Ribbentrop had got close to Wallis Simpson in the circles of Lady Cunard and Lady Astor, and had been able to influence her. Many people were well aware of this and the matter was even raised in the House of Commons. Speaking in the debate on the Abdication on 10 December, the communist MP and dedicated anti-monarchist, Willie Gallacher, observed: 'The King and Mrs Simpson do not live in a vacuum. Sinister processes are continually at work . . . The Prime Minister told us he was approached about a morganatic marriage . . . but he did not tell us who approached him . . . It is obvious that forces were encouraging . . . what was going on. [. . .] I want to draw your attention to the fact that Mrs Simpson has a social set, and every member of the cabinet knows that the social set of Mrs Simpson is closely identified with a certain foreign government and the ambassador of that foreign government.' [Hon. Members: 'No, no']. 'It is common knowledge . . .' Gallacher retorted, and went on to say that the only answer was for the monarchy to be abolished altogether.

On his abdication Edward and Mrs Simpson were granted the title of Duke and Duchess of Windsor, but had to leave Britain immediately. Their wedding took place quietly in France, on 3 June 1937. Meanwhile, 'Bertie', the eldest of his three younger brothers, ascended the throne as King George VI, with his wife Elizabeth as queen.

One of the first big projects the Windsors undertook in 1937 was a trip to National Socialist Germany. Now would come the meeting that Edward had wished for: as Duke of Windsor he visited Adolf Hitler, Chancellor of the German Reich, albeit not in Berlin, but at his private residence, the Berghof, near Berchtesgaden in Bavaria.

In the notes that Stephanie jotted down for her ghost-writer Rudolf Kommer, she points out that she played a major part in the planning and realisation of the ducal visit to Germany, though officially Fritz Wiedemann and Hitler's deputy, Rudolf Hess, were responsible for it. Stephanie's maid, Wally Oeler, later gave a detailed account to friends of hers in Berlin: 'He [Wiedemann] was the one who officially invited the Duke of Windsor to Germany, as soon as they heard that he wanted to come over for a visit . . . Anyway, express airmail letters written in pencil were going back and forth, and there were telephone conversations nearly every day.'

During their twelve-day visit in the second half of October 1937, the Duke and Duchess of Windsor were the official guests of Dr Robert Ley, the head of the German Labour Front. The travel and all the costs of their stay in Germany were paid for from German government funds. It was billed as a 'study-trip' to look at the country's social institutions. But behind this there was another agenda. After the humiliating treatment his wife had received from the British, the duke wanted to show her a country that would extend her a truly 'royal' welcome. The men in power in Berlin expected that in the not too distant future the former king of England would return to the throne 'under their patronage'.

The first call the Windsors paid was on Hermann Göring, at his extravagantly enlarged country house, Karinhall, on the Schorfheide heath, north-east of Berlin. The same evening, Foreign Minister von Ribbentrop gave a dinner for his guests at the very grand Horcher restaurant in Berlin. Paul-Otto Schmidt, chief interpreter at the Foreign Ministry, sat between the Duchess of Windsor and the actress Marianne Hopper. Goebbels found the duke a 'nice, friendly young man, clearly equipped with sound common sense'; the propaganda minister became 'really fond of him'. 'His wife is unassuming, but distinguished and elegant; though without any "side", a real lady . . . Magda is charmed by them too. Especially his wife.'

Then on 22 October, the Windsors visited Adolf Hitler in his mountain-top retreat, the Berghof. They only stayed a few hours, yet the visit provoked violently conflicting opinions in Britain, France and the USA. The tour of the German Reich by a former British monarch was taken to be a proclamation of solidarity with National Socialism.

Wiedemann picked the guests up at the railway station in Berchtesgaden, where a large number of press correspondents had gathered, among them Winston Churchill's son Randolph. After a short stroll along the shore of the Königsee lake, the party drove up to the Berghof, where Hitler came down the steps in front of his house and greeted his guests warmly. Hitler's mistress, Eva Braun, would have dearly loved to be introduced to the duke and duchess. But that was ruled out by Hitler, and she had to stay in her room.

To judge from the notes made by the interpreter, Paul Schmidt, the whole conversation that followed was very non-political. The duke, clearly well-disposed towards Germany, was very appreciative of the country's progress in the social sphere, for example the workers' welfare arrangements in the armaments company, Krupp of Essen. The duchess only contributed occasionally and with great reticence to the conversation, mainly when a topic of particular interest to her as a woman was raised.

After the Windsors' visit to Germany the Nazi press sang the praises of the duke and duchess. The newspapers recounted the touching story of how, when leaving Germany at the frontier, she pressed the entire contents of her purse into the hand of an SA man. 'It's for the KdF' [the 'Strength through Joy' organisation, which provided free holidays and recreation for industrial workers], were apparently her parting words.

The next time Stephanie von Hohenlohe met the Führer, she asked him what impression the duchess had made on him. 'Well, I must say she was most ladylike', Hitler replied. The princess was very pleased that, under the aegis of her friend Fritz Wiedemann, the Windsor visit had gone off to Hitler's complete satisfaction.

CHAPTER SEVEN

Trips to the USA and their Political Background

Stephanie von Hohenlohe loved travelling. Not only did she drive by car all over Europe with friends but she also found herself being lured by America. Although her first two trips to the USA appeared to be of a private nature, it turns out that even then she made contact with people in the press, who would later be useful to her when she went into exile there. She made her third trip to the States in the company of Hitler's adjutant, Fritz Wiedemann, and his wife Anna-Luise. Her fourth trip under the Third Reich was a political 'assignment' for Wiedemann.

In 1931, and again at the beginning of December 1932, Stephanie had travelled to New York, where she had been received by Kathleen Vanderbilt and her stockbroker husband, Harry Cushing Jr. From the first moment, Stephanie moved in America's high society circles and was deluged with invitations. At these parties she met Dr Rudolf Kommer, the agent of theatrical impresario Max Reinhardt, as well as the art collector Jack Hay Whitney, the composer Cole Porter, hotel owner Honoré Palmer, car manufacturer Walter P. Chrysler, and her relative by marriage, Prince Alfred Konstantin Chlodwig von Hohenlohe-Waldenburg-Schillingsfürst (1889–1948) and his wife Felicitas. Stephanie stayed at the Ambassador hotel; many of her friends gathered in her apartment there and though Prohibition was still in force alcohol flowed freely.

She spent Christmas in Wedgwood, Pennsylvania, with Alice and John C. Martin, owner of the *Saturday Evening Post* and *Ladies Home Journal* magazines, a newspaper, the *Philadelphia Ledger*, and other titles in the Curtis Martin Press. They proved to be amazingly influential hosts, who took the princess very much to their hearts.

At that time no-one could guess that after the Second World War Stephanie would work as a journalist on Martin's papers.

However, this trip ended with a bombshell. When Stephanie arrived on the liner at Southampton on 2 January 1933, she was collected in a Rolls-Royce by her mother. She seemed extremely nervous, and the joy at seeing her daughter's return was for some reason clouded. Stephanie soon discovered why. While she had been away in America, a German newspaper, the *Neue Freie Presse*, had run a story on 24 December 1932 under the headline 'Princess Hohenlohe arrested in Biarritz as a spy'. It said:

As reported in [the French newspaper] *Liberté*, a certain Princess von H [ohenlohe] has been arrested in Biarritz by the French political police, on charges of espionage and anti-French propaganda. It was claimed that the Princess had been engaged in intense correspondence with Lord Rothermere. These letters have been confiscated. Official sources in Paris, the Ministry of the Interior and the German embassy refuse to give further details. The local authorities in Biarritz immediately denied the report. However, *Liberté* claims it can confirm the mysterious arrest. The paper even claims to know that an application for bail has been turned down . . .

A day after Stephanie's arrival in England, on 3 January 1933, the following 'defence' appeared in the German press, in the form of an extremely poorly researched article:

Princess Stefanie [*sic*] Juliana zu Hohenlohe-Waldenburg-Schillingsfürst, about whom recent reports have appeared in certain French newspapers, to the effect that she had been arrested in Biarritz, arrived in Southampton yesterday from New

York on board the MS *Europa* and immediately drove to London. The Princess, who spent December in New York, is absolutely appalled by these reports in the chauvinistic French press. Last year she only spent a few days in Biarritz and travelled direct from there to the United States. The whole affair appears to be a plot engineered by the Poles against the Princess. The Princess is blamed for the publishing policy of Lord Rothermere, who, in a series of articles in the *Daily Mail*, has been arguing for a return of the Polish Corridor to Germany.[1] Princess Hohenlohe, who is a friend of Lord Rothermere, frequently accompanied him during his stays in Berlin to meetings with German politicians.

The fact is that in 1932 Stephanie had not spent a single day in Biarritz. She had long ago given up her villa there. She had travelled to New York from Southampton, not from France.

On her return to London, Stephanie immediately rang Lord Rothermere and asked his advice about what to do in this situation. He saw no reason at all for her to react either to the inaccuracies or the libellous statements in the article. But Stephanie's son Franz certainly believes that was bad advice.

After the original story had appeared, Rothermere had instructed his Paris bureau to gather information. In the end, it proved to be a matter of barefaced blackmail. Photographs, letters and telegrams, purporting to come from Rothermere, were offered for a modest sum. But since all the documents, and even a cheque bearing Rothermere's signature, proved to be forgeries, Rothermere, on the advice of his lawyers, took no action against the blackmailers. Stephanie was finally able to recall that, during her time in Paris, a 'peculiar' man had tried to sell her documents of some kind, but she had turned the offer down. Nonetheless, at the end of it all, the word 'spy' clung to the Princess.

In 1937 Stephanie succeeded in persuading Fritz Wiedemann to join her on a trip to the USA. Hitler certainly gave Wiedemann his blessing, but did not entrust him with any political mission. Nonetheless, Wiedemann managed to make it look as if he were on official business, since the American ambassador in Berlin, William E. Dodd, cabled the State Department on 16 November 1937: 'Wiedemann . . . is travelling to Washington for the purpose of consultations with the German Embassy on matters concerning the Reich.'

Wiedemann had booked a first-class cabin from Cherbourg to New York, on the German liner *Europa*. He paid for his own ticket, and those of his wife Anna-Luise, the Princess and her personal maid, all from the 'special fund' that had been put at his disposal. Even as he was leaving from Berlin's Lehrter station at about midnight, several American reporters had gathered despite the lateness of the hour. They wanted to know whether Wiedemann was being sent to take soundings among the German-American League. But Wiedemann said nothing.

Though Stephanie von Hohenlohe travelled in the company of the Wiedemanns, there was on board a strikingly handsome 41-year-old American baritone named Lawrence Tibbett, who at the time was adored by his female fans. Stephanie had first heard him sing at the Royal Opera House, Covent Garden, where she called on him in his dressing-room. The two of them hit it off, and from that developed a plan to travel to America on the same ship.

For the whole five-day crossing, Stephanie and Tibbett were inseparable. The fact that they spent the last night together in Stephanie's cabin was indiscreetly revealed later by Wally Oeler, Stephanie's personal maid. Until the end of June 1937, this young woman had been in service with Frau von Siemens in Berlin's lakeside suburb of Wannsee. When Stephanie was looking for a maid, Wiedemann was able to help her. He arranged a permit for Wally Oeler to leave Germany and, on behalf of the Princess von Hohenlohe, sent her a third-class train-ticket from Berlin to Paris. This was the beginning of her nomadic life with the princess, which she frequently talked about to her friends. Wally Oeler was astonishingly well informed and kept a journal. Thus, the question is raised as to whether the young woman could have been a Gestapo informer, even though, or precisely because, she was employed through the good offices of Fritz Wiedemann.

The party's arrival in New York on 25 November 1937 was hardly what they had been expecting. It was not just the German Consul-

General, Dr Hans Borchers, who came to greet them. A large press contingent was waiting for them, as were seventy-five policemen, some mounted, and a crowd chanting hostile slogans. They carried banners reading: 'Out with Wiedemann, the Nazi spy' or: 'I'm Wiedemann, Hitler's agent, and I've come to destroy democracy.' Security men had to hustle the new arrivals into waiting taxis.

Wiedemann then condescended to address a few words in English to the journalists. He said he was convinced that the opportunities for a lasting peace in Europe were better than a year before. He hoped to be received by President Roosevelt. But most of all, he just wanted to get to know the country he had heard so many good things about.

The travellers stayed for one night at the Waldorf-Astoria hotel, where Lawrence Tibbett had also checked in. The next day they took the train to Washington. During the journey, sandwiches were served by a coloured steward, a fact that caused Wally, the maid, considerable amazement. She had to force herself to eat the sandwich, since in Germany an 'abhorrence of negroes' had been inculcated into her.

In Washington the travelling party stayed at the German embassy. Wiedemann did indeed have several discussions with the ambassador, Dr Heinz Dieckhoff. The latter was very concerned that Wiedemann should convey to the Führer the 'unvarnished truth about the potential strength of the United States'.

Fritz Wiedemann was also received by Hugh R. Wilson, who would later be the USA's last pre-war ambassador to Germany. Wiedemann was meant to provide him with some information about his future posting to Berlin. At the particular suggestion of President Roosevelt, Wilson was primarily interested in the German Labour Service and the organisation known as *Kraft durch Freude* (Strength through Joy). At all events, in spring 1938, Wilson set off for Berlin, full of good intentions. His spell of duty did not, however, last very long. Because of his protest against the anti-Jewish atrocities in November 1938, he was recalled and never returned to his post.

In the American capital, Wiedemann also met his friend Dr Hans Thomsen, the German chargé d'affaires in Washington. He was the son of a wealthy Hamburg merchant, and a qualified lawyer, who had built a considerable career for himself.[2]

The Wiedemanns continued their journey and left Washington for Chicago. There Wiedemann made contact with the German-American League. This was a highly pro-Nazi association of American citizens of German extraction. These were people who believed they could be of service to their former homeland by founding an organisation whose ideals were in sharp contradiction to those of their new democratic country. As one member of the League in Chicago told Wiedemann: 'Of course I'm an American citizen and I've sworn the Oath of Allegiance. But if it should come to war, the bonds of blood are sure as hell stronger than any oath!' Finally, Wiedemann's journey took him to the West Coast, to San Francisco.

Meanwhile, Stephanie von Hohenlohe was accompanying her new lover to his concert performances in Philadelphia and Chicago, so that she could celebrate his success with him. But in the bitterly cold 'windy city' of Chicago, she contracted double pneumonia. She was so much in love with the new object of her adoration that she had wandered through the city dressed only in a party frock with a fur stole over her shoulders.

All the party foregathered in New York for the homeward voyage. In the Waldorf-Astoria, there was a stormy erotic encounter between Wiedemann and the 'lady diplomat', as Wally Oeler told some friends: 'One day, at 3 o'clock in the afternoon, we wanted to get into our room. The chamber-maid, a waiter and I reached the bedroom, and the door was open. There was Captain Wiedemann having his pleasure with her, and they didn't even notice the three of us. The other Germans in the hotel were so outraged by this that they said the fellow should be reported for racial dishonour, because they knew perfectly well that the princess was born Jewish. I think one of them went and told the Frau Captain [Wiedemann's wife], but she did nothing about it. I acted as if I knew nothing. That man W[iedemann] behaves so badly, and yet he claims to be Hitler's right-hand man.'

Wally Oeler also complained bitterly to her relatives about the behaviour of her employer during the trip: 'In spite of my repeated requests, she didn't pay me a penny of my wages, and what's more my overcoat didn't arrive on the ship in time, so I didn't have anything warm to wear in America, in all that pitiless cold. In Chicago I collapsed from cold in a blizzard, because the wind there had such strength that it simply swept you away. Then your legs feel so weak that you don't want to stand up again.'

The princess was well known for not always paying her staff on time. An English chauffeur, who drove her for weeks all around Europe, never received his pay. On the contrary, he often spent his own money on the princess. Since it never occurred to her to reimburse him, he simply took her car away. Wally Oeler allowed herself to be fobbed off time and again, but since she very much wanted to go on living in the princess's interesting world, she held her peace.

The princess brought back from the States a number of handsome books on American architecture, which she sent to the Führer as a Christmas present. On 28 December 1937 Hitler replied from the Obersalzberg to her Christmas letter:

My dear Princess!

I would like to thank you most warmly for the books about American skyscraper and bridge construction, which you sent me as a Christmas present. You know how interested I am in architecture and related fields, and can therefore imagine what pleasure your present has given me.

I have been told how staunchly and warmly you have spoken up in your circles on behalf of the new Germany and its vital needs, in the past year. I am well aware that this has caused you a number of unpleasant experiences, and would therefore like to express to you, highly esteemed Princess, my sincere thanks for the great understanding that you have shown for Germany as a whole and for my work in particular.

I add to these thanks my warmest best wishes for the New Year and remain, with devoted greetings,

Yours,
Adolf Hitler

On 31 December 1937 a telegram was despatched from the Obersalzberg to Princess Hohenlohe at the Dorchester hotel in London: 'A happy New Year and best love. Fr.' It seems that Stephanie would have to see in the New Year without her lover, but no doubt in pleasant company, with the champagne flowing freely. But Fritz Wiedemann was certainly not bored that New Year's Eve. At that time, on the Obersalzberg, Hitler's powerful adjutant was very close to Eva Braun's younger sister, Gretl. Wiedemann conceived a great affection for this still unmarried sister of Hitler's mistress.

Stephanie made another trip to the United States in February 1938, this time on express instructions from Wiedemann. She travelled once again on the MS *Europa* with her maid and a new friend, Madame Charalambos Sinopoulos, the wife of the Greek ambassador in London. Needless to say, all three travelled at the expense of the German Reich. But this time she came across a man who did not succumb to her charms. He was Ralph Ingersoll, the publisher of *Time* magazine in New York. Before she left, Wiedemann wrote to her in London:

Dear Princess,

As promised I am enclosing an article, which we can assume would have a favourable impact, if it were to be published in *Time* magazine. As you know, Herr Ingersoll owes us a favour. So that you can see our position on this question, I am also sending you the document sent from Hamburg to Herr Feldmann on 29 January. This paper, which in fact contains important hints, is based on the mistaken assumption that *I* wanted to sign the article. There is no question of that. As far as I'm concerned, anyone who wants to can sign this article. The important thing is that it gets published. So, please do your best and don't disappoint us!

With the German salute
Your very devoted servant
Wiedemann
Adjutant to the Führer

The four-page article entitled 'Hitler as Architect', was written by Helmuth von Feldmann, a member of Goebbels' staff. It culminated in this crass statement: 'As a statesman Hitler is an architect, as an architect he is a statesman.' This was meant to convince people that Hitler was in favour of peace, for surely all the magnificent buildings he created were not meant to be destroyed in another war. However, the pro-Hitler article did not in fact appear, since the princess was unable to get an appointment with the publisher during her eight-week stay.

Full of longing, Stephanie sent a telegram to her 'dear Fritz'. She was feeling so unhappy about the painful separation from him. She missed him terribly. But at the same time she kept in close touch with her other lover, the opera singer Lawrence Tibbett, who was on tour in Cleveland. She met him several times there.

Then, however, *Time* did draw the public's attention to Adolf Hitler in a dramatic way. At the end of 1938, the magazine chose him as 'Man of the Year', and on the front cover he was billed as 'an unholy organist' who played on the 'organ of hatred'.

While Stephanie had been in America, a great deal had changed in Europe. Austria, her homeland, had been incorporated into the German Reich. At dawn on 12 March 1938 Hitler ordered units of the Wehrmacht to cross the frontier into Austria. Two days later he made his appearance on Vienna's Heldenplatz and announced to thunderous cheers 'the entry of my homeland into the German Reich'. A plebiscite held on 10 April confirmed with an overwhelming majority the annexation of the 'Ostmark', as the country was now called. Even the leader of the Austrian socialists, Karl Renner, publicly voted 'yes' and Cardinal Innitzer of Vienna also greeted the *Anschluss* 'with joy', and had the churches 'decorated' with swastika flags. Before the *Anschluss*, Stephanie von Hohenlohe was known as an agent of the German Reich, and people knew that she was 'hostile towards the present Austrian government'. This fact had been reported to the Foreign Office by the British ambassador in Vienna. Now Stephanie was back from the United States, there was a Greater German Reich – and Stephanie's 'adversary', Joachim von Ribbentrop, was Reich Foreign Minister.

CHAPTER EIGHT

Rivals for Hitler's Favour: Stephanie and Unity

The Austrian princess, Stephanie von Hohenlohe, was to become the most serious competitor of Unity Mitford, the British Fascist. By this time, Stephanie was forty-seven years old and, always dressed with striking elegance, she stood high in Hitler's estimation. But the 24-year-old Unity had made no less an impression on the Führer. Whether he was in Munich or Bayreuth, Berlin or the Berghof, he always liked to have her close to him.

The two women already knew each other from pro-German gatherings in London and had met several times at the Nazi Party rallies in Nuremberg. But neither was particularly 'amused' by the other.

The national rallies of the NSDAP, the Nazi Party, had been held in Nuremberg every year since 1927, and they exerted a great fascination on the public at large. They were meant to show the whole world that *Führer und Volk* were as one. The most solemn moment always came in the evening, when searchlights created a vaulted 'cathedral of light' over the parade ground. It was hugely impressive when thousands of uniformed men marched past to martial music, their arms raised in the Nazi salute, and then, as total silence returned once more, listened mesmerised to the Führer's words. Enthusiasm for the Third Reich then welled up in their souls. Those taking part in the rallies had been selected by their local party organisers. On the podium sat special guests of the Führer, both German and foreign.

Stephanie was deeply impressed by this 'orgy of dedication' with its quasi-religious character. It was in 1935 that she first attended a Nuremberg rally, as the representative of Lord Rothermere. On 2 July 1937, Fritz Wiedemann informed the *Reichsleiter* and 'dear party colleague', Martin Bormann, that on the Führer's instructions Princess Hohenlohe had to be invited to the 'National Labour Rally' in Nuremberg. At the same time Bormann was alerted to the fact that the lady was likely to suggest that another important personage from England should be invited.

Stephanie brought an English friend of hers, the journalist Ethel Snowden, widow of Philip (Viscount) Snowden, the former Chancellor of the Exchequer in the Labour governments of 1924 and 1931, and later Lord Privy Seal, who had died in 1937. Lady Snowden wrote for Rothermere's *Daily Mail*. Goebbels, in his diary for 14 September 1937, noted about her: 'Lady Snowden writes an enthusiastic article on Nuremberg. A woman with guts. In London they don't understand that.' It was mainly Ethel Snowden's Jewish friends who were unable to forgive her for being so eager to accept the way the Nazis presented themselves. Another member of Stephanie's party at the rally was Wiedemann's wife.

The 'Reich Party Congress of Greater Germany' on 5 September 1938 saw the princess once more take her seat on the VIP dais at Nuremberg. In advance of the event, Wiedemann had sent Stephanie's son, Franzi von Hohenlohe, the tickets for the Party Congress, and for the parade of the Reich Labour Service and also, of course, the necessary transit permits.

What displeased the princess at this party rally was the fact that she had to share the dais with the British fascist, Unity Mitford, and her parents, Lord and Lady Redesdale. Unity Valkyrie Mitford (1914–48) and her five sisters were the famous, not to say notorious, but never uninteresting Mitford girls.[1]

Unity, who had first visited Munich with her sister Diana in August 1933, became an ardent devotee of Hitler, to whom she was introduced in February 1935, in his favourite Munich restaurant, the Osteria Bavaria in Schellingstrasse. She apparently found out that he frequented this hostelry from none other than Stephanie von Hohenlohe.

Unity was fascinated by National Socialism, but at a very naïve level: she simply loved all the parades, the songs, and the good-looking young men in their uniforms. And she liked wearing a black shirt with a short skirt and matching black elbow-length gloves.

In this outfit, with her statuesque figure and thick blonde hair, she resembled one of those warlike maidens after whom she had been named. That 'crazed Valkyrie' as her sister Nancy described her, had, through her acquaintance with Hitler, suddenly been given a feeling of great importance, so that she had no difficulty in buying his anti-Semitic propaganda and repeating it readily on every occasion that presented itself. 'The Yids, the Yids, we've got to get rid of the Yids!' Unity had recorded this refrain on wax in a studio at Harrods department store and took it with her to Germany.

Another man for whom Unity conceived a deep affection was Julius Streicher, publisher of *Der Stürmer*, and one of Nazism's most sadistic Jew-baiters. At his invitation, in June 1935, Unity went to a demonstration on the Hesselberg hill, near Dinkelsbühl, south-west of Nuremberg, the 'sacred mountain of the Franks', where she publicly declared her fascist convictions and hatred of the Jews. She addressed a crowd estimated at 25,000 and told them of her loyalty to Hitler.

Fritz Wiedemann was watching the young Englishwoman very closely; in his work for the Führer, he frequently had dealings with her. On a rather despairing note, he remarked 'Strange as it sounds, Unity Mitford also had considerable influence . . . being a friend of Hitler. She did her own country a disservice by giving him the idea that defeatism was rife in Britain. Everything that Mitford told Hitler he took as gospel; on the other hand, those people who had made a correct assessment of Britain could not get their views accepted. In this, as in everything else, he only believed what he wanted to believe.'

Unity Mitford complained vehemently to Hitler about his obvious fondness for Stephanie von Hohenlohe, despite the fact that the woman was a Jewess. As Princess Carmencita Wrede told Unity's biographer later: 'She said to Hitler: "Here you are, an anti-Semite, and yet you have a Jewish woman, Princess Hohenlohe, around you all the time." Hitler did not answer.'[2]

It is striking that Hitler showed no reaction and said not a word when Unity confronted him with Stephanie's Jewish origins. His silence may mean that she was working for German intelligence, or was supplying him with information that he simply could not afford to be without. And precisely what game Unity herself was playing is still not entirely clear, even today.

Unity hated the Hohenlohe woman, calling her a 'rusée', a wily manipulator, 'who reported to Lord Rothermere exactly what Hitler was planning'. She also admitted freely that she was unspeakably jealous of the princess.

Unity feared the great influence that the older woman was exerting on her beloved Führer. What the two women were really competing over was which of them could attract more attention and achieve greater propaganda value in Britain.

Unity was incandescent with rage when she learned that Hitler had presented Stephanie with a large signed photograph of himself. She herself had received a small portrait in a silver frame, which she showed to everyone and kept on her bedside table, even when travelling in a sleeping-car. Furthermore, the jealous Unity could not fail to notice that Stephanie wore the Gold Medal of the Nazi Party. Unity for her part had only been given the normal decoration by Hitler, a round, white enamel badge with a black swastika surrounded by the words 'Nationalsozialistische DAP', which all party members wore pinned to their lapel.

When the 1937 Party Rally took place, Unity Mitford was already under surveillance by the SS, who suspected her of espionage. The head of the SS, Heinrich Himmler, could not stand the Englishwoman, and nor could Hitler's chief adjutant, Wilhelm Brückner. The latter disliked the uncomfortably close relationship between Hitler and Unity and later objected: 'What if she's an agent of the British Secret Service, cleverly placed right under our noses? We should be more cautious, mein Führer!'

On 3 September 1939, the day that Britain declared war on Germany, events rapidly gathered pace. Only a few days earlier the British Consul in Munich had again urged Unity to leave Germany, as hordes of her fellow-countrymen were doing. Yet she continued to cherish the illusion that she was under the Führer's protection and stayed on in Munich. If Unity's escapades had at first only raised a smile, many of Hitler's entourage stopped laughing when they heard that she had met with Hitler on no less than 140 occasions.

The correspondent of Reuters' news agency, Ernest Pope, who had stayed close on Hitler's heels, claimed that Unity had been tireless in passing on to Hitler anti-Nazi remarks by Germans and others who were hostile to his regime, and had thus become 'the most dangerous woman in Munich'.

On the day war was declared Unity tried to commit suicide. She sat on a park bench in Munich's famous Englischer Garten, pointed a revolver at her head and fired. But she survived, since the bullet lodged in the back of her skull. As a matter of 'Reich secrecy' she was rushed to a hospital in Nussbaumstrasse. On 8 November the errant Englishwoman received a visit from the Führer, who promised to make all arrangements for her return home.

In a specially equipped railway carriage of the German Reichsbahn, she travelled with a doctor and nurse to the Swiss capital, Bern. From there her mother collected her and took her back to England. In 1948, after long years of infirmity, she suddenly contracted meningitis and died. Thus, in the end, she too became a victim of the war.

CHAPTER NINE

Wiedemann's Peace Mission

'Göring and Halifax' is the heading that Stephanie wrote over her notes about the political mission she undertook with Fritz Wiedemann. In London, on 27 June 1938, the princess received a telegram from Wiedemann requesting her to come to Berlin immediately: 'Audience Wednesday or Thursday.' She guessed that on one of those days she would have the long-planned meeting with Field-Marshal Göring. Since she had to attend a wedding in Berlin anyway, she flew there immediately.

The princess stayed, as usual, at the Adlon hotel in Berlin, and arranged for a limousine from the Reich Chancellery to drive her out to Karinhall, Göring's imposing country house north-east of Berlin.

In the course of her two-hour 'pilgrimage' from the capital to Karinhall, Stephanie prepared herself mentally for the meeting with the Reich Minister of Aviation and commander-in-chief of the Luftwaffe, the man she described as 'conservative, most un-Nazi of all Nazis'. She recalled that the astute Joseph Goebbels had called him 'an upright soldier with the heart of a child'. But she had been told that what he really meant was: 'An upright soldier with the *brain* of a child.'

Stephanie saw in Göring the courageous pilot and possible successor to Adolf Hitler.[1] There was no man in Germany about whom the Führer spoke with such respect, admiration and gratitude. 'What would I be without Göring?' Hitler had confessed to the princess. And he went on: 'What would I have achieved without him? . . . I may have great ideas but it is Göring who translates them into reality.' With tears in his eyes – and they were real tears, Stephanie noted – Hitler begged Göring not to drive his car at such a reckless speed.

Stephanie von Hohenlohe was extremely well informed about the career of Hermann Göring. She brooded over the course of his turbulent life, recalled the successful pilot who, during the First World War, had shot down between thirty and forty enemy aircraft, and by the end of the war was in command of the famous 'Richthofen Circus' fighter squadron. He had been awarded Germany's highest military decoration, the *Pour le Mérite*, whereas Hitler 'only' had an Iron Cross. During Hitler's Munich *putsch* in November 1923, Göring had been severely wounded. His treatment with morphine went on far too long, and he became addicted. But the princess also recoiled from the terrible things he had done. She knew of the events surrounding the so-called Röhm *putsch* in June 1934, the murder of the former Reich Chancellor, Kurt von Schleicher, and his wife, and other hideous crimes in which Göring was heavily implicated. Suddenly, she had the feeling that she did not want to drive out to Karinhall after all. But then she wondered whether she should sit in judgement over the Field-Marshal. Might she not even have an opportunity to exert a moderating influence on this 'apocalyptic monster'? Now she felt like the Devil's Advocate. All the good things that came into her mind in connection with this 'corpulent Nazi Lohengrin' gained the upper hand.

Stephanie had heard countless stories and jokes about the Field-Marshal's overweening vanity, his elaborate wardrobe, his collection of jewellery, his passion for pomp and parades. Despite his great obesity, he was known as the 'prancing pierrot'.

As the chauffeur drove her through the entrance gates to the Karinhall estate, Stephanie decided to be friendly towards Göring, regardless of what fancy dress he might be wearing, and also to avoid showing any fear of the lion-cubs which he kept as pets. 'That was how I finally met the Number One of Hitler's twelve apostles.

He was given that nickname in 1928, when he was elected as one of the twelve National Socialist Party members to sit in the Reichstag.' The princess imagined Göring one day joining the ranks of Germany's legendary folk-heroes, like Till Eulenspiegel or Götz von Berlichingen.

Göring talked to Stephanie about his personal ambitions, his efforts on behalf of Germany, his relationship with Hitler and other top Nazis. In the course of their conversation she could not help sensing signs of disharmony within the party.

Göring was keen to visit Britain. He remarked emphatically that 'it was no bluff, that Hitler would soon declare war'. Only he, Göring, could prevent this, if he could just speak to [the British Foreign Secretary] Lord Halifax in London. Tensions within the party would prevent him from travelling there. Stephanie was to arrange a suitable meeting, but von Ribbentrop must know nothing about it. (Ironically, it was just before her visit to Karinhall that she had had the meeting with Ribbentrop, at the Kaiserhof hotel in Berlin.) Göring was anxious that Lord Rothermere should not find out about it either.

The princess was more than willing to make preparations for this mission, since it was her lover, Wiedemann, who was to take soundings in a preliminary meeting with Halifax in London. She asked her best friend, Ethel Snowden, to approach Halifax, a fact confirmed by Halifax in his diary:

On Wednesday, 6 July, Lady Snowden came to see me early in the morning. She informed me that, through someone on the closest terms with Hitler – I took this to mean Princess Hohenlohe – she had received a message with the following burden: Hitler wanted to find out whether H.M. Government would welcome it if he were to send one of his closest confidants, as I understood it, to England for the purpose of conducting unofficial talks. Lady Snowden gave me to understand that this referred to Field-Marshal Göring, and they wished to find out whether he could come to England without being too severely and publicly insulted, and what attitude H.M. Government would take generally to such a visit.

In just three days Stephanie succeeded in arranging a secret meeting between Lord Halifax, Sir Alexander Cadogan, and Hitler's adjutant, Fritz Wiedemann. She then alerted Berlin. In his official diary for 17 July, the British Foreign Secretary wrote this about his conversation with Princess Hohenlohe:

> Princess H. said that W[iedemann] would be quite happy to spend Saturday and Sunday, 16th and 17th, privately and only come to see me on Monday morning. We therefore agreed on 10 a.m. at 88 Eaton Square. I did nothing more than establish that the sole purpose of W[iedemann]'s call was to discuss the actual visit itself. Without going into detail, I merely pointed out that it was obvious that G[öring]'s visit, should it take place, would be generally known about and that it was doubtless desirable to assure him in advance that it would not be without result.

Wiedemann left Germany secretly and stayed with the princess in London. Then came the meeting with Lord Halifax. On 18 July 1938, with Prime Minister Neville Chamberlain's 'permission', Wiedemann was received by Halifax at his private residence in Belgravia. Wiedemann claimed he had come to London 'with Hitler's knowledge', but that Ribbentrop had not been informed. He wanted to establish whether 'a highly placed German figure might come here as soon as possible in order to conduct wide-ranging talks on Anglo-German relations. He hinted that this person was Field-Marshal Göring.'

Wiedemann apparently went on to state that 'the Field-Marshal was very keen on this idea', and that Hitler desired good relations with Britain. However, the Führer had instructed him personally to inform Halifax that at present the critical problem was the suppression of the Sudeten Germans by the Czechs.[2] 'If, in the foreseeable future, a satisfactory solution cannot be found, I will simply settle the question by force. Tell Lord Halifax that!'

A visit by Göring to London, as proposed by Wiedemann, was, however, rejected by the British Foreign Secretary on the grounds that the problem of the Sudetenland had not yet been resolved. But

Wiedemann refused to let the matter drop. He insisted that Göring be invited, since Halifax had been Göring's guest in Berlin in 1937, on the occasion of a field sports exhibition. Halifax then countered that 'any such *rapprochement* with the German government' would have to be brought to the attention of the French government.

Having accepted the British refusal, Wiedemann 'stressed most vehemently that Herr von Ribbentrop must not be apprised of the matter until it was absolutely unavoidable. He added in confidence that Herr von Ribbentrop's standing with the Führer had long since ceased to be what it had once been.'

In a memorandum dated 11 August 1938 Halifax made reference to his conversation with Wiedemann, stating:

> The Prime Minister and I have thought about the meeting I had with Captain Wiedemann last month. Of especial importance to us are the steps which the Germans and the British might possibly take, not only to create the best possible relationship between the two countries, but also to calm down the international situation, in order to achieve an improvement of general economic and political problems . . .
>
> Our hopes have recently been shattered by the conduct of the German press, which, it seems to us, has not hesitated to incite public opinion in a dangerous manner over every incident that occurs either in Czechoslovakia or on the frontiers.

The French ambassador in Berlin, André François-Poncet, conveyed the following message to Paris: 'The idea that Captain Wiedemann should be received by Lord Halifax was cooked up by Princess Hohenlohe, who is extremely well known to the secret services of all the Great Powers, and who at the moment seems to be serving the interests of Britain, although Captain Wiedemann, who enjoys the closest relations with her and frequently visits her in London, is of the opinion that she chiefly feels herself committed to the interests of Germany.'

This statement by the highly respected diplomat was nothing if not explosive. The princess – 'extremely well known to the secret services of all the Great Powers' – did not allow even a man like François-Poncet to know for whom she was really working – or spying. He was not the only one who enquired about her activities without reaching any firm conclusion. In his report, the French ambassador pointed out that Wiedemann, who was moderately intelligent and well-meaning, was also naive, and spoke very little English. Wiedemann did in fact speak reasonable English, but he was clearly not capable of conducting such a delicate political mission in a foreign language. This meant that throughout the whole conversation with Halifax, Stephanie von Hohenlohe acted as interpreter. This was an astonishing state of affairs, which turned her more and more into a secret agent.

Stephanie later had this to say to her ghost-writer, Rudolf Kommer, about the ill-fated exercise: 'Very shortly afterwards, I learned that as soon as Ribbentrop heard the news from London, he went straight to Hitler and protested in the strongest terms about this interference by the Field-Marshal, the Captain and myself, and that he succeeded in completely changing Hitler's mind . . . Ribbentrop's star was at that time in the ascendant, but the rumblings of war were getting nearer. For me this chapter was closed.'

At all events the princess's suite in the exclusive Dorchester hotel, overlooking Hyde Park, where she had been living since 1936, became a London 'base' for Nazis. It was possibly an outpost of German espionage as well. That was certainly the impression gained by the British ambassador to Austria, Sir Walford Selby, who had followed the Viennese woman's route to becoming an 'international adventuress'. He warned his government against her: 'There is no doubt that German propaganda was very active in London during those years. The Austrian government was watching these manoeuvres with the deepest disquiet, especially those of Princess Stephanie von Hohenlohe, who they knew was an agent of Hitler.'

To Ribbentrop, Wiedemann presented the subject of the Göring visit as though it had been Halifax and not he who had broached the matter. His report ended with the extravagant claim: 'Lord Halifax asked me to convey his regards to the Führer and to tell him that he, Halifax, would like, before he died, to see his work culminate with the Führer entering London at the side of the King of England, amid the cheers of the population. He then accompanied me to his front door, where we said goodbye to each other very warmly.'

Yet this doorstep farewell yielded less pleasant results. A newspaper reporter had been watching the two men. The next morning, as Wiedemann boarded the plane at Croydon aerodrome, he saw a banner headline in a left-wing newspaper announcing that Hitler's adjutant had had a secret meeting with the British Foreign Secretary. The anonymous author of this explosive piece was in fact a man named Willi Frischauer. Coincidentally, he was the uncle of Eduard Frischauer, the second husband of Stephanie's half-sister, Gina Kaus. Willi Frischauer had published a successful monthly magazine in Vienna until he was forced to emigrate. At the time in question he was writing for the *Daily Herald* and was extremely interested in the political 'career' in London of his Viennese compatriot, Stephanie von Hohenlohe. Writing stories about her was always a lucrative occupation. What is more, Frischauer knew Stephanie 'socially' from her Vienna days, when she had worked with his friend, 'Feichtl' Starhemberg, so he claimed, on 'all kinds of international wheeling and dealing – arms, finance and political intrigue'. 'Feichtl' was the brother of a leading figure in pre-*Anschluss* Austria, Count Rüdiger Starhemberg, Vice-Chancellor of the republic and commander of the Home Defence Force.

Needless to say, the sensational revelation from London quickly reached Berlin. In the middle of a press conference at the German Foreign Office on Tuesday morning, someone burst in with the news that Wiedemann had been to see Halifax. It was a bombshell. As Wiedemann wrote in his memoirs: 'I must confess that it was an embarrassing matter for Ribbentrop, and he immediately put through a phone-call to Hitler.'

The foreign press reacted promptly, as Goebbels noted in his diary: '23 July 1938 . . . Wiedemann's visit to Halifax on the Führer's instructions continues to dominate the foreign press more than ever. A welter of rumours.' In Goebbels' view, the whole business had been 'unduly exaggerated by the British press. The Führer has no particular intention other than simply to soothe the British.'

On 22 July 1938 the Czech ambassador in London, Jan Masaryk, wrote in great indignation to Prague: 'If there is any decency left in this world, then one of these days there will be a big scandal when it is revealed what part was played in Wiedemann's visit by Steffi Hohenlohe, *née* Richter. This world-renowned secret agent, spy and confidence trickster, who is wholly Jewish, today provides the focus of Hitler's propaganda in London. Wiedemann has been living with her. On her table stands a photograph of Hitler, signed "To my dear Princess Hohenlohe – Adolf Hitler" and next to it a photograph of Horthy, dedicated to "a great stateswoman".'

It was with very mixed feelings that Wiedemann flew back to Berlin, and since Hitler happened to be staying 'on the mountain', he went straight on to Berchtesgaden. When he landed there at about 5 o'clock in the afternoon, he was told that the Führer had gone for a walk with the English fascist girl, Unity Mitford, and was expected back shortly before dinner.

When Hitler returned, a little before 7 p.m., he summoned Wiedemann to hear about the trip. Wiedemann began cautiously with the greetings from Halifax and his hope one day to see Hitler in London as a guest of the king. He was just starting to say: 'As to Göring's visit . . . ', but he got no further. Hitler cut him off immediately. 'It's out of the question now . . . Gentlemen, will you come in to dinner, please!' Wiedemann himself found it scarcely credible that, even later on, he was unable to return to the subject.

Thus Wiedemann had no choice but to send a message to Lord Halifax, after a decent delay, saying he regretted that his mission had failed. He wrote later: 'In Hitler's mind – given his great uncertainty about Britain – the page had turned once again.' Wiedemann was not sure whether Unity Mitford had 'whispered something' to the Führer, or whether he felt that 'a raising of Göring's political profile was more unwelcome than ever'.

Ribbentrop demanded a written report from Wiedemann on his visit to Britain. Outwardly, that was the end of the matter as far as Wiedemann was concerned. But he freely admitted that Ribbentrop 'never forgave my attempt to meddle in his foreign policy'.

In his autobiography Herbert von Dirksen, who was Germany's ambassador in London at the time, once again went over the events leading to Wiedemann's London mission:

> The most important political event of that summer was an attempt at rapprochement, undertaken from the German side, which sheds the brightest of lights on the methods of Hitlerian diplomacy – its multi-tracked approach, its bypassing of official channels, its dishonesty and lack of consistency, as well as the complete inability to attune itself to the mentality of the other side . . . the motivation for the London mission seems to me to stem from two sources: on one hand Göring's desire for prestige and his wish to maintain peace through an understanding with Britain; and a parallel initiative by a clever woman on the other. This woman, Princess Hohenlohe, a Hungarian by birth,[3] divorced from her husband, who had lived for years in London, was able, by reason of her acquaintance with Wiedemann, to gain access to Göring and even to Hitler. The latter had received her for a conversation lasting several hours, a distinction that he notoriously denied the official representatives of the Reich abroad. But since Princess Hohenlohe was a clever woman who was working for peace, this opportunity to exercise influence on the Führer was only to be welcomed. Under her guidance, Wiedemann trod the polished parquet floors of London. Since his mission was completely in line with my own endeavours, and he loyally kept me informed about everything worth knowing, I did all that was possible to promote the success of his mission.

Dirksen recalled that Ribbentrop had not discussed Wiedemann's mission with him, other than to warn him to be cautious in dealing with Princess Hohenlohe. 'I replied that I had considered her above suspicion, since the Führer had granted her the honour of an audience in order to hear her views on Britain. Thus it was that this amateurish attempt to reach a compromise with Britain, made on the highest authority in Germany, ended in a tangled thicket of personal intrigue.'

CHAPTER TEN

Mistress of Schloss Leopoldskron

On 21 July 1938 the London *Evening Standard* printed a story in the 'Londoner's Diary' column headed 'Friend of Hitler'. It read:

Princess Hohenlohe Waldenburg-Schillingsfürst, who is believed to have arranged Captain Wiedemann's meeting with Lord Halifax, and who acted as Wiedemann's hostess in London, plans to acquire Schloss Leopoldskron near Salzburg, as a holiday home. The mansion was requisitioned [by the Nazis] after the annexation of Austria.

The Berlin journalist Bella Fromm wrote about Stephanie at the time: 'Breaking up the Wiedemann marriage was a mere bagatelle in comparison with the work of the Stephanie–Wiedemann team on behalf of the National Socialists. It was just tough on Frau Wiedemann that she was wounded and inconsolable. For these exceptional services Stephanie was rewarded by Hitler with Schloss Leopoldskron near Salzburg, once the home of that world-famous genius of the theatre, Max Reinhardt.'

In London the princess had frequently been in contact with Dr Rudolf Kommer, Max Reinhardt's agent, regarding his projects in Britain and the United States. Kommer told Stephanie how Reinhardt's property, Schloss Leopoldskron, had been confiscated by the Gestapo as being 'owned by a person hostile to the people and the state', and that it was now to be used for Nazi purposes. He advised her to take an interest in it. The German tax authorities had imposed a fictitious mortgage on the mansion, which could have led to the assumption that Max Reinhardt was in debt. This was simply not true.

As Stephanie von Hohenlohe had wanted all along, in March 1938 the expropriated Schloss Leopoldskron was made available to her by Hitler and Göring as a personal residence and 'political salon', in recognition of her work as an intermediary with Lord Halifax. As another of Stephanie's biographers puts it: 'The man pulling the strings in this travesty, in which a Jewish woman was rewarded for her services to National Socialism with the property of a Jew deprived of citizenship, was none other than Hitler's adjutant, Fritz Wiedemann.'[1]

The actress Helene Thimig, who later married Reinhardt, wrote in fury: 'What a macabre joke: Reinhardt's creation – now a palace for the Nazis! And this Aryanised palace has been placed under the management of the Jewish Princess von Hohenlohe!'

Max Reinhardt (1873–1943) was one of Germany's greatest actors and theatre directors – in fact he pioneered directing as an independent artistic profession. He had bought Schloss Leopoldskron in 1918, and restored it in the most exquisite style. In collaboration with the poet and librettist Hugo von Hoffmannsthal, he founded the Salzburg Festival, which opened in 1920 with *Everyman*.

Hitler always showed a great interest in things theatrical. As Goebbels wrote: 'He praises great figures like Mahler or Max Reinhardt, whose abilities and services he does not dispute. In interpretative arts the Jew does sometimes manage to achieve something.'

In 1933 the Nazis offered Max Reinhardt (whose real name was Goldmann) 'honorary Aryanship', a suggestion he rejected as outrageous. Reinhardt saw in 'Adolf the Colossal' a man who sits 'like the flea in Aesop's fable, on the cartwheel of time, unaware of who is driving the cart. He buzzes proudly: what a lot of dust I am stirring up!' On 5 October 1937 Reinhardt travelled to America, this time not as a tourist but as an immigrant. A short time earlier a Nazi supporter had thrown a bomb into the hall of Schloss Leopoldskron.

Also living temporarily in the Schloss was Reinhardt's theatrical agent, Dr Rudolf Kommer who, ironically, would later become Princess Stephanie's ghost-writer. In 1941, at the request of Stephanie's son Franz, Kommer had once more summarised the events surrounding Schloss Leopoldskron, admittedly from his own viewpoint, and with the aim of helping Stephanie resist the threat of deportation from the USA.

Dear Princess Hohenlohe,

I hear from Franzi that you are unable at the moment to get at your letters and documents from 1938, and that you wish to clarify matters relating to Schloss Leopoldskron, Prof. Max Reinhardt and myself. I will hurriedly give you a brief survey of the facts:

(1) Approximately two months after the German occupation of Austria (in March 1938) I was informed by Prof. Reinhardt's housekeeper at Schloss Leopoldskron, that the Schloss had been requisitioned in March and was being handed over to a Nazi military organisation. This would have meant the physical destruction of assets of great artistic value. When I was definitively informed by prominent Nazi lawyers that there was no legal protection of any kind in Nazi Germany for Prof. Reinhardt (or for myself), I thought about how this architectural jewel might be rescued from the barbarians. When I saw you in London in June 1938, I suddenly remembered that in previous years you had repeatedly tried to buy Schloss Leopoldskron from Prof. Reinhardt. I therefore suggested that you travel to Salzburg and either buy or rent the Schloss from the Nazi authorities. I naturally hoped that your personal connections would be of help to you in these efforts. You succeeded in obtaining a five-year lease from them and thus halted their plans to turn the beautiful baroque property into barracks. It was an extremely kind act towards Prof. Reinhardt on your part, and not a hostile one, as some ill-informed newspapers reported.

(2) You additionally offered your help and support, in a spirit of genuine friendship, in rescuing Prof. Reinhardt's (and my) personal property from Schloss Leopoldskron. It would take too long to describe here our long-term plans, which the outbreak of

war put an end to, but it is sufficient to explain what in fact was successfully done. In August 1938 I received in London 26 crates containing my library (some 6,000 volumes), papers, pictures and items of personal clothing. A few months later Prof. Reinhardt received in Hollywood, Cal., a quantity of books, china, silver, furniture etc. etc. from Schloss Leopoldskron. This was all organised by you in the most generous fashion, and I will always be profoundly grateful to you . . .

In the hope that your persecution by the press, which arises from a complete misinterpretation of your personality, will soon come to an end, I remain most devotedly and gratefully

Yours,

Rudolf K. Kommer

There are some things in this letter which lack credibility. For one thing, the statement that the princess actually wanted to buy the mansion is not correct. She just did not have the money to do so. The American press also refused to accept this explanation. It is true that Stephanie sent a small part of Reinhardt's personal possessions back to him. Her son had the task of dealing with the shipping formalities. On 28 October Wiedemann received this note from Franz: 'Dear Fritz . . . I enclose for your attention a list that I have carefully made of the items that are being returned to Professor Reinhardt. It is admittedly not complete, and I fear I will have to trouble you again in a few days with the second section. Although it looks very long, there aren't an awful lot of things there: and Steph need not have been so horrified when she visited the house.'

On 24 November he received the list back, signed off by Wiedemann, and with it the necessary authority from the Führer himself to export the articles belonging to Max Reinhardt: 'The Führer has ordered that all personal possessions of the former owner of Leopoldskron, Professor Max Reinhardt, be returned to him without delay. Prince Hohenlohe is authorised by me to carry out this instruction from the Führer. Accordingly, no special approval from the Currency Office is necessary, nor is confirmation by the tax authorities, or approval by any other authority or administrative department.'

Reinhardt's son, Gottfried, dealt at length in his biography of his father with the fact 'that the one-time Princess Stephanie Hohenlohe – alias Fräulein Richter from Vienna' – had 'moved into Schloss Leopoldskron as châtelaine, by the good grace of Hitler'. However, he states, inaccurately, that 'the woman who wore the Gold Medal of the Nazi party was the second wife of Herr Wiedemann, the German consul in San Francisco who, even before America's entry into the war, had been expelled from the country for Nazi intrigues. She owed her entrée into international politics to the British newspaper mogul, Lord Rothermere, whose *idée fixe* had been to smooth the path for a return of a Hohenzollern to the throne of Germany. Her thinking must have been more realistic than that, since she soon switched her allegiance from a second Kaiser's empire to the Thousand Year Reich. What is more, her "seizure of power" at Leopoldskron did not lack far-sighted realism either: for internal purposes, Hitler's loyal neighbour [Austria] was administering German national property, which had been disgracefully sold off to a foreigner; outwardly the emigrant princess was acting as trustee of the property on behalf of its racially alien owner. Through her Kommer regained possession of his library. She also sent personal effects from Leopoldskron to Max Reinhardt in California, though admittedly it was only junk. She had obtained the Gauleiter's permission to do this. The double game this lady played became another bone of contention between Max Reinhardt and Kommer, who accused Max of ingratitude towards the lady.'

But Max Reinhardt retorted: 'I could never imagine that someone on such distant terms with me as the Princess would ever have moved to Leopoldskron on my account. You are also wrong in your assumption that I should think it worthwhile exposing the Princess as Jewish. Her outward appearance made it clear for all the world to see. Furthermore, since her aristocratic friends repeatedly stressed the particular piquancy of her Mosaic faith in her relationship with the Almighty (in Berchtesgaden), I have never thought otherwise. However, I am more than ready to believe her capable of adopting any other faith . . .'

The first cultural highlight following the annexation of Austria was the Salzburg Festival, which began on 24 July 1938. The leading figures of the Nazi regime now ruling the country they called Ostmark had put in an appearance in 'this fair German city'; the châtelaine of Leopoldskron was not, however, invited. Goebbels thought it important that the Salzburg Festival should become a genuine Reich festival. But with an eye on the Bayreuth Festival, in future 'no Wagner would be played' at Salzburg. Even so, the first Salzburg Festival of the Nazi era opened not with a Mozart opera, but with Wagner's *Die Meistersinger von Nürnberg*.

The party members in Salzburg did not like the new mistress of Schloss Leopoldskron. However, since the local Gauleiter's office naturally carried out the wishes of the Führer, conveyed to them by Wiedemann and supported by Field-Marshal Göring, the provincial governor, Dr Albert Reitter, was instructed to put the Schloss at the princess's disposal.

At all events the terms of occupancy were to be made absolutely watertight. Legally the position was that the Schloss was the property of the Province of Salzburg and that 'Her Princely Highness' was only granted rights of occupancy. The German Foreign Minister received a letter from his press attaché with the following justification: 'Since the person of the Princess Hohenlohe was judged critically in the former country of Austria, the provincial government has assured itself the freehold of the Leopoldskron estate under the property register. The criticism of the princess rests on the fact that Princess Hohenlohe has a bad reputation among the people of Salzburg, who have known her since her days as a girl from Vienna.'

The new châtelaine had the Schloss converted, regardless of expense. Since she had, from the very start, planned to hold large receptions there, an oversized electric cooker had to be installed, as well as a large refrigerator and all the most modern electrical kitchen appliances, for which in turn a transformer was necessary. A central heating system was installed. Since Stephanie enjoyed playing sports she had a tennis-court built. The extravagantly laid out gardens swallowed up money. In addition to all this there were very high staff costs.

The enormous costs of renovation and furnishing were not borne by the Province of Salzburg but by the central government in Berlin. To cover himself when making the payments, Wiedemann wrote that there were so many bills which, 'as the Führer himself says, increase the value of the Schloss, and since the Schloss is now state property, this is money well spent'. After Wiedemann had departed for San Francisco (see p. 105) his friend General Bodenschatz only settled these exorbitant invoices with reluctance. Finally, the Reich Party Leader, Martin Bormann, took over the payment of craftsmen's invoices, up to the summer of 1939.

As the princess was being attacked on many sides, Wiedemann had drafted a suitable document for her:

10 June 1938. Princess Stephanie von Hohenlohe is personally known to the Führer. She has at all times stood up for the new Germany abroad in a manner worthy of recognition. I therefore ask all German authorities concerned with domestic and foreign affairs to take every opportunity to show her the *special* appreciation that we owe to foreigners who speak up so emphatically for today's Germany.

Captain Wiedemann (Retd)
Adjutant to the Führer

As soon as the princess had established herself in Schloss Leopoldskron, she began to play the hostess. She succeeded in bringing a whole string of fairly important French, Britons and Americans to Leopoldskron, always with equal success: the guests were delighted by what they saw and, once they were home again, wrote about how good the Salzburg Festival was and that no better music could be heard than in Germany.

One guest whom Stephanie found very agreeable was the American conductor Leopold Stokowski; she discussed with him putting on open-air opera productions in the grounds of her mansion. Other guests were the theatre critic Philip Carr and Mrs Carol Carstairs, the wife of a prominent New York art-dealer. The world of French culture was represented by the president of the Paris

Mozart Society, Mme Octave Hombert, and Charles Bedaux, a right-wing confidant of the Duke of Windsor, who often holidayed at the nearby Schloss Mittersill, to play golf or tennis.

Stephanie was disappointed that the Führer never visited his 'dear princess' at Schloss Leopoldskron. Nor did Hermann Göring, who also had a residence on the Obersalzberg, just across the border in Germany. The most frequent guest was Fritz Wiedemann, though usually accompanied by his wife and three children.

The respected diplomat Herbert von Dirksen was one of those who often visited Stephanie at the Schloss; he came with his stepmother Viktoria von Dirksen, as members of Berlin's high society all knew each other well. And Stephanie often had herself photographed with the ambassador. From 1928 to 1933 Herbert von Dirksen had been the German ambassador in Moscow, then from 1933 to 1938 in Tokyo. Finally, he went to London in 1938 as Ribbentrop's successor, representing Germany at the Court of St James. As early as 1940 he was put out to grass.

His stepmother, Viktoria, was the second wife of the widowed and retired ambassador and privy counsellor, Willibald von Dirksen, who died in 1928. When she first met Hitler in Berlin, Viktoria was forty-eight and he was thirty-three years old. Before long Berlin was calling her the 'Mother of the Revolution' and 'Mother of the Movement'. Viktoria von Dirksen's 'Thursday soirées' – a regular political fixture – were held in her grand town house in Margaretenstrasse. Her carefully chosen guests included the Bechsteins, owners of the piano business, who had been among Hitler's earliest supporters in Munich. Hitler himself very rapidly rose to be the 'adornment' of the political salon. Viktoria's brother, Karl August von Laffert, as well as her son-in-law Werner von Rheinhaben, permanent secretary at the Reich Chancellery from 1920 to 1933, were also members of this circle.

Anyone who talked to Viktoria von Dirksen would be repeatedly informed about her 'diplomatic activity'. Even in private company, she would make enthusiastic speeches about the greatness of the Führer. One of Viktoria's 'speeches', made during a boat excursion on the Wannsee lake with members of the diplomatic corps, was summarised thus by the French ambassador, François-Poncet: 'All in all, Madame, you are to Germany what Joan of Arc would have been to France, had she not been burned at the stake just in time.'

One of Stephanie's 'conquests' during her young days in Vienna also visited her at Schloss Leopoldskron. He was Fritz Schönbichler, tall, fair-haired, good-looking and with piercing blue eyes. He was still a good friend of hers, and a brilliant pianist, who enchanted everyone with his playing.

At this point decisions had to be made about a professional career for Stephanie's son Franzi, who was still at Oxford University. His ambition was to join the German Diplomatic Service and, exploiting his acquaintance with Fritz Wiedemann, it was to Hitler's adjutant that he now turned for assistance.

Leopoldskron 5.2.1938

Dear Captain Wiedemann,

I am enormously sorry to hear that you have got to have a knee operation in the next few days. I hope it all goes off well and that you will soon be able to return to your sporting activities.

Meanwhile, I would like to take this opportunity, while you are laid up and perhaps have a little less to do, to put a request to you.

Would you be kind enough to answer a few questions that I have wanted to ask you for a long time?

First of all, what preparations, examinations or formalities are necessary for the German diplomatic service?

Are foreign qualifications such as the French 'Baccalauréat' or the British 'Diploma of Responsions' and 'Degree of Bachelor of Arts' recognised for a career as a German diplomat? I would also very much like to know, if an entrance examination is obligatory, whether one can take this before doing military and labour service.

I would be hugely obliged to you, dear *Herr Hauptmann*, if you could answer these questions as soon as possible. My address is 51 High Street, Oxford.

But now I must not bother or detain you any longer.

I am most grateful to you in advance and remain, with very best wishes for a speedy recovery,

Your sincerely devoted
Franz Joseph Hohenlohe

The very next day, Wiedemann forwarded the prince's letter to a senior counsellor named von Kotze in the German Foreign Office in Berlin, asking him to send Franz the papers he requested. Wiedemann added that the Führer was aware that the princess's son was thinking of joining the German Diplomatic Service. The reply written by 'Wiedi' – as Franz called him – gives precise information about the entry requirements for the Diplomatic Service he was so keen to enter.

However, it seems that Franz did not fulfil all the requirements, for on 25 October 1938 Wiedemann confirmed that, at Stephanie's request, he had spoken to a Dr Ilgner of the giant chemical concern, I.G. Farben. The young prince was now to send his application papers there with all speed. Wiedemann also advised Franz to give his name as a reference, when it came to the question of his Aryan ancestry – 'after I have looked at the papers myself, of course'.

Wiedemann went on to explain: 'Basically, I agree with your mother that you should grab this opportunity to join I.G. Farben. It offers plenty of prospects without closing any doors to you later on. Furthermore, Dr Ilgner feels it important, as does your mother, that you should do short-term military service . . . If I were you, I would also mention in your letter that at the moment your nationality is still Hungarian, but that you intend to apply for German nationality.'

Wiedemann's connection with I.G. Farben went back a long way. This was because of his extremely close relationship with Lilly von Schnitzler, wife of a main board director of I.G. Farben, Georg von Schnitzler. In 1934 the von Schnitzlers' daughter married Dr Herbert Scholz, who made a textbook career for himself in the Nazi Party. In connection with Stephanie's son, it is interesting to read a letter dated 23 November 1938 from Wiedemann to 'His Excellency Ambassador Döme Sztojay, Berlin'. In it he asks that the enclosed flask of lavender perfume from Princess Hohenlohe be passed on to

Herr Scholz, who was by then adjutant to the Regent of Hungary, Admiral Horthy. In this way Princess Stephanie did a little to help her son's job application, along with a gift to Schnitzler's son-in-law.

As for the 'short-term military service' mentioned in 'Wiedi's' letter, Franz asked for further details. It was a form of military service for men over twenty-four years of age. These men were occasionally called up for brief exercises lasting four to eight weeks. Thus Franz could take up his post with I.G. Farben without delay.

So that the young prince need not walk anywhere, two cars were placed at his disposal by Daimler-Benz AG in Munich – an open Type 170V IIIA sports car, and a supercharged cabriolet. But in December 1938 the firm wanted to have both cars back. Fritz Wiedemann, now promoted to *Brigadeführer*, immediately replied to say that both the prince and the princess wanted to go on using the cars over Christmas. Not until early in the new year would he be in a position to state how much longer the cars would be needed.

On 8 October 1938 Stephanie sent a letter personally addressed to State Counsellor Gritzbach, in which she suggested that art objects from Austria might be sold for hard currency to an interested group abroad. The reply she received was that the letter had been forwarded to the person responsible for such matters, the Reich Minister for Science and Education, Bernhard Rust.

The ministry, in the person of a principal secretary named von Normann, then sent Wiedemann a detailed statement of its position, which Wiedemann did not, however, agree with. He wanted the matter put before Field-Marshal Göring, particularly in view of Germany's urgent need to acquire foreign currency.

Stephanie was staying at the Adlon hotel in Berlin when her Hungarian lawyer, Dr Ernö Wittmann, wrote telling her about the interest expressed by an eminent British art dealer, Lord Duveen, which Wittmann had in turn discussed in Paris with Duveen's agent, Dr Simon Meller: 'Meller is of the opinion that should Berlin be inclined to sell any art objects of the 18th century, such as Watteau's paintings in Potsdam (especially *L'Enseigne de cher Guersain*), his syndicate would be happy to buy them and would pay well – and possibly also some 13 Rembrandt paintings of Jews! It would be a good thing if you could deal with this business in Berlin.' The princess had no difficulty in taking on this assignment. She had a sound understanding of art and was a shrewd negotiator, but time was against her – as would soon become clear.

One very special guest at Schloss Leopoldskron was the British politician and shipowner, Lord (Walter) Runciman. In 1938 he was Britain's official intermediary in the dispute between the Czech government and the Sudeten German Party (see p. 218 endnote). In the summer of that year he was sent to the Sudetenland to sound out sentiments there, and it was suggested to Princess Stephanie – probably by Wiedemann – that she should invite him to Leopoldskron as well. The groundwork was laid and Runciman spent several delightful days at the Schloss.

When he returned to England after a three-week stay in Czechoslovakia, he reported to the British government that 'Sudetenland is longing to be taken over by Germany, and the Sudeten Germans want to return to their homeland'. As the journalist Bella Fromm remarked, the princess had done a good job.

The press also linked Stephanie's name with the Munich Agreement, one of the first ever summit conferences, which took place on 29 and 30 September 1938: the heads of government or of state from Britain, France, Italy and the German Reich met to discuss Hitler's demand for the annexation of the German-populated Sudetenland. Until its incorporation into the new Czechoslovakian state in 1918, the region had been part of the Austro-Hungarian Empire; Hitler reasoned that since the *Anschluss* of Austria into the German Reich, Germany had a legitimate claim on this territory. Since May 1938, Hitler had been conducting an unprecedented war of nerves, by using the Sudeten German Party under Konrad Henlein, the so-called 'Reich Commissar for the Sudetenland', to raise the pressure on Prague ever higher with their demands for autonomy, accusations of Czech atrocities and threats of military action.

Finally, the British premier, Neville Chamberlain, anxious to salvage his appeasement policy, had several meetings with Hitler and accepted Mussolini's proposal for a four-nation conference. Without inviting the victim – Czechoslovakia – to the table, the Munich conference served to disguise the fact that Britain and France were giving way to the German dictator. The Munich Agreement of 30 September 1938 decreed that Czechoslovakia must hand over the territory in question to Germany between 1 and 10 October and in return received vague promises of an international guarantee. True, Hitler gave the assurance that this was his 'last territorial demand', yet he had long ago resolved to 'smash the rump Czech state'.

Chamberlain proclaimed his 'success' as a victory for peace, ignoring the profound shock caused in Moscow by the accommodation that the Western Powers reached with Nazi Germany. From Munich, there was a direct path to the Nazi–Soviet Pact of 23 August 1939, and thus to the Second World War, which broke out less than two weeks thereafter.

Fritz Wiedemann had written to Lord Rothermere at that time: 'It was her [Princess von Hohenlohe's] preparation of the ground that made the Munich Agreement possible.' The fact that the princess played a not inconsiderable part in bringing about this political event in Munich was also highlighted by the press. Although she did not see it that way herself, the princess wanted to send her congratulations to the British prime minister and the German Reich Chancellor. Staying at that particular moment at the Adlon in Berlin, she wrote to Adolf Hitler:

There are moments in life that are so great – I mean, where one feels so deeply that it is almost impossible to find the right words to express one's feelings. – Herr Reich Chancellor, please believe me that I have shared with you the experience and emotion of every phase of the events of these last weeks. What none of your subjects in their wildest dreams dared hope for – you have made come true. That must be the finest thing a head of state can give to himself and to his people. I congratulate you with all my heart.

In devoted friendship
Yours sincerely
Stephanie Hohenlohe

CHAPTER ELEVEN

Wiedemann's Dismissal: Stephanie Flees Germany

Early in January 1939 the game of hide-and-seek around Princess Stephanie and Fritz Wiedemann came to an abrupt end. Hitler found out that Wiedemann was Stephanie's lover.

But it was not only the love affair that led to Wiedemann's dismissal. Stephanie often sensed a distinct sullenness in Wiedemann. He accused her of knowing nothing of life in the German Reich except what she saw from her suite at the Adlon hotel. As Stephanie's son Franz tells us, his mother had even talked to Wiedemann's wife about her husband's very obvious problems. Anna-Luise Wiedemann described his 'outbursts of screaming' at home, if things were going badly at the Reich Chancellery. She would have much preferred to go back to their farm in Fuchsgrub. But Wiedemann was against that, chiefly because he did not want to damage their children's future prospects.

Since the *Kristallnacht* pogrom against Germany's Jews on 9 November 1938, there had scarcely been any more proper conversations between Hitler and Wiedemann. When Wiedemann wanted to talk to Hitler about this or that weakness in the system, the Führer simply did not listen. So it is not surprising that in Goebbels' diary, as early as 24 October 1938, we find this entry: 'The Führer tells me incidentally that he really has to get rid of Wiedemann now. During the [Munich] crisis he apparently did not perform well and lost his nerve completely. And when things get serious he has no use for men like that.'

Wiedemann had long suspected that he would soon be dismissed: 'I just hung on until Hitler sent me into the wilderness.'

When Wiedemann came into the Reich Chancellery on 19 January 1939, his colleague Julius Schaub said he was to go to see 'him' immediately. Hitler was standing in the conservatory. As Wiedemann later recorded, the Führer told him: 'I have no use for men in high positions – by that he probably meant Schacht[1] – and in my immediate circle – that meant me – who are not in agreement with my policies. I am dismissing you as adjutant and appointing you Consul-General in San Francisco. You can accept the post or decline it.' Wiedemann replied briefly that he accepted the position.

The recent biographer of Hitler, Ian Kershaw, describes the relationship between the Führer and his personal staff: 'Genuine warmth and affection were missing. The shows of kindness and attentiveness were superficial. Hitler's staff, like most other human beings, were of interest to him only as long as they were useful. However lengthy and loyal their service, if their usefulness was at an end they would be dispensed with.'[2]

The dismissed adjutant certainly did not want to earn less than he had been up till then – 1,500 Reichsmarks a month. Hitler assured Wiedemann that consuls were well paid and that in financial matters he would always see him right. In the end, Wiedemann succeeded in negotiating a better salary than that of his predecessor Baron Manfred Killinger. He was to receive 4,000 Reichsmarks a year more than Killinger, on the grounds that he had served for four years as the Führer's personal adjutant.

Wiedemann later described how, during this dressing down that lasted only a few minutes, Hitler constantly tugged at his own nose while gazing at the ceiling with a bored expression; the Führer also spoke to him about his relationship with the princess and said he must break it off immediately, since she was 'under suspicion'.

Goebbels once again commented that 'Princess Hohenlohe now turns out to be a Viennese half-Jewess. She has her fingers in everything. Wiedemann works with her a great deal. He may well have her to thank for his present predicament, because without her around he probably would not have made such a feeble showing in the Czech crisis.'

Wiedemann was forced to accept a further humiliation. He now had to take orders from his arch-enemy, the Foreign Minister, Joachim von Ribbentrop.

On 13 January 1939, shortly before Wiedemann's dismissal, the *Reichsführer* SS and head of the Gestapo, Heinrich Himmler, produced further damning revelations. He submitted a report to Hitler, which had been received from an undercover agent of the German Secret Service in England and contained credible evidence that for some considerable time Princess Hohenlohe had been working for British intelligence. This news was enough to send Hitler into a terrible rage, and he ordered a warrant to be issued for the princess's arrest. In hand-written notes by Stephanie that still exist, though they are undated and scarcely legible, we read this sentence: 'Gratitude of the Nazis: [I] was to have been arrested in Berlin a year ago.' However, the warrant was never enforced.

Nevertheless, material on the princess was also being gathered by the office of Himmler's second-in-command, SS *Gruppenführer* Reinhard Heydrich. But in late 1938 a report was made by SS *Obersturmführer* Bielstein of Department III, for his departmental chief, SS *Oberführer* Jost. It was pointed out to Jost that the file on the 'Princess Hohenlohe case' was not being maintained in the regulation manner. Documents had not been sent to the correct offices. Thus Heydrich had received a report on the princess's racial origins, which had *not* been drafted by the department responsible for Jewish Questions, run by Adolf Eichmann. This report had been 'full of inconsistencies'; and 'only an expert in this field' could give 'a really conclusive assessment'. One of Eichmann's staff, SS *Obersturmführer* Hagen, then gave his 'professional verdict: half-Jewess.'

Once Hitler had been informed of the close liaison between his adjutant and Stephanie von Hohenlohe, it emerged that his closest henchmen had long been privy to the open secret. Each of them now did his bit to show up the princess, even more than Wiedemann, in a far from favourable light.

Wiedemann found out to his great astonishment that the military intelligence service, the Abwehr, had also taken a close interest in him and his mistress. Admiral Wilhelm Canaris,[3] head of the Abwehr and attached to the Armed Forces High Command, was on cordial terms with Wiedemann. Thus it is no surprise that as early as the end of July 1938 Wiedemann was invited for a chat with Canaris. The Abwehr chief had no choice but to warn Hitler's adjutant about the intrigues that were clearly building up against him. Afterwards Wiedemann immediately discussed this with Stephanie, who was planning to sue the newspapers that had published defamatory articles about her. To help her in this, Wiedemann turned once more to Admiral Canaris, writing to him on 29 August 1938, at the Reich Ministry of War in Berlin:

Dear Admiral,

(1) I enclose a report from an agent, which may interest you. It comes from the famous Lescrinier.

(2) Princess Hohenlohe wishes to put an end once and for all to the gossip about her, and to answer the latest reports by foreign newspapers, by picking on one of the papers and taking legal action to force it to withdraw the false statements. As her legal adviser she has chosen the attorney Dr Sack, whom of course you know.

However, in order to pursue this action, I would be most obliged to you, *Herr Admiral*, if you could for the time being pass over to me all the newspaper reports about Princess Hohenlohe that have appeared in the last six months. I need hardly mention that I – who am always named in connection with the princess – also have a certain interest in seeing these matters finally laid to rest.

With a German salute!

Your very devoted

Wiedemann – Adjutant to the Führer

In his book *Der Mann, der Feldherr werden wollte* ('The man who wanted to command') Wiedemann described his posting as he wanted to see it: 'Just a few weeks earlier Colonel Oster,[4] who had particularly good contacts with the Foreign Ministry, told me that I was to be appointed Consul-General in San Francisco. The posting there was the final gesture of personal benevolence that Hitler showed me, as his former subordinate. For, when I returned from my trip to America in the autumn of 1937, I had told those who would listen: "Anyone who wants to do me a good turn can send me to San Francisco as Consul-General." This had even reached Hitler's ears. Ribbentrop actively supported my posting, since he had always suspected me of wanting to become Foreign Minister one day. He was happy to get rid of me in this way.' However, Ribbentrop had spelled out very clearly to Hitler that Wiedemann was closely involved with the Jewish Hohenlohe woman.

The diplomat Ulrich von Hassell,[5] who in 1938 was dismissed as Germany's ambassador to Rome, noted in his diary for 25 January 1939: 'I hear, incidentally, that Wiedemann has also been brusquely shown the door by H[itler] in person, interestingly also with the parting words: ". . . should you wish to accept the post." From a senior source I learned additionally that H[itler] told him he wanted to spare him any conflict between his own opinions and "those of the Führer". This would confirm my suspicion that Ribbentrop, with whom W[iedemann] was in considerable disagreement, is behind it all.'

Another diplomat, Reinhard Spitzy, who had been First Secretary at the German embassy in London since 1936, gives an unvarnished account of those events: 'However, our ambassador quickly noticed that Wiedemann was plotting with Hitler against him and Madame [Ribbentrop's wife] immediately declared him to be one of their most dangerous enemies. It wasn't long before Ribbentrop did in fact succeed in shooting Wiedemann down in flames, as he charmingly put it.' Spitzy goes on to write about Wiedemann's acquaintance with Princess Stephanie and recalls that she was described as the daughter of a Jewish dentist. Ribbentrop then really began to 'turn on the heat' and soon Wiedemann was 'out of the game'.

Leni Riefenstahl, the actress and film-maker whom Hitler so admired, recalled that Wiedemann's 'relationship with Hitler became more distant because of his half-Jewish girlfriend'.

From the day of his dismissal Wiedemann only entered the premises of the Reich Chancellery one last time. Shortly before his departure for the United States in early March, Hitler summoned him once more and walked up and down the drawing-room with him. Later Wiedemann found out from a friend that Hitler already regretted having dismissed him. Wiedemann was unable to say anything negative about his employer. Hitler had always treated him kindly, Wiedemann said, and never gave him any assignment that would have brought him into conflict with his conscience.

In his memoirs Wiedemann only makes very brief mention of his mistress, Princess Stephanie. Once when Forster, the Gauleiter of Danzig, had returned from a trip to England and reported that there 'they were thinking of inviting Göring for a visit . . . I immediately phoned a friend of mine, Princess Hohenlohe, and asked her to find out how much truth there was in this rumour'. And then again in connection with Stephanie's plan to set up a personal meeting between Hitler and Rothermere. There is not a single word about his love for her. And yet his greatest concern was to know that his mistress and her son Franzi were safe in Schloss Leopoldskron.

He confided to Göring:

I ask you to protect my honour and to intercede with the Führer in my behalf. When I took my leave of the Führer, he warned me against Princess H. in the interest of my future career. The Führer does not believe the princess can be relied upon and thinks that various anti-German articles in the foreign press can be traced back to her.

I have informed the Führer

(1) that I vouch absolutely for the princess's integrity and loyalty to the Third Reich and its Führer . . .

(2) that of course I have given the princess, as a foreigner, no information that might not be in the national interest.

I cannot prove these things, but on the other hand I *can* prove that the princess had a decisive influence on the attitude of Lord R[othermere] and thus of the *Daily Mail* . . .

After my departure, my enemies and those who are jealous of me will once again impugn my honour. I am defenceless against them. But I would like to be justified to some degree in the eyes of the Führer.

From a wide variety of sources, Hitler knew more about his staff than he let on. The Luftwaffe adjutant Nicolaus von Below confirms that it came as a complete surprise to everyone else, when they heard one day that Wiedemann had been dismissed without reason and transferred to the Foreign Service. True, von Below was glad he would not have to meet Wiedemann again. He found the man inscrutable and had always been suspicious of his high-profile links with foreign diplomats and politicians.

Although Wiedemann's dismissal created quite a stir in the German and foreign press, it appears that in Salzburg Governor Reitter knew nothing about it. Nor could he have guessed that the princess would leave Schloss Leopoldskron more or less overnight. As late as 18 January 1939 the provincial governor informed Stephanie that Professor Joseph Gregor of the National Library in Vienna had approached him about the Max Reinhardt library in Leopoldskron. Gregor, who claimed to be a leading historian of modern theatre, was entirely in favour of keeping the Reinhardt library locked away in Leopoldskron. Yet he was of the opinion that it should not remain a dusty exhibit, but that it could be of use to those interested; and selected scholars of repute should from time to time be allowed access to it for research purposes.

Governor Reitter doubted whether the princess, for all the generous hospitality she had brought to Leopoldskron, would agree to the professor's request to be allowed to visit her and discuss the matter.

Reitter's letter was not answered by the princess but by Wiedemann, from Berlin. He informed Reitter that the library belonging to Professor Max Reinhardt 'has been restored to him on the express orders of the Führer'.

At the end of January the princess, together with her mother, left Leopoldskron en route for London. The dream of the châtelaine to live in one of the most magnificent parts of the Ostmark had proved a brief one. She travelled with only a few personal belongings, but then gave her lover in San Francisco the task of arranging for everything else to be sent on to London after her. This operation took a long time. At the end of August 1939, the Governor of Salzburg province, Dr Reitter, assured Wiedemann, now in San Francisco, that he would make every effort to deal with the matter to his fullest satisfaction. In fact, the housekeeper at Schloss Leopoldskron, Frau Gwinner, who had been employed there in Reinhardt's day, was able to say exactly what belonged to the princess. Yet since there had been differences between the princess and the housekeeper, Frau Gwinner does not seem to have been prepared to offer much assistance.

Schloss Leopoldskron now became the residence of the local Gauleiter – until the Americans arrived in Salzburg at the end of the war. After the war the Schloss was given back to the Reinhardt family. Today it is the property of 'The Salzburg Seminary – A Community of Fellows'.

As far as Stephanie's widowed mother was concerned, Stephanie counted herself lucky that, at the end of the 1938 Salzburg Festival that summer, her mother married the ninety-year-old Hungarian, Kalman Negyessy de Szepessy, in the little provincial town of Boldva in Hungary. The 'groom' imposed no conditions whatsoever on his 'bride'. He remained in Hungary, while Ludmilla Richter returned to Leopoldskron as the Baroness Kalman de Szepessy. This meant that, like Stephanie herself and her son, Ludmilla also held a Hungarian passport. Stephanie knew more than enough about anti-Semitism at the highest level. On 9 November 1938, as already mentioned, the pogrom known as the *Kristallnacht* took place. This night of terror, echoing to the sound of shattering glass, spread with unremitting brutality right across the German Reich which, since 12 March 1938, had of course included Austria; 91 people were murdered and countless others injured, 191 synagogues were torched, some 7,500 shops were smashed up and looted, and nearly every Jewish cemetery vandalised. No fewer than 30,000 Jews were thrown into concentration camps. That was just the beginning; the night of pogroms was followed by unparalleled discrimination against Jews, and their progressive exclusion from the community – culminating in their death in the gas chambers.

Unfortunately Stephanie was unable to arrange permission for her aunt Olga, her mother's younger sister, to travel with her to England. Soon after Ludmilla's wedding, her sister Olga was arrested. She died in the Theresienstadt concentration camp on 27 September 1942.

CHAPTER TWELVE

The Lawsuit against Lord Rothermere

Stephanie von Hohenlohe returned with her mother from Salzburg to London where, as her son Franz confirms, she owned four houses. Exactly a year earlier, in January 1938, the princess had received her final cheque from Lord Rothermere in payment for her activities, together with the news that he no longer wished to employ her. Rothermere wanted to terminate her contract, since it might be 'misunderstood' if he were to continue his efforts to bring about an understanding between Britain and Germany. He had already told Stephanie this verbally, after she had given him a detailed report on the Blomberg-Fritsch[1] crisis.

Wiedemann found it inconceivable that Rothermere would want to go on taking Hitler's side. Stephanie warned Rothermere, although at that point he had already sacked her:

It's important to know what is currently going on in Germany. The Germans are going through a serious crisis. Changes are taking place, which are of the greatest importance for the future of Europe. All the conservatives are being thrown out and only extremists are keeping their jobs or being recruited . . . You must be very careful in future. To be quite frank, I do not see how it will be possible for you, under these new conditions, to continue to support Hitler in future and at the same time serve the interests of your own country.

She cleverly added: 'Hold on to this letter, so that it will be evidence of how accurately I have kept you informed. I'm serious; don't throw this letter away.'

A professional collaboration lasting seven years, and a once very intense personal friendship, had come to an end. Rothermere told Stephanie that 'he did not contemplate any more political missions'. However, through Wiedemann, she continued to be precisely informed about the correspondence between Rothermere and the Reich Chancellery, and knew that the press baron was certainly maintaining his contact with Hitler. Stephanie was pretty desperate, since the cancellation of Rothermere's payments placed her in considerable financial difficulties. As she herself wrote, she had always been very lavish with money and so had thrown away the chance to be 'one of the richest women in the world'. As soon as it became known that she was no longer His Lordship's emissary, her own 'market value' would drop significantly.

Placed in this predicament, Stephanie now hit upon an odd idea. She wanted to find out what Rothermere really thought about her. The next thing that happened was that a certain Baron Theodor Geyr von Schweppenburg, a minor official in the German Foreign Office, travelled to London, under the pretext of needing to speak to Rothermere in connection with an article he intended to write for a journal, the *Deutsch-Englische Hefte*. He carefully recorded his discussion with Rothermere and presented it to his lady 'client':

At the end I mentioned in passing that I had picked up certain hints from an American journalist, to the effect that a big publisher in America was interested in publishing a story in which Lord Rothermere's relationships with women, and in particular with Princess Hohenlohe, would be alluded to, with the intention of identifying Lord R.'s sources of political information. Lord R. seemed very embarrassed; he immediately said: 'Haha! I haven't seen the Princess for 14 months. I wish you would tell Herr von Ribbentrop that I consider her a very indiscreet woman. I don't think he likes her and I believe she was not received at the embassy in London, when he was ambassador here . . .' I

immediately changed the subject and asked him what he thought
of the political situation. He gave only a brief opinion and added:
'But you *will* tell Herr von Ribbentrop, won't you, that I have no
communication with Princess H. and that I consider her very
indiscreet!' I told Lord R. that I had no opportunity to see Herr v.
Ribbentrop, and that I was only one of his numerous staff, to
which he replied that he would give me a present for Herr v.
Ribbentrop (some 400-year-old Augsburg silver), and that when I
handed it to him I could pass on Lord R.'s message. 'Perhaps you
can also take with you a present for the Führer?' The Baron
declined the request.

Following Geyr von Schweppenburg's mission, Stephanie von
Hohenlohe decided to sue Rothermere. Unfortunately she had no-
one at her side at that moment, who might have been able to
dissuade her from this rash course of action.

She sought out the most prominent law firm of the day, Theodore
Goddard & Partners, who three years earlier had handled the
second divorce of Mrs Wallis Simpson, so that she would be free to
marry the former King Edward VIII. Even before coming to court,
the costs to be met were considerable, and of the £800 she had to
deposit in advance, £600 had already been used up. Stephanie was
asked to make further payments, but she did not do so. Five days
before the case was due to be heard, she was given an ultimatum.
She had to deposit a further £500. She managed to scrape together
another £200 and covered the balance with a post-dated and
unsecured cheque.

The case against Rothermere began on 8 November 1939 and
lasted six days in a crowded courtroom of the King's Bench Division.
The plaintiff claimed that in 1932 Lord Rothermere had promised to
pay her, as his European political representative, an annual sum of
£5,000 for the rest of her life. Furthermore, he had agreed to restore
her good name, since certain foreign newspapers had described her
as 'a spy, a vamp and an immoral person'. Stephanie also made it
clear to His Lordship that, should she lose the case, she would not
turn down an offer from an American publisher to publish her

memoirs, with particular emphasis on the political activities of Lord Rothermere, and his numerous improper liaisons with women.

In Germany Goebbels was following events closely: 'A case is being heard in London between Rothermere and Princess Hohenlohe over a retainer which this "lady" is demanding from him. In it, all sorts of embarrassing details are being trotted out. Some of them about Wiedemann, too. Even so, I do not believe the Hohenlohe woman has been spying. Sometimes she has spoken up for us.' Joseph Goebbels, Minister for Propaganda and National Enlightenment, and one of Hitler's henchmen considered to have an astute mind, was clearly uncertain as to whether the princess had been a spy, and if so, for whom.

Lord Rothermere, for his part, stated that his campaign for friendship with Nazi Germany 'was before Hitler ran amok'. When asked if the princess had acted as his 'ambassador', he retorted 'I am not a sovereign state yet'. He denounced as 'preposterous' the suggestion that he had agreed to support the princess 'for the rest of her life', and added: 'There was no opportunity of "giving" her money because she was always asking for it . . . She was always pestering and badgering me, so I sent her away to Budapest and Berlin.'

'But it was surely a little tough on Hitler?' the princess's counsel suggested.

'Oh, I'm not sorry,' Lord Rothermere replied. 'Hitler richly deserved it.'

The court-case did not leave Fritz Wiedemann unscathed either. In particular, a letter from him to Lord Rothermere was mentioned, in which he pleaded the cause of the princess. The Reich Foreign Minister, Ribbentrop, immediately requested a cabled report and, if possible, a copy of the letter or, failing that, a precise indication of its contents.

During the hearing, Lord Rothermere's defence counsel produced a trump card. He was in possession of the letter in question, which Fritz Wiedemann had sent to Lord Rothermere in the autumn of 1938, on behalf of his mistress, and which, although marked 'strictly secret and confidential', the barrister read out to the court.

Wiedemann informed Rothermere that the princess had approached him with the request to obtain Herr Hitler's consent for the correspondence between himself and Lord Rothermere to be submitted as evidence in a possible lawsuit. 'Your Lordship knows how very much the Führer values the princess's work for the improvement of relations between our two countries . . . It was she who gave you an introduction to the Führer. A fact for which he is equally grateful . . . Under these circumstances, and taking into consideration the Führer's noble and generous nature . . . I have no doubt that he will give her his permission to use the correspondence in question as evidence that she was in your service, since he will take the view that, in so doing, he will be helping her in her clash with a powerful man. Even though it is exceptionally awkward for him.'

It is known that Rothermere reacted very angrily to this letter from Wiedemann and threatened to go and see Hitler in Berlin, in order to tell him about this 'business Wiedemann and Hohenlohe have cooked up'. Thereupon Wiedemann indicated that as far as he was concerned there was no more to be said.

When the judge gave his decision every last seat in the courtroom was occupied. Mr Justice Tucker ruled against the princess. The claim she had made for a lifelong retainer fee was, he said, without justification. There was no evidence that her former 'employer' had ever made such a promise.

Lord Rothermere generously bore all the legal costs. But he refused to make any future payments either to her or her son. He did not even want her to go to the United States, but to stay in Europe. It is possible that he feared there would be further revelations on her part, which could be damaging to him at the very moment when he wanted to renounce his efforts on Hitler's behalf. At about that time, Rothermere published his book, *My Campaign for Hungary*, with a foreword by Winston Churchill. It did not contain a single word about the princess or her role as an intermediary.

On 3 September 1939, three days after the German assault on Poland, Britain declared war on Germany, and things which hitherto had been whispered about the princess often enough, were now spoken out loud: Stephanie von Hohenlohe-Waldenburg-Schillingsfürst, Jewish by birth, was a close friend of Hitler and was the Third Reich's most prominent propagandist abroad.

Now the American news magazine, *Time*, picked up on the events surrounding Stephanie von Hohenlohe in London. It reported an incident at the Ritz hotel, of which Princess Stephanie had been the focus. She had already become inured to abuse. But in the Ritz there was a sensational scene: when she walked into the hotel, she immediately caught the attention of four society ladies, the Duchess of Westminster, Lady Stanley, Lady Dufferin and Mrs Richard Norton. 'Even before the princess could be escorted to her table, mutterings could be heard from these *grandes dames*. Then the tranquillity of the dining-room was broken by a loud clear voice: "Get out, you filthy spy!" However, without batting an eyelid, the princess took her seat and the ladies went on with their meal. But when they left the room Mrs Norton stopped and informed the head-waiter that in future she and her aristocratic women-friends intended to dine elsewhere, for as long as the princess continued to be allowed into the Ritz.' Thus, Stephanie's financial predicament was further aggravated by social ostracism.

She had to admit to herself that, because of losing her lawsuit, no-one would want anything more to do with her, 'an unattached woman'. So in December 1939 she decided to leave London for America. She had realised long ago that Hitler was heading for a world war. Many American friends sent her invitations, although in the American newspapers, too, people could read that she was 'a spy, a glamorous international agent and a girl-friend of Hitler'.

Four days after judgement had been given against her in her case against Lord Rothermere, she wrote him a 'begging letter', which Lady Snowden – still a good friend of Stephanie – personally handed to the press baron. It read:

I don't know if you planned to ruin me, but in any case you have succeeded. This letter to you is the culmination of your victory over me. I will try to be as unmelodramatic as possible, which is not easy, since you have turned my life into a horror-play. One kind word to me from you could have prevented everything. You never had a better or more devoted friend than me. I would have gone through fire for you, and my devotion to you was like that of a faithful dog. You knew that, you knew it very well. And you knew it when you came to court. It was the cowards around you, the ones who hate me, who confused your sense of justice and turned you against me, which, as you know, I do not deserve.

Your barristers and solicitors, seventeen of them all told, and all your other friends, filled half the court when the case was being heard, while I was only accompanied by my 78-year-old mother, since my son has abandoned me, because he could no longer tolerate the passive resistance which arises from the allegation that I am a spy, and from my reputation as a spy. You had millions, I only had £250 – that was all I had left after my lawyers had milked me dry, and I had been forced to exist for two whole years without the income on which I had built my life. The fact that I am still in the land of the living today, is only due to my wanting to spare my boy from being the victim of a further sensation – his mother's suicide. But my indescribable misery will perhaps make me forget even this consideration.

'I say all this without trying to plead for your sympathy,' she wrote, yet she did precisely that. She appealed to Lord Rothermere as the father of a son, to think of her son as well, and not to 'ruin' his future. Then she resorted to another form of guile. She told Rothermere about the amazing financial offers the press had made to her, and their downright 'perverse' interest in the part of her life she had spent with him. She would never, of course, give any interviews or write any articles about it, she said, but added threateningly that she hoped she would never have to. She asked him to spare her from complete social humiliation and to guarantee her a carefree life, at least for the next three years. Should he no longer wish to communicate with her directly, he could do so through her one selfless friend, Lady Snowden.

Stephanie ended her letter: 'You hold the lives of two human beings in your hands, that of a young man full of hope for the future, and mine, which you have robbed of any future. – It is for you alone to decide what shall become of these two lives! S.H.'

At that time Rothermere would in fact have been prepared to finance Stephanie's upkeep, together with her mother and her personal maid, in somewhere like Mallorca, but certainly not in the United States where her lover was awaiting her.

Princess Stephanie and Lord Rothermere, who had attracted so much attention through a number of spectacular political initiatives, were never to meet again. Rothermere died in Bermuda scarcely a year after the court case.

As *Time* magazine put it: 'The curtain swiftly fell on the comic-opera lawsuit of Her Serene Highness Stephanie Hohenlohe-Waldenburg-Schillingsfürst versus Viscount Rothermere.'

CHAPTER THIRTEEN

The Spy Princess as a 'Peacemaker' in the USA

'One of the most fanatical exponents of National Socialist ideology . . . was Stephanie, Princess Hohenlohe-Schillingsfuerst, the "princess" in quotation-marks, because she was not born in silk and satin. She became a princess by marriage. . . She was one of the first female agents sent abroad by the Nazis before they came to power.'

This statement comes from the German-Jewish journalist, Bella Fromm, who from 1939 onwards lived in exile in the USA. In the unpublished writings she left on her death, Fromm goes into more detail about Nazi espionage activities in the United States during the Second World War. She wanted to reveal how effective and widespread the operations of Hitler's women agents had been. Many of those involved in political intrigue in the US were second generation German-Americans, others were visitors from Germany. The women Bella Fromm knew to be Nazi spies included Lily Barbara Stein and Elizabeth Dilling from Chicago, and a Brooklyn waitress named Hedwig Engemann. The American aviatrix Laura Ingalls was in close contact with two of Himmler's most dangerous operators, Baron Kurt Ludwig von Gienanth and the German cultural attaché, Richard Sallet. Since these two Nazis held diplomatic passports, it was a long time before their anti-American activities were discovered. In addition to these, there was the 'beautiful Nazi spy', Inga Arvad, who hit the headlines by becoming romantically involved with the young John F. Kennedy.

'Hitler's spy princess', Stephanie von Hohenlohe, turned her back on Europe in December 1939. 'By this time even I was convinced that Hitler had chosen the path of destruction.' She and her mother headed for a country that was still neutral and where her friend Fritz Wiedemann was now working as Consul-General in San Francisco.

If the princess in fact wanted people to believe she had left England voluntarily, this was not wholly correct. As a precaution, her friend in London, Ethel Snowden, got an MP to put down a question in the House of Commons early in December, asking whether His Majesty's Government intended to expel the princess 'in view of her close relationship with the German Reich Chancellery'. However, since it had come to the notice of the Home Secretary that the lady in question, a Hungarian citizen, had already taken steps to leave the country in the next few days, he for his part did not propose to take any action.

So it was that on 11 December Stephanie, under the assumed name of Mrs Maria Waldenburg, boarded the SS *Veendam* at Southampton with her mother, and reached New York eleven days later. The American journalist Helen Worden, who wrote for the *New York World-Telegram* and knew the princess, was on the quayside and described her arrival: 'Her auburn hair was combed straight back. She wore a silver-fox turban with a provocative pink rose perched on it, a three-quarter length silver-fox coat, a black dress of silk jersey (an Alix model), and black kid Perugia sandals with sky-blue platform soles. Gorgeous diamond ear-clips were fastened on her small, pretty ears, and a scintillating diamond clip lightened her dark dress.'

This elegant outfit and extremely high-heeled shoes, not to mention the falsification of her age – she claimed she was six years younger than she was – certainly did not deceive the immigration official. He recognised her because, ever since Wiedemann's arrival, the FBI had put out instructions that Princess Hohenlohe was to be kept under observation. She was only carrying a visitor's visa, but the fact that she was travelling with 106 pieces of luggage did not suggest that she intended to leave the USA again in the near future. Not only was the FBI notified of her arrival; so were the leading newspapers.

Stephanie von Hohenlohe in her evening finery, 1932. (*Ullstein Bilderdienst, Berlin*)

Archduke Franz Salvator, the natural father of Stephanie's son Franz, with his wife, the Archduchess Marie Valérie, youngest daughter of the Emperor Franz Joseph of Austria. (*Author's archive*)

Stephanie with her son Franzi, 1915. (*Private collection, Prince Franz von Hohenlohe*)

Stephanie in 1914. (*Private collection, Prince Franz von Hohenlohe*)

Stephanie as a volunteer nurse, 1916. (*Private collection, Prince Franz von Hohenlohe*)

Stephanie on the Riviera, outside the Carlton hotel in Cannes, 1928. (*Private collection, Prince Franz von Hohenlohe*)

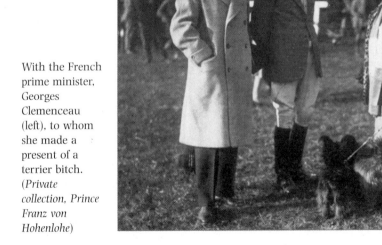

With the French prime minister, Georges Clemenceau (left), to whom she made a present of a terrier bitch. (*Private collection, Prince Franz von Hohenlohe*)

The Regent of Hungary, Admiral Horthy (in office 1920–44), who did his best to resist Nazi intimidation before and during the Second World War. (*Private collection, Prince Franz von Hohenlohe*)

The British newspaper magnate Lord Rothermere (left), with Joachim von Ribbentrop, in London in December 1934. At this time Ribbentrop was Hitler's foreign policy adviser but had no official status in the German foreign ministry. He spent three weeks in London meeting influential people. (*Ullstein Bilderdienst, Berlin*)

Stephanie in London, 1932. (*Private collection, Prince Franz von Hohenlohe*)

Stephanie with her guests at a hunting-lodge near Fuschl, in the Salzkammergut, near Salzburg. Left to right: Captain Donald Malcolm, Stephanie, Christopher Rhodes, Lady Hyde, the Comte and Comtesse Boisrouvray and Stephanie's son Franzi. (*Private collection, Prince Franz von Hohenlohe*)

Stephanie with Archduke Franz Salvator and Lady Melchett. (*Private collection, Prince Franz von Hohenlohe*)

A visit to the Berghof, Hitler's private residence, in January 1936. Seated, Stephanie von Hohenlohe and Magda Goebbels; behind, left to right: Lord Rothermere, Ward Price (of the *Daily Mail*), Adolf Hitler, Fritz Wiedemann, Joseph Goebbels. (*Private collection, Prince Franz von Hohenlohe*)

Stephanie with Fritz Wiedemann. (*Private collection, Prince Franz von Hohenlohe*)

Lady Astor addressing a meeting on women's rights in London, 1933. (*Ullstein Bilderdienst, Berlin*)

14, BRYANSTON SQUARE,
LONDON, W. 1.
TELEPHONE: PADDINGTON 7773.

12. –I. –37

Sehr geehrter Herr Reichskanzler,

Unser Abschied war so
schnell und im bei sein so vieler
Menschen — das ich kaum Zeit
hatte Ihnen richtig für Ihre
Gastfreundschaft zu danken. —
Sie sind ein charmanter
Hausherr — dazu noch Ihr schönes
excellent geführtes Haus in dieser

Stephanie's letter to Hitler, dated 12 January 1937, thanking him for his hospitality at the Berghof on 6–8 January. (*Bundesarchiv Coblenz*)

Adolf Hitler with Unity Mitford in Munich, 1937. (*Ullstein Bilderdienst, Berlin*)

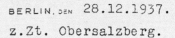

ADOLF HITLER

Hochverehrte Prinzessin !

    Für die Bücher über amerikanische Hoch-
und Brückenbauten, die Sie mir als Weihnachts-
geschenk übermitteln liessen, sage ich Ihnen recht
herzlichen Dank. Sie wissen, wie sehr ich mich
für Architektur und die damit zusammenhängenden
Gebiete interessiere und können daraus ermessen,
welch' grosse Freude mir Ihr Geschenk bereitet.

    Ich habe mir ferner berichten lassen,
wie aufrecht und warmherzig Sie auch im vergan-
genen Jahre in Ihren Kreisen für das neue Deutsch-
land und seine Lebensnotwendigkeiten eingetreten
sind. Ich weiss wohl, dass Ihnen manche Unannehm-
lichkeiten daraus erwachsen sind und möchte Ihnen
deshalb, hochverehrte Prinzessin, aufrichtigen
Dank sagen für das grosse Verständnis, das Sie un-
serem Volke im ganzen und meiner Arbeit im beson-
deren immer entgegengebracht haben.

    Ich verbinde mit diesem Dank meine herz-
lichsten Wünsche für das neue Jahr und verbleibe
mit ergebensten Grüssen

Letter from Hitler to Stephanie, thanking her for her Christmas present, some books about American architecture and civil engineering. (*Hoover Institution Archives, Stanford*)

Stephanie with Fritz Wiedemann, sailing on the *Europa* to America. (*Private collection, Boris Celovsky*)

Schloss Leopoldskron, near Salzburg, which was expropriated by the Nazis and occupied by Stephanie in 1938–9. (*Ullstein Bilderdienst, Berlin*)

Stephanie in the Waldorf Astoria hotel, New York, 1939. (*Private collection, Boris Celovsky*)

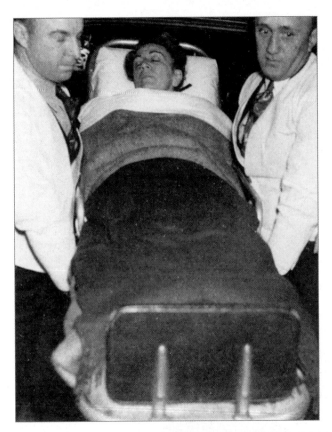

With sirens wailing, Stephanie is carried on a stretcher through San Francisco to a hearing before the immigration authorities. (*Private collection, Boris Celovsky*)

Stephanie with Lemuel Schofield, head of the US immigration authorities, who became her lover. (*Private collection, Boris Celovsky*)

Stephanie von Hohenlohe, the 'lady with connections'. (*Private collection, Boris Celovsky*)

Drew Pearson, a leading US columnist in the 1950s and 1960s, who collaborated with Stephanie on her biggest publishing coups. (*Ullstein Bilderdienst, Berlin*)

Axel Springer (1912–85), founder of one of Germany's largest postwar press empires, who employed Stephanie in her later years. (*Ullstein Bilderdienst, Berlin*)

Karl-Heinz Hagen, editor of the German magazine *Quick*, in his interview with President Kennedy, organised by Stephanie and Drew Pearson. (*Private collection, Prince Franz von Hohenlohe*)

Stephanie's last resting place in Meinier, near Geneva. She was in fact born in 1891. Even in death she lied about her age. (*Private collection, Boris Celovsky*)

Any number of press people immediately took an interest in Stephanie. She and her mother had booked a suite at the Waldorf-Astoria hotel. A mob of photographers descended on the princess and wanted to get pictures of her in her rooms. In interviews in the hotel lobby Stephanie announced that she had left Britain in order to write her memoirs in peace and quiet, at the request of her literary agents Curtis Brown & Co.

In 1976, when Brown himself was asked what he recalled about the princess, he well remembered this lady who had 'a great deal of charm. Like everyone who left Germany at that time, she wanted to write a book. About scandal among the top Nazis, no doubt . . . You ask whether money was discussed? She talked of little else!'

The first call she made on arrival in New York was to her lover in San Francisco, Fritz Wiedemann, who wanted to cross the continent to see her straight away. However, she preferred not to be seen so soon with a well-known Nazi.

On the afternoon of Christmas Day, Stephanie and her mother moved to the quieter but no less prestigious Plaza hotel, where she took a smaller room, with no telephone; but the press soon turned up there too.

Very soon after her arrival, Stephanie received a letter from Harry Bull, the publisher of Town & Country magazine. He enquired whether she, as a 'celebrity', could write a series of articles for his international readership. One of the articles was to be entitled 'The Intelligence of Adolf Hitler'. Harry Bull wanted to know whether the Führer always relied on his intuition, or was only guided by 'cold' logic. Did he possess anything that could be described as a sense of humour? Was he the type of man who thinks in a calculating, businesslike way? Why did he spend so much time in Berchtesgaden and give the government and foreign envoys the bother of travelling to the Bavarian Alps with their concerns? Then he was also interested in Stephanie's prediction of the length and outcome of the present war. However, the princess was unable to summon up the enthusiasm to write these articles.

Since Stephanie was unwilling to give endless interviews, the pressure from reporters became ever more burdensome, and she hoped the interest in her would soon die down. But Alan Collins, who ran the New York office of the Curtis Brown literary agency, wrote to her on 12 January 1940: 'It's not enough for your only answer to be always: when is this ever going to stop? It will only stop when the newspapers, who want an interview, at least have a chance to see you. I know this is tiresome – but it's just the price you pay for being famous.'

Three days later, on 15 January 1940, the following internal memorandum was sent to the editor of *Town & Country*, a Hearst magazine, by its publisher, Harry Bull:

The point of the Princess Stefi story is that since she says our material is totally erroneous and gives a false impression of her, she should tell the true story herself.

She says that up to 1932 she was a private citizen and cannot understand why she has become so celebrated and misunderstood. In order to clear herself, she should start with a little sketch of her youth, marriage, early private life, and then her connection with Lord Rothermere and the political situation which brought her into prominence.

If Princess Stefi was photographed ten thousand miles from where she really was, she can explain this; she could point out that she had not been in Czechoslovakia for some ten years, but that the newspapers had conceived some fantastic legend, and there seemed no way to stop it.

While everyone wondered what was going on when she lived at Leopoldskron, the princess says she was trying to save things – furniture, etc. – for Reinhardt, and that she did many kind things for emigrés through her connections.

The Hungarian to-do was something on which she worked at Rothermere's directions, and she did the same in bringing him together with Hitler in Berlin – or did she have no association with this meeting?

In other words she will have to go a little bit into some of the legend in order to explain that it is not true, and where she was.

All we would really like is a straightforward sketch of her life and the true story of the activities that brought her so much uncalled-for publicity. She is obviously a misunderstood woman and that should be the key to the story. I should think 3,000 words would be adequate . . .

If she would like, we could get Harry de Pauer to help her put the material into shape, or we could send over Rosamund Frost, who speaks excellent German, and would do an editorial job on it from the viewpoint of the *Town & Country* office.

Harry Bull's next step was to explain to Stephanie that the 'twist about the misunderstood woman' – since that was supposedly how she saw herself – could be effectively worked up by the magazine. Furthermore, everything that appeared about her in *Town & Country* would hopefully stoke up demand for her forthcoming memoirs.

On 22 January 1940 even that highly respected newspaper, the *New York Times*, stooped to publishing a detailed article under the headline 'Princess plays role in Nazi diplomacy'. Referring to 'secret preparations' for the military invasion and dismemberment of Czechoslovakia, in which Stephanie was said to be involved, the article went on: 'The Princess is without doubt the star among a whole group of female members of the former German aristocracy, who have been recruited by Hitler for a wide variety of operations, many of a secret nature. They have been acting as political spies, propaganda hostesses, social butterflies and ladies of mystery.'

The anonymous writer generously conceded that only a few women were fitted for such activities. But Stephanie had all the qualifications. She was thoroughly familiar with the ways of the world and was fluent in several languages. Her most outstanding ability was that of coaxing secrets out of people while diverting all suspicion away from herself. The key sentence ran: 'On orders from the Nazi party, Princess Hohenlohe has placed the heads of Lords, Counts, and other highly placed personages at the feet of Hitler.'

Always with an eye to her as yet unwritten memoirs, Stephanie was anxious to become acquainted with Sinclair Lewis, one of the most important American novelists of the day. In 1930 he was the first American to receive the Nobel Prize for Literature, and since 1928 had been married to Dorothy Thompson, a leading American journalist, whom Stephanie had already met in England. She also hoped to use the actress Marion Davies, whom she had met in Germany, as a way of getting access to her lover, the newspaper magnate, William Randolph Hearst. Stephanie even tried to get in touch with two of the most prominent anti-Nazi emigrés from Germany, Marlene Dietrich and Erich Maria Remarque, author of the anti-war novel *All Quiet on the Western Front*. However, both of them refused since they knew all about Stephanie's strong links with National Socialism. Later, when she met Charlie Chaplin, she expressed surprising enthusiasm for his film satire on Hitler, *The Great Dictator*, which was premiered in New York on 15 October 1940.

Curtis Brown's man in New York, Alan Collins, gave the princess precise instructions on how best to approach the material she had gathered for her memoirs. She was neither to play up nor play down her own part in events, but 'concentrate on what you saw and your reactions thereto'. More important than the mere narration of events would be 'your judgement as to what made people act the way they did'.

She was to have a ghost-writer, Rudolf Kommer, the former agent of the theatre director Max Reinhardt, who had quit Hitler's Germany in May 1940 and now, like Stephanie, was living in a New York hotel.[1] At a time when German armies were sweeping across Holland, Belgium and Luxembourg, Kommer and Stephanie had lengthy discussions about the political situation in Europe. In the middle of May, after one of these conversations, Kommer put his thoughts into a letter:

Dear Princess,
Our conversation yesterday has given me much to think about and I am sure you will not mind if I set out my views again.
    There are moments when opinions can and must change profoundly. The invasion of Holland is just such a moment in world history, and here in the United States you can see by the day, no, by the hour, what a complete turnaround is happening. Yesterday America's entry into the war was an entirely taboo

subject – today it is already under discussion. Overnight it can become a reality.

Anyone who does not believe in a German victory, i.e. in the total collapse of Europe, and who has the fate of the German people at heart, must somehow take a stand today. It is wrong to think that men like Rauschning[2] and Thyssen[3] are not listened to . . .

If the crazy and criminal plans for reducing each other to rubble are to be foiled where Germany is concerned[4] – and this seems to be the critical problem for Europe in the next few years – then Germany must emerge from the war intact. However, this is only possible if a sensible end is put to the war, from the German side, before it ends in horror. This means that we cannot just watch with our arms folded until Nazi Germany is annihilated, or it has annihilated the West; we must somehow get rid of this total insanity and apply common sense and humanity again. Whether this can or will happen, I don't know. What we need are true patriots in Germany, who can win the trust of the German people, and true German patriots outside Germany who can win the trust of Germany's present opponents. These two groups must be in communication with each other. Is this feasible? I don't know. At all events, men like Bruening,[5] Rauschning and Thyssen will be the principle assets in the regeneration of Germany.

It was for this reason alone that I made the case yesterday at such wearisome length for *nailing one's colours to the mast*. Whether this is done publicly with *éclat*, or quietly, but with overwhelming conviction, in private – makes no difference. If the future Germany is not to arise under another dictator, if that Germany, which even today under the eyes of the Nazis exists in some inchoate and unrecognized form, is to spring into life neither stunted nor disadvantaged, then its diplomatic representatives, so to speak, must today place their credentials before the world. But in order to win its trust, we must somehow show our colours. The day will come when it is too late to do this.

Today it is a painful question of honour, whether one is for or against the Monster – and questions of honour do not wait long for an answer.

Perhaps, my dear Princess, you can now better understand why I pressed you so strongly. There are still a few idiots who misunderstand you. Admittedly – you can't hang an 'anti-Hitler' placard round your neck. But you know exactly who this is all about. The world is ablaze and neutrality is something absolutely unrealistic. Those who are lukewarm will be damned whatever happens. Show your true colours – that is the watchword!

With very best wishes, in all devotion

Yours

Rudolf K. Kommer

While the princess devoted herself intensively to marketing her memoirs, and had still not seen her beloved Fritz, he himself had become truly smitten by another 'lady spy'. In San Francisco, the British Consul-General, P.D. Butler, had learned of a claim by American military intelligence (G-2) that they were 'in possession of evidence that Wiedemann and a Baroness Reznicek are leaders of an alleged conspiracy, the purpose of which is to overthrow the present German government and arrange for Wiedemann's return to Germany, in order to set up a new regime'. The lady in question was a journalist, Baroness Felicitas von Reznicek, who was suspected of various undercover activities. She had joined the Nazi Party in May 1933, soon after Hitler seized power.

Wiedemann and the baroness, fourteen years his junior, had met and fallen in love at a cocktail-party in San Francisco. Since Wiedemann had been dumped by Hitler, it seems that Felicitas von Reznicek was working on a way to enable him to jump across to the other side. The British ambassador in Washington, Lord Lothian, was informed that the baroness had an interesting proposition for the British government, namely that Wiedemann was seeking 'asylum in Britain' and was willing to co-operate immediately and in every way with the British government. But from the embassy there was no reaction whatsoever to Wiedemann's offer.

In February 1940 Baroness Reznicek was unexpectedly ordered 'home to the Reich'. Which authority had previously despatched the journalist to San Francisco is not at all clear. Wiedemann claimed that she was not from the Foreign Ministry but from one of the other 'departments'. Felicitas von Reznicek kept on delaying her departure from California, because she did not want to be separated from Wiedemann. In May she finally left the country on a Japanese ship. She was accompanied by Wiedemann's daughter, who had been entrusted to the baroness for the long journey back to Berlin, via Japan, China and the Trans-Siberian railway.

We must assume that Stephanie knew nothing about her lover's liaison and that the baroness had left the field clear for her, before Stephanie finally reached San Francisco in late March. Wiedemann had even hoped she might arrive sooner, as his letter of 3 March 1940 shows:

I was pretty disappointed that you didn't come this weekend. It would have been so lovely, and now we must put it off for at least a week, as I have a lot to do in the next few days.

As regards your book and your questions, I am in complete agreement. Your questions, especially, are very clearly formulated. But before we do any more work on this, we must talk about it first. You must surely realise that the whole world will know you have certain information that you can only have obtained through me. You must, after all, think of my position. Several books have already been published, which deal with exactly the same subject; so readers will only be interested in something extraordinarily sensational. Perhaps we could promote you as 'the first woman to write a book about . . . [Hitler]' But it has to be more than sensationalism. You have too good a name for that kind of thing. In short, we have to talk about all this. Writing letters can lead to too many misunderstandings.

If those reporters make it too difficult for you to come here by car (and I'm almost convinced that's true), then you could come by train. You ought to take a sleeper and then you'd arrive here in the morning. If you're not among the very first passengers off the train, and if Mirle [Wiedemann's daughter, Anne-Marie] picks you up, I can't imagine there would be any complications. It's not so easy for me to get to LA as it's not in my area. And if I'm caught outside my patch, I can be fired on the spot. And you can imagine that my dear boss [Ribbentrop] would take great delight in doing that. So come here soon!

All my love

F.

It was in the romantic holiday resort of Carmel on the Pacific coast, 90 miles south of San Francisco, that Fritz and Stephanie fell into each other's arms, almost a year after Hitler had imposed this separation on them. Wiedemann wanted to please her and handed her a 25-page manuscript containing his own thoughts and notes for the chapter in her planned memoirs, to be titled 'Hitler through a woman's eyes'. He had even gone to the trouble of writing a foreword for Stephanie's book. It goes without saying that Wiedemann was the princess's best source for the intimate details of Hitler's life.

From that moment on, the Austrian woman and her Bavarian lover were under observation, wherever they went and literally round the clock. It started with a nocturnal rendezvous in the General Grant National Park. FBI agents submitted exhaustive reports, in words and pictures, to their chief, J. Edgar Hoover, who recorded even the most trivial detail for posterity. After her first meeting with Wiedemann – having put her mother and son into a small hotel in San Mateo – Stephanie flew to Philadelphia to offer her manuscript to friends, for publication in local newspapers. On 28 May she returned to California. She landed at Burbank, outside Los Angeles, where Hoover's FBI spooks were waiting for her.

From Burbank she took another plane north to Fresno and booked into a hotel under the name of 'Mrs Moll'. Before going up to her room, no. 624, she asked at the reception desk if there was any post for her. Soon after that she received a phone-call, which was made from a public call-box. The people listening in to the call only understood the words 'Hello, darling', since the rest of the conversation was in German. But they were able to 'decipher' one phrase: 'Restaurant Omar Khayyam'. 'Mrs Moll' and Fritz Wiedemann then met there and lunched apparently undisturbed, little knowing that meanwhile the princess's hotel room was being thoroughly searched by the FBI.

After their meal, the princess checked out of the hotel and drove with Wiedemann in a blue 1940 Chevrolet convertible, east along Highway 180, towards the General Grant National Park. As was customary, at the entrance to the park they had to sign a visitors' book. The entry read: 'Fritz Wiedemann, Consul-General in San Francisco.' After a brief tour of this park, the couple drove on to the Sequoia National Park, where at 5.30 p.m. they arrived in Kaweah Camp. There they rented a chalet as 'Mr and Mrs Fred Winter' from San Francisco.

'After an evening meal in the coffee-shop belonging to the camp, and run by Mr Koch, a fanatical Nazi supporter, the subject and Wiedemann retired to their cabin for the night at about 9.30 p.m. With the co-operation of the park wardens the agents secured cabin No. 545, from which anyone entering or leaving No. 582 could be observed. Surveillance of cabin No. 582 was maintained throughout the entire night. At 8 a.m. on 30 May the subject Hohenlohe and Wiedemann left their cabin and drove straight to the General Grant National Park, where they had breakfast.' Despite this romantic bliss, the princess claimed years later, when being interrogated by the FBI, that intimacy never occurred between her and Wiedemann. That night, as only one cabin had been assigned to them, Wiedemann had, she said, slept in the car.

Their tour took them back to the coast, to the Café Lucca in Santa Clara and then on to the San Francisco suburb of Hillsboro and 1808 Floribunda Avenue, the residence of the German Consul-General. It was there that the Wiedemanns lived, and from now on, with Frau Wiedemann's agreement, so did Stephanie von Hohenlohe and her mother.

So as to have better protection from the press in California – by now Stephanie was being described as the new Mata Hari – Wiedemann made an official declaration to the Foreign Ministry in Berlin: 'One of the circumstances under which my wife and I have taken the Princess as a guest into our home is that she is about to publish her memoirs, for which various publishers have offered her advances of up to $40,000.'

Soon after Wiedemann's arrival in the USA, a report on his sphere of activity appeared in *Time* magazine: 'Fritz Wiedemann, Adolf Hitler's tall, burly 47-year-old "Man Friday", who as personal adjutant to the Führer, has already had to carry out a number of sensitive missions in Europe, was last week dispatched to a new post. He will act as Germany's Consul-General in San Francisco. Captain Wiedemann's job will be to calm ruffled German-American relations and make the Nazi regime more palatable to a far from friendly USA.'

As early as 2 January 1940, the US Treasury Secretary, Henry Morgenthau Jr received the following report from one of his officials, John Wiley:

> An informant on [the Wall Street banker] Mr Kuhn's staff reported a while back that the German Consul-General in New York, Borchers, was saying that Wiedemann has been given the job of keeping America out of a war with Germany, since both Hitler and Wiedemann are worried that Germany could repeat the Kaiser's historic error of bringing America as a combatant into the German war. Wiedemann and Stephanie worked closely together on the 'non-violent' solution at Munich and we may suppose that they are now expected to perform a similar task in the United States. Borchers went on to say that Wiedemann has been sent to San Francisco as a future German ambassador, should one need to be appointed; this would suggest that Wiedemann is not *persona non grata* with Hitler.

However, Wiedemann maintained that he was definitely *persona non grata* with Ribbentrop and that he had been sent to America because Hitler no longer trusted him.

There is a very revealing picture of Fritz Wiedemann's activities in the USA to be found in the Federal German Archives in Koblenz, in the record of a lawsuit in California, in which a certain Alice Crockett sued Wiedemann for a sum of money. This American woman living in San Francisco claimed to have been employed by the German Consul-General and accused him of being the head of an espionage network operating in the USA and the western world.

Alice Crockett had found out that the German government had transferred a sum 'greatly in excess of $5 million, to be used in espionage activity in the United States and the Western Hemisphere'.

A number of men and women, whose names the plaintiff did not know, were on Fritz Wiedemann's payroll. The German government and Wiedemann also employed 'Princess Holenhole' [*sic*]. Her job was to 'contact and pay the aforementioned employees the aforementioned sums of money for espionage activity on behalf of the Government of Germany and the defendant, Fritz Wiedemann.'

From San Francisco, Fritz Wiedemann made numerous trips to Mexico, usually to exchange secret documents. Alice Crockett went with him to Mexico herself, in the first week of April 1939. And Stephanie von Hohenlohe also travelled to Mexico, though without Wiedemann's knowledge.

Wiedemann was meant to devote special attention to the Panama Canal Zone and to find out ways of making the canal impassable to United States shipping.

The plaintiff further claimed that Wiedemann had the task, 'as head of German espionage in the United States and Western Hemisphere, to promote strife and class hatred in the United States', and that he 'did employ ruffians to stir racial hatred . . . and did pay the said ruffians from the funds of the German government . . . and that the defendant Fritz Wiedemann did encourage strikes of all types and kinds of industry . . . for the purpose of undermining the strength and ability of the United States to prepare to fight for the national defence'. Fritz Wiedemann's 'spy-ring' included numerous factory supervisors, foremen and workers, especially in the steel and armaments industries. The persons named were paid by Fritz Wiedemann.

Alice Crockett had also been told by Wiedemann that he 'directed the activities of the German-American Bund (League) . . . and was active in secretly storing large quantities of ammunition in the USA, and more particularly in the eastern portion of the United States and New Jersey; that this ammunition was to be used by members of the German-American Bund in fighting against the government of the United States.'

But Wiedemann was not working alone. On the east coast, German propaganda was in the hands of Dr Friedhelm Draeger, based in New York. Under him, the New York office was run by Dr Mathias Schmitz, while the head of propaganda on the west coast was Hermann Schwimm. Alice Crockett's deposition did not mention the names of anyone else working for Wiedemann.

However, it seems that Wiedemann told Crockett he was working with the famous transatlantic aviator, Charles A. Lindbergh. Wiedemann used him to lull the Americans into a false sense of security from attack by Germany. Because of his high reputation with the American public, Colonel Lindbergh was 'the best propagandist in America for Germany and Nazism'. Wiedemann told the plaintiff that Lindbergh was 'working for and with the Nazis'. Wiedemann also worked with Henry Ford, and the Ford Motor Company, which had important investments in Germany, in 'furthering the German and Nazi cause in the United States'.

According to Alice Crockett's submission, Wiedemann had 'serious misunderstandings . . . with high officials of the German government and the Nazi Party, including the Führer, Adolf Hitler himself, Joseph Goebbels, the head of propaganda, Field-Marshal Göring, and others whose exact names and titles are unknown to the plaintiff'. The issue was usually whether Fritz Wiedemann, as head of the propaganda section, was capable of performing his tasks adequately.

Since Wiedemann was anxious to know 'whether his work was being done to the satisfaction of the German government, the Nazi Party and the aforementioned high officials', he sent Alice Crockett to Berlin on 1 May 1939. There she visited Hitler, Goebbels, Göring and other senior military and party officials. Everywhere she found satisfaction with Wiedemann's activities. In respect of her services, Wiedemann had agreed to pay Alice Crockett the sum of $500 per month plus expenses. As she had worked for six months and incurred expenses of $5,000, Crockett was claiming a total of $8,000, but she asserted he had not even paid a part of this. She therefore asked the court to award her this sum of money, together with her legal costs. It appears that the court ruled in the plaintiff's favour. In the notes left by the journalist Bella Fromm, there are also indications that Wiedemann was heavily involved in espionage and that the Panama Canal played a certain role in this, as did the building up of a German-Japanese spy network.

Ever since Stephanie had been back at Wiedemann's side again, there were intense discussions about the political situation, and how this terrible war in Europe might be ended. In New York, Rudolf Kommer had sent her off with some ideas which she was very keen to put into practice.

Hence, on 27 November 1940, there was a meeting in suite 1024-1026 of the Mark Hopkins hotel in San Francisco between two men and a woman: the person who joined Fritz and Stephanie for 'peace talks' was Sir William Wiseman, former head of the British Secret Service in the western hemisphere and now a partner in the prestigious Wall Street banking firm of Kuhn, Loeb & Co.

The object of this conspiratorial encounter was to work out a plan for persuading Hitler to make a separate peace with Britain. Stephanie von Hohenlohe had the experience and ability to take on the role as intermediary between London and Berlin. She was firmly convinced that Adolf Hitler would be delighted to see 'his dear princess' again. Wiedemann suggested that she should travel on her Hungarian passport through Switzerland to Berlin and personally present Hitler with an Anglo-German peace plan. In her own unpublished memoirs Stephanie genuinely saw herself as the woman who wanted to stop the war and who could have been a peace broker. She initially believed that her efforts, together with those of Wiseman and Wiedemann, would meet with success and that the war would be over by the beginning of 1941. Her son Prince Franz even published an essay to this effect, entitled 'The Woman who Almost Stopped the War'.

The three 'peacemakers' were clear in their own minds that the fighting had to be stopped and that the moment for this could not be more favourable. The man best suited to do this, they thought, was the British Foreign Secretary, Lord Halifax, whom both Wiedemann and Stephanie knew very well.

The question also arose as to who in Germany would back such a peace plan. The first name to be mentioned was that of Crown Prince Wilhelm, then came the Chief of Police in Berlin, Count von Helldorf,[6] and the Chief of the Army General Staff, General Franz Halder.[7] (Stephanie even mentioned the Gestapo and SS chief, Heinrich Himmler, as a possible ally, on the grounds that he was a 'royalist', which gives an indication of how out of touch she was with the realities of Nazi Germany.) It was not particularly clever to mention the other names in the hearing of a member of British intelligence, since it revealed the identity of potential German resistance fighters who might be unwittingly exposed.

Trustingly, Wiedemann also informed Sir William that the German embassy in Washington and all official German establishments in the USA had received instructions from Berlin not to do anything that might mobilise American public opinion against Hitler and the Third Reich. However, Wiedemann expressed the belief that National Socialism, if only by reason of its revolutionary nature, would inevitably come into conflict with the USA.

The 27 November meeting, which had been preceded by shorter discussions between Wiseman and Wiedemann, or Wiseman and Stephanie, was bugged by the head of the FBI's San Francisco office, N.J.L. Pieper, recorded on tape and later transcribed as an 111-page document. On 13 January 1941 President Franklin D. Roosevelt received a 30-page summary of the meeting of the 'peace envoys' in California.

Hoover's summary includes this account of the princess's contribution to the discussion:

> The Princess stated that she had not seen Hitler since January 1939. Wiseman then suggested that Hitler might think she was going to Germany on behalf of the British. In reply to this remark, the Princess stated she would have to take that chance but that Hitler was genuinely fond of her and that he would look forward to her coming, and she thought Hitler would listen to her.
>
> When asked by Wiseman just what she would say to Hitler, she replied, 'I must say more than "war is terrible and must stop".'

She stated she would make Hitler see that he was 'butting against a stone wall' and make him believe that at the opportune moment he must align himself with Britain and that such an alliance would bring a lasting peace.

The Princess stated that she would set forth three powerful arguments: First that Hitler had failed to conquer Britain [two months earlier the RAF had beaten off the German Luftwaffe, and Hitler's plans to invade Britain were postponed indefinitely. *Tr.*]; secondly that the alliance with Russia [i.e. since the Nazi–Soviet Non-Aggression Pact of August 1939. *Tr.*] and Italy was of little importance compared to an alliance with Britain which would bring about a lasting peace. She stated also that 'Mussolini is a clown, the laughing-stock of the whole American nation'. [. . .]

She continued that the third point in her discussion with Hitler would be to point out the strength of the American nation and that 'anybody that told Hitler that the German Reich was stronger than the United States, was telling damn lies'.

Stephanie pointed out to her colleagues that President Roosevelt was already technically in breach of US neutrality by sending fifty destroyers to Britain at America's expense. A few days later, on 8 December, Winston Churchill sent a long and historically decisive letter to President Roosevelt, asking for America's financial and material assistance in waging the war against Nazism. He ended the letter: 'If, as I believe, you are convinced, Mr President, that the defeat of the Nazi and Fascist tyranny is a matter of high consequence to the people of the United States and to the Western Hemisphere, you will regard this letter not as an appeal for aid, but as a statement of the minimum action necessary to achieve our common purpose.'

Roosevelt himself did not think much of the endeavours of Wiseman, Wiedemann and Princess Stephanie, yet he gave them some consideration. Firstly he thought Hitler unpredictable; secondly Sir William Wiseman was known to be the mouthpiece of a political group in Britain headed by Lord Halifax. These individuals were pinning their hopes on being able to bring about a lasting peace between Great Britain and the German Reich.

It emerged from the report to Roosevelt that none of the three 'peacemakers' trusted each other. It can be assumed that Wiseman wanted to persuade Wiedemann to sign a statement in which he would betray his frank opinion of Hitler. In the two reports that Wiseman had sent to the British embassy, he represented Wiedemann as a genuine and serious opponent of Hitler and an honourable Bavarian officer. Yet in the discussions Wiedemann seemed very inept and frequently lapsed into German, until the princess forced him to conduct this vitally important conversation in English. Towards the end of the meeting, it was agreed that they should bypass the British Ambassador in Washington, the Marquess of Lothian, and send their peace proposal direct to 10 Downing Street. The princess remarked that Churchill knew her personally and knew of 'the other reports' that she had delivered in the past.

But, as we now know, events had already overtaken Stephanie and her well-intentioned peacemakers. Despite Britain's perilous position, Churchill's government had rejected all earlier peace feelers put out by Germany. Churchill believed that, even without direct military intervention by the USA, its economic support would gradually turn the tide. As he wrote elsewhere in his 8 December letter to Roosevelt: 'If . . . we are able to move the necessary tonnage to and fro across salt water indefinitely, it may well be that the application of superior air-power to the German homeland and the rising anger of the German and other Nazi-gripped populations will bring the agony of civilisation to a merciful and glorious end.'

CHAPTER FOURTEEN

Stephanie's Fight against Expulsion and Internment

In November 1940 Princess Stephanie's temporary visa expired. She tried to get it renewed on the grounds that, given the current political situation, she would rather remain in the United States and stay with friends. But her application was refused. The head of the FBI, J. Edgar Hoover, blocked it. And he informed his subordinates about the lady:

> Stephanie von Hohenlohe-Waldenburg, who uses various aliases, is very close to Fritz Wiedemann, the German Consul-General in San Francisco . . . and in the past has been suspected by the French, British and American authorities of working as an international spy for the German government . . . The princess is described as extremely intelligent, dangerous and cunning, and as a spy 'worse than 10,000 men' . . . I would like to stress emphatically that in my opinion this woman's visa ought not to be renewed. I would further suggest that she be deported from the United States at the earliest possible moment.

Stephanie's son now had an excellent idea. His mother should go through the formalities of marrying one of her long-time friends. He should of course be an American, and then, as his wife, she could not be deported. Franzi was thinking here of Donald Malcolm, though Malcolm did not accept an invitation to come to California.

Instead he suggested that Stephanie should travel down to Mexico, which she later did, but only for a few days.

On 14 December Stephanie and Fritz Wiedemann met for the last time in their love-nest, the St Francis hotel. Three days later a police officer informed the princess that her temporary residence permit was not being renewed, and that she had to leave the country within four days, that is to say on 21 December.

The events leading up to Stephanie's deportation were also being closely followed at the Reich Chancellery in Berlin. Joseph Goebbels commented with glee in his diary for 22 December 1940: 'We remember the "Princess" who is today destitute and has been deported from the USA. Wiedemann has completely fallen for her, sexually.' At that moment Goebbels was sitting with Hitler in the air-raid shelter of the Reich Chancellery, as the air-raid siren had just sounded. The Führer said he did not believe the Americans would enter the war. They were afraid of Japan.

Prince Franz, Stephanie's 26-year-old son, was earning his living in New York as an artists' and photographers' model. As soon as he heard about his mother's deportation he gave an interview to the tabloid *PM*, in which he understandably presented his mother in the best light. All the same, he felt it was not a good thing for her to be living in the home of the German Consul-General. He said she had no connection whatever with the Nazis, and was not even in favour with them any longer. He was anxious to tell the public that 'incidentally, she is not Jewish, has not had any cosmetic facial surgery, and is certainly not 120 years old'.

On 27 December Stephanie decided, with her mother, secretly to leave the extremely hospitable Wiedemann home. She was fortunate, once again, that an old friend of hers, Vilma ('Mimi') Owler Smith, lent her an apartment in a building on Forest Avenue in Palo Alto. Mimi Smith also organised an attorney for her, Joseph J. Bullock. The first thing the lawyer did was ask a woman doctor to sign a certificate stating that neither the princess nor her mother was well enough to travel. Armed with this document and with an affidavit from Stephanie, Bullock headed for Washington on New Year's Eve.

Stephanie's affidavit makes astonishing reading:

I hereby expressly declare that I am not and never have been in sympathy with Germany or the Axis Powers in their present state of war, and that all my sympathies lie with the kingdom of Great Britain and its people. Further: that without any basis a misleading, false and libellous smear on my good name has been published, purely due to the fact that I was perhaps unwise enough to have accepted the invitation of the German government's representative in San Francisco, to be his house-guest. As soon as I recognised this fact, I left the residence of the person in question and have had no further contact with this person.

Thus, within a few days, her lover had become an anonymous 'person'. Stephanie felt that Fritz Wiedemann could have done a great deal more for her in fighting her threatened deportation. And her new 'best friend', Mimi Smith, chimed in as well. She now took over the 'negotiations' with Wiedemann, and the first thing she tried to do was get money from him for Stephanie. When that failed, she threatened blackmail, needless to say under Stephanie's guidance. She would inform the German embassy in Washington of the fact that Wiedemann had been in contact with the British authorities.

Yet Wiedemann refused to be cowed and simply drew a line under the love affair. He was unable to accede to the princess's wish for further financial contributions. What is more he asked her to repay all the money he had lent her from his personal account since her arrival in the United States, a total of $3,003. In a sad letter he bade farewell to his mistress:

I am choosing this somewhat unusual route, in order to be reasonably sure that my letter will in fact reach you; after the experience of recent days, this seems necessary. After you left I tried for two whole days to get news of you by telephone. The guardians of your hiding-place were so good that I did not succeed. I don't know whether we will ever get a chance to discuss the bitterness of the last few days, like sensible human beings. The heavy blow that struck you like a bolt from the blue does much to explain your behaviour. I do know that you no longer wish an approach on my part and that you will do everything to avoid it. Even so, I cannot simply draw a line under the years which, thanks to you, were among the richest and most wonderful of my life. I know that today you will treat me with cold disdain when I tell you that, wherever a call from you reaches me, I will be there for you, just as far as my strength allows.

I still have to answer your last letter personally. You asked me for a sum of money that I no longer possess. You, or possibly your friend who acts for you, seem to think I can, like a cashier at a bank, withdraw funds that do not belong to me, i.e. embezzle them. I refused and replied that I would try to get the money for you, if you were to hand over your shares as collateral. I assume this was not an unreasonable demand, since your representative, whom you have only known for a few days, was trustworthy enough for you to give her the key to your safe. Secrecy was guaranteed, as I discovered in a conversation with a representative of the Bank of America. If the worst happened the papers could have been deposited in the safe in my office.

I regret having given you the funds a year ago, which you have been in need of in the last few days. Had I not done so then, I could have given them to you now and then I would not have had to be reproached by you for failing you at this crucial moment.

This brings me to the point that still has to be sorted out between us. I've given you the entire savings that I have here. It was money put by for my family for an emergency, if I ever have to leave here, which may very soon be the case. The shares and jewellery *you* own are today worth many times more than what I have. I emphasise that I don't need the money today, nor even tomorrow. But maybe one day I'll need it in a hurry. For this reason I must know your address, or that of your representative, who has the job of sending me the money. I have written to [Donald] Malcolm about it. He has not replied to me, and I obviously can't force him to. Do you want to put me and my family in a situation where we need the money urgently and can't find you because we don't know where you live? The only thing I am asking of you is to tell me whom I can approach in order to get back the sum of money you owe me. There must be someone who can confirm to me that they are acting for you. You may be quite sure that I won't ask you for repayment, as long as I don't need the money urgently.

I have given you the following sums:

	$
A year ago in New York	1,500.
Here for a trip to NY	850.
Christmas 39, for Franz's trip to NY	60.
A cheque that was not honoured	20.
Telephone calls to NY in last few weeks	73.
On our very last day	500.
	3,003.

7 April

According to the archives, this large sum was never repaid by the woman whom Wiedemann still loved.

In the end, after her son Franzi had made a plea on her behalf, the Hungarian embassy in Washington took up her case, as she was a Hungarian citizen, and obtained a twenty-day postponement of her deportation. Stephanie could stay in the country until 11 January 1941. The plan was that on that day she was to sail on the passenger-ship SS *Exeter* from New York to Lisbon. But the princess's health was not good. In her mind, the only thing left to do was to write directly to the US president, Franklin D. Roosevelt. In a long letter she related half her life story and invoked her acquaintance with his mother, whom she had twice met socially: once in Paris and once in Salzburg. Finally, in well-chosen words, she came to the matter in hand:

Please allow me to appeal to you as a man, and as president of a free country. Permit the authorities to grant me a reprieve. Give me time to restore my good name for the sake of my son, whose future is in jeopardy. Grant me the same privileges that this land of freedom would grant to anyone who is not guilty of an unjust or disloyal act. Please spare me the humiliation of having to leave this country under such oppressive circumstances, as though I were a criminal.

Most sincerely yours,
Stephanie Hohenlohe

Yet on 9 January the princess was informed by her attorney that all efforts to save her from deportation had failed. She had a nervous breakdown and threatened suicide. A Catholic priest was summoned, and her friend Mimi tried to reach President Roosevelt by phone. Franzi hastened to California from New York. The warrant for Stephanie's forcible deportation had been signed by the head of the Immigration and Naturalization Service, Major Lemuel Schofield, who had recently taken over responsibility for the Hohenlohe case. However, if the princess could deposit a bail fee of $25,000, she would be spared detention. Mimi agreed to pay her bail.

Stephanie was then informed that the hearing in connection with the enforcement of her deportation order would take place on 17 January at 10 a.m. in the offices of the Immigration Service. At the appointed time Stephanie von Hohenlohe arranged to be transported there in an ambulance with siren wailing, and then carried in on a stretcher. The press were already there and one reporter managed to snatch a photo of her. The inevitable chaos ensued, and Schofield decided immediately to adjourn the hearing to the princess's apartment in Palo Alto.

Although the princess had to make her statements under oath, the information she gave was very vague. She was represented by her two attorneys, Bullock and White, and her son had arrived from New York again. An official doctor was called in from the US Department of Health. The investigating officer, Earl A. Cushing, questioned Stephanie about the purpose of her stay in the United States. The reason she gave was: to write her memoirs. After a brief intervention by her lawyer, White, the interrogation of the visibly exhausted princess was interrupted and adjourned. Nonetheless the immigration authorities ordered an 'extremely discreet surveillance of the subject'.

There was also a message from the Secretary of the Treasury, Henry Morgenthau Jr, to say that he was anxious to see the princess deported: 'Britain, the country she came from, refuses to "take her back". The State Department indicates that Japan would be prepared to issue her with a transit visa, always provided that Russia co-operates, since that would be the only way she could be deported to Hungary, of which she is a citizen. I have issued instructions that this should happen as quickly as possible.'

Another lawyer was called in to say that he had obtained forty-two refusals of a visa for the princess, and thus it was impossible for her to leave the United States.

The whole business about 'the Hungarian woman' irritated the president himself. On 7 March 1941 F.D. Roosevelt gave his Attorney-General Robert Jackson an unambiguous directive: 'That Hohenlohe woman ought to be got out of the country as a matter of good discipline. Have her put on a boat to Japan or Vladivostok. She is a Hungarian and I do not think the British would take her off. That is their lookout anyway. F.D.R.'

At this point, on Saturday 8 March, Schofield had the princess arrested at her apartment by officials of the Immigration and Naturalization Service (INS). He planned to 'ship her across the Pacific to Siberia'.

A week later Schofield visited her in the INS detention centre in San Francisco. It was the worst thing the 48-year-old Lemuel Bradley Schofield, married with four children, could have done. He fell fatally in love with his 'prisoner'. There was no way she was going to be sent to Siberia. He intended to examine her case again thoroughly, to see if she really was a Nazi agent. Even Jackson, the Attorney-General, played a benevolent role, and finally on 19 May the princess was a free woman. However, the following conditions were imposed on her:

(1) She must at all times keep the district director of the INS informed of her place of residence.
(2) She is not allowed any contact whatsoever with the German Consul-General in San Francisco.

(3) She may not, without the knowledge and approval of the relevant INS district director, have any direct or indirect contact with a representative of a foreign government.

(4) She must establish residence in a small town with no airport.

(5) On request, she must report her address to the INS district director and answer all questions put to her relating to her activities.

(6) She may not, without the consent of the INS district director responsible for her place of residence, give any lectures, or interviews to the press, nor issue any public declarations of documents or any other statements.

On 1 July Stephanie and her mother moved from Palo Alto to the Raleigh hotel in Washington DC, where Schofield was also staying, though he was unaware that the FBI were preparing a report about this. 'When Schofield was in the hotel . . . he spent the whole time with Princess Hohenlohe, either in her room or his. On one or two occasions it was obvious that Princess Hohenlohe had spent the whole night with Major Schofield, as she was found in his room at 8.30 or 9 a.m.'

Franzi von Hohenlohe had again put in a plea for his mother's release. Back on 16 April he sent this telegram to the president's wife, Eleanor Roosevelt:

WOULD NOT HAVE BEEN SO BOLD AS TO WIRE UNDER ORDINARY CIRCUMSTANCES BUT SINCE YOU ARE IN CALIFORNIA COULD YOU POSSIBLY GRANT ME THE FAVOR OF A SHORT MEETING BEFORE YOUR RETURN EAST VERY SINCERELY
PRINCE FRANCIS HOHENLOHE 360 FOREST AVE PALO ALTO.

He received this prompt reply:

16 April 1941

My dear Prince Hohenlohe,

Mrs Roosevelt asks me to say that she received your message while she was in California, but her time was so short she could make no appointments.

Very sincerely yours,
Secretary to Mrs Roosevelt

Wiedemann's days as Consul-General in San Francisco were also numbered. On 16 January 1941 President Roosevelt had ordered the closure of all official German premises in the USA. Their staff had to leave the country by 14 July that year.

But Wiedemann did not want to return to the German Reich. Like the princess, he now offered his services to the Americans. He was prepared to reveal everything he knew as a former intimate of the Führer. It came to the ear of the FBI chief, Hoover, that Wiedemann had made an offer to the Hearst publishing group '. . . to put his entire knowledge of the Nazi situation at their disposal, provided he is allowed to remain in the USA'. Hearst was willing to pay Wiedemann the sum of $15,000. Hoover contemplated keeping Wiedemann on as a defector and double agent. But the State Department and ultimately President Roosevelt himself turned this idea down. Wiedemann had to leave the USA.

Wiedemann relates in his memoirs how in July 1941 he returned to Berlin via Lisbon, and two days later was called in to a meeting with the Foreign Minister, Ribbentrop. He wanted to hear Wiedemann's views on America and whether it would enter the war. Wiedemann could only reply in the affirmative.

Wiedemann was able to spend ten days on holiday at his farm in Fuchsgrub. Then in November 1941 Hitler posted him as Consul-General to the Chinese seaport of Tientsin. On Ribbentrop's orders, his wife and children were not allowed to travel to China with him. He remained there until 18 September 1945, some weeks after the Japanese surrender, when he was captured by the US army and later taken to Washington. Prior to this he was subjected to a lengthy interrogation, recorded in a 100-page document. Anyone looking for the princess's name will only find it briefly mentioned twice. When questioned about his time as German Consul-General in San Francisco, Wiedemann stated that he had received 'a great deal of information through his good friend Princess Stephanie Hohenlohe'. The interrogating officer, Colonel Heppner, asked Wiedemann to spell the name and also wanted to know if she was American-born. Wiedemann replied: 'No, Hungarian. She lived in London for a long time and was an intermediary between Rothermere and Hitler.'

In Washington DC Stephanie enjoyed relative freedom but had serious financial worries. So she decided to look for a way of making some money. She discussed this with Major Schofield who, in late July 1941, sent a confidential memorandum to the newly appointed Attorney-General, Francis Biddle: 'Princess Hohenlohe has suggested making a public statement about the dangers threatening this country and the whole world, and at the same time demonstrating the weaknesses of Hitler and his policy, and showing how he might possibly be overthrown.'

The princess would be prepared, Schofield went on, to write a series of articles either under her own name or anonymously. She could speak in German, French and Italian, in short-wave radio broadcasts beamed from America to Germany and the occupied countries. She could reply to the isolationist speeches by Lindbergh and his supporters, she could write pieces for various magazines and give lectures to women's clubs, as well as at other meetings and historical seminars. She could also be useful in producing foreign language propaganda.

Schofield summarised his conversations with Stephanie in a memorandum:

(1) Her personal experience of Hitler over six years enables her to draw a true-to-life picture of Hitler and his methods. She can describe his falsity, his treachery and his cunning. She can show him up for what he is, not an audacious conqueror, but a sly and crafty crook who does not hesitate to apply the crudest methods to achieve his ends; and who only attacks when he is sure of his absolute superiority, when he has got his opponent politically, morally and physically on the ropes. In order to achieve his purposes, he resorts to the cheapest trickery and does not even shrink from murder. Princess Hohenlohe can underpin all this with numerous statements that he has made to her, as well as the political views he has personally expressed.

(2) By reason of the precise knowledge she has of the situation in Europe, she can make a particularly strong point of the fact that the President must be given the most extensive powers in order to

stand up to Hitler and to be able to co-ordinate all operations in this country. This is absolutely necessary, even if it means temporarily giving up some of our democratic ideals. If you want to preserve and guarantee the future liberty of this great democracy and of the individual, then you must now curtail some of these democratic ideals.

(3) Princess Hohenlohe can make it clear that it is idle to hope that Hitler could ever be mollified and persuaded to enter into civilized international relations. A peace treaty negotiated with him means the end of democracy, as his many broken treaties and promises demonstrate. She can prove by what he has said to her that he has no time for 'old-fashioned morality'; he described holding to an agreement that is no longer of use to him, as 'the ideas of those gentlemanly old liberals.' He told her his policy was to alter his behaviour according to the demands of the moment, to suit his requirements at the time: 'They can't nail me down!' She can show how stubborn Hitler is when he wants to achieve a goal, that he never abandons his objective, he simply changes his methods in order to achieve it. He himself admitted he lets people believe he has given up his plan; but in reality he has only altered the way he intends to carry it out.

(4) Based on her experience, she can confirm that America is the only power strong enough to thwart Hitler's plans to impose his order on the world.

(5) She can make it clear that our country must act to protect itself. Hitler will not rest until he has destroyed our economic system and has infiltrated our country with his own doctrines. Chiefly because we are helping Britain. For this reason, if for no other, Hitler will get his revenge and will do everything in his power to destroy and subvert our nation. Once, in the princess's hearing, he boasted that he never forgets and never forgives 'those who stand in his way'. He once told her the war was principally a political and psychological one, rather than a war of armaments. The greatest mistakes made up to now, he said, were those due to ignorance of countries, their customs and characteristics and especially the mentality of their leaders.

(6) [-]

(7) The Nazis' methods should be made to look ridiculous. Their radio broadcasts and newspaper reports should be exposed as deceiving the German people.

(8) No-one in the world is working as hard for peace as the President, no-one has the power he has to bring this peace about. America must speak and act in a warlike manner in order to impress and intimidate the Nazis. It is unpatriotic to criticize the President, since that jeopardizes his efforts to prepare the American people and the nation's resources for the worst that may happen. Nothing helps the Nazis more and gives Hitler more personal pleasure than publicly expressed opposition to the President, strikes and other signs of disunity.

(9) We should not put so much stress on how powerful Germany is. The Nazis are not invincible. They have been able to win so far, not because of their military skill but mainly because of their numerical superiority. While others were preparing for peace, Hitler was making his dispositions for war. If things change and armaments are more equally distributed, Hitler can be dealt a crushing defeat.

(10) There are many signs that Hitler is gradually weakening and beginning to have doubts. That can be seen in his Russian campaign. In May 1938 a report appeared in the British press, that Czechoslovakia was mobilizing out of fear that Hitler might be planning an invasion of Russia. At the time Hitler had poured scorn on this idea in a conversation with the princess: 'Do you think I'm a fool? I would never dream of attacking Russia, except as a desperate last resort, if the Reich was in great danger.'

The list of Stephanie's ideas is a fascinating blend of analysis with a little wishful thinking, and the understandable aim of presenting herself as a great protagonist of America.

This report was locked away by Attorney-General Biddle, and was meant to be kept secret, especially from J. Edgar Hoover. But some anonymous person leaked the memo to the FBI chief, who was furious. Where was all the detailed information on espionage that the princess could have provided in the interests of national security? What is more, on 18 August Francis Biddle had told the FBI he had instructed Schofield to send the princess back to California.

But Stephanie moved with her mother, and for part of the time her son, to a little white house in the Washington suburb of Alexandria, Virginia, to be closer to her new lover, Lemuel Schofield, who. wrote her a charming love-letter: 'Everything about you is new and different and gets me excited', he wrote on his typewriter. 'You're the most interesting person I've ever met. You dress better than anyone else, and every time you come into a room, everyone else fades out of the picture . . . Because of you I do so many crazy things, because I'm mad about you. Now you know.'

However, Hoover was soon on the trail of the couple and on 24 October he had someone find out the identity of the owner of 612 Beverly Drive, Alexandria, which was not difficult. Major Lemuel Schofield was frequently seen there visiting the princess, and as the house was extremely small, the old baroness, Stephanie's mother, left the scene during these trysts and went to stay in a hotel.

On 8 December, the day after squadrons of Japanese bombers attacked and destroyed a large part of the US Pacific Fleet in Pearl Harbor, Stephanie and her mother went to a movie. At the time they were staying with friends in Philadelphia. After leaving the cinema they were surrounded by FBI agents. The princess was arrested immediately, but not her mother. In FBI raids right across the country Germans, Italians and Japanese, now the enemy, were taken into custody. Although Stephanie's passport stated that she was a Hungarian citizen, she was classified as German and taken to the internment camp in Gloucester City, New Jersey. A hearing before the complaints commission ruled against the princess.

On 13 February 1942 the Attorney-General, Francis Biddle, signed an order for 'the internment of Princess von Hohenlohe-Waldenburg, German citizen, resident in Alexandria, Virginia, as she is a potential danger to public security and peace in the United States'.

While this was happening, Hoover ordered his agents to search the princess's home from top to bottom. As none of these men knew any German, they took her mother's handwritten cookbook, thinking it was Stephanie's diary. Also in the house they found the Gold Medal of the Nazi Party, which Hitler had conferred on Stephanie. It was photographed and confiscated.

The princess had to spend seven months in the Gloucester City internment camp. She wrote melodramatically about her sufferings there:

> The living conditions there were appallingly unhygienic and inadequate in every way. Twenty women occupied a single room, which was filthy, and also served as a dump for old furniture, dirty, worn-out mattresses, and mountains of dusty old papers. For weeks we had no bed-linen or hand-towels; instead we were given old rags. The floor was made of stone, icy cold and damp.
>
> The wind blew from all sides through the ten big windows, and most of the time the heating did not work. The doctor advised us: 'Keep your feet off the floor if you don't want to catch pneumonia. This is no place for women.'
>
> We spent our time sitting on our beds, fully clothed, with our overcoats on. There was no furniture in the room except for our beds, a table and a bench. During the night the warders made the rounds twice and shone torches in our faces, to count us. Sleep was impossible under those conditions.
>
> We had six drains in the room which, because of the faulty sewage system, flooded the room whenever it was high tide on the Delaware river. Sometimes the stench was unbearable.
>
> I had to share the room with prostitutes and sluts with venereal disease . . .
>
> For months on end our food consisted of nothing but beans, fatty meat and meat-balls. We didn't eat the fatty meat, and just the smell of the meat-balls made us ill.
>
> For the first two months we weren't allowed to leave the room. After that we were able to spend about half an hour each day, except Saturdays and Sundays, on a dirty, covered balcony.

In the *New York Times* of 8 August 1942 there appeared a detailed story about a Lutheran pastor in Hartford, Connecticut, who was taken to court for carrying a message for the interned Princess Stephanie von Hohenlohe – though he denied that he actually delivered the message. The Reverend Schlick was called upon to hold services in the camp and the princess asked him to smuggle a message out for her.

The pastor said that he had first met the princess, who was known to be 'a very dangerous foreign woman', on 8 February in the camp. Three weeks later, when he was on another visit, she gave him a letter to take to a clergyman in Philadelphia. But the Reverend Schlick got cold feet; he told the princess he could do nothing for her. During the trial the pastor was asked whether he imagined the immigration authorities knew what he was doing. After all, he had been helping a 'dangerous foreign woman' in the course of his duties. Schlick confirmed that he was unaware of that and apologised. It was too late to be sorry, the judge retorted. Schlick admitted that he had joined the German-American Bund in 1923, at a time when the organisation was known as 'Friends of the New Germany'. He left the Bund in 1935, after Hitler came to power. The outcome of the trial has not been recorded.

Thus the princess gradually became more and more desperate. In a thoroughly dejected mood she wrote on 15 December 1942 to Sir William Wiseman:

My dear Sir William
You will recall the lunch you invited me to in your apartment in July 1940. On that occasion I told you that certain people in Washington had misinterpreted the motive behind the meeting between you and Mr Wiedemann. And not only my own motives, but also your personal intentions. You will also recall that you were very anxious to clarify your position, both in your interest and mine, as you put it. For that reason you got in touch with a highly placed official in Washington, who arranged a meeting for you with Attorney-General Biddle. However, when you got to Washington

you were told he had suddenly been taken ill, or had to leave town suddenly (I have forgotten the details now). Nonetheless, you had a long interview with the Attorney-General's personal assistant and gave him a detailed account of yourself, your views, and the role you played in the last war (which was apparently not known), as well as about your motives and activities in this particular case. You explained that, before arranging the meeting with Mr Wiedemann, you had been to see a Mr Butler, head of the British Purchasing Commission in New York, the body which was chiefly engaged in acquiring war materials. Mr Butler (I think that was his name) in turn got in touch with the Foreign Office in London, in order to find out whether you should be involved in this matter, i.e. whether your intervention was considered useful and desirable. The answer was affirmative.

As far as I know, you met Mr Wiedemann twice. The first meeting took place in your suite at the Palace Hotel in San Francisco. I was not present, but saw you the same evening shortly before you left for New York. On that occasion you told me how affected you had been by Mr Wiedemann's obvious keenness and sincerity, and you thanked me for making the meeting possible. You stressed that your government would not fail to show its gratitude, when the time came. The second and last meeting took place some months later, again at a dinner in your hotel suite. That time I was there. You gave a detailed report to the Washington official. You even showed him a telegram you had received from official quarters in London, thanking you for your useful work and acknowledging your valuable reports. You offered to disclose these reports, if desired. You went on to emphasise that my article on the subject was in no way a hostile act, that, on the contrary, my activities had been extremely praiseworthy, and that my intention had been exclusively to serve Britain and the cause of democracy. You said – and I quote: 'If you made a mistake, then so did I.'

I am reminding you of all this, because my reason for writing is to ask you to write an affidavit for me, confirming it all. I also think it would be a good thing if you mentioned that, when you visited London in the summer of 1940, you met Lord

Rothermere's son; that he had come to see you because he was interested in my book, and that he asked you to support his father in his efforts to avoid any publicity. When, after returning to New York, you saw Lord Rothermere on several occasions, you reported to me about how hostile and embittered he felt towards me. You warned me of his attempts to discredit me, and you told me he was seeking the co-operation and support of influential people in America, to lend more weight to the whole thing.

I will not prolong this letter by describing my feelings, especially my dismay at the fact that you, knowing my difficult situation and all the background and detailed circumstances, have not felt obliged to submit such a statement on your own initiative – you should at least be familiar with the Queensberry Rules! To avoid any further hesitation on your part, I would like in any case to stress that it is only the consideration I owe my son, that might persuade me to take any further steps.

Stephanie Hohenlohe

Sir William never replied.

The only visitor Stephanie had was her mother. Although she was only supposed to stay for half an hour at the most, she arrived in the morning and did not leave until the evening. What is more, the old lady drove up in the chauffeur-driven official car belonging to the man she hoped would soon be her son-in-law, Lemuel Schofield. This meant that, despite all orders from above, Schofield was still in regular contact with Stephanie. When Hoover and Roosevelt heard about this, all hell broke loose. The president wrote to Hoover on 17 June 1942: 'Once more I have to bother you about that Hohenlohe woman. This time I am told that her son has been in a detention camp but has written to his mother that Uncle Lem (Schofield) has arranged to get him out in a short time. I really think that this whole affair verges not merely on the ridiculous but on the disgraceful. Is that woman really at Ellis Island? F.D.R.'

In a further letter the president again expressed his anger: 'If the immigration authorities do not stop once and for all showing favour to Hohenlohe, I will be forced to order an enquiry. The facts will not be very palatable and will go right back to her first arrest and her intimacy with Schofield. I am aware that she is interned in the Gloucester centre, but by all accounts she enjoys special privileges there. The same is apparently true in the case of her son, who is being held on Ellis Island. To be honest, this is all turning into a scandal that requires extremely drastic and immediate action. F.D.R.'

On 16 February 1942, Prince Franz was arrested while visiting friends in Katonah, NY. The New York press now began sniping at him. 'We hear from Ellis Island that Prince Hohenlohe was arrested Monday night. He was immediately taken to the immigration office, where he is now awaiting interrogation by the Aliens Office. His mother, Princess Hohenlohe, is a close friend of Captain Fritz Wiedemann, Hitler's Number One, who was an envoy in America before the war. She is said to be in custody in an internment camp for enemy aliens in western Pennsylvania.'

Prince Franz was held at Ellis Island until 10 July 1942, when the hearing finally took place in New York. Five weeks later he was transferred to Camp McAlester in Oklahoma. His next sojourn was at Camp Kennedy in Texas. On 1 May 1942 he had written to his mother from Ellis Island:

Lemmy [referring to Lemuel Schofield] came here for the weekend and found me in good health. I think it's very nice of him to visit me here. We are allowed to go for a walk twice a day in the yard. It was of course me who asked him to come, not because I had anything particular to say to him, I simply wanted very much to see him again. He said he was very sorry to find me locked up here and he hoped I would be out soon. Despite all their efforts, the FBI haven't been able to come up with anything against me. He asked me if I needed anything and what he could do for me. But Mrs Parks supplies me with everything imaginable, from fruit and flowers to stamps and toiletries, so at the moment I don't need anything.

After President Roosevelt had intervened once again, Attorney-General Biddle had no choice but to take action. He transferred the princess to Camp Seagoville, 12 miles from Dallas, Texas, where there was no-one for miles around who could have been any help to her. But Biddle had miscalculated. Schofield resigned from his government position and was now working for a thriving law firm. This meant he was free to look after his mistress all the time.

Being transported from Gloucester to Seagoville between 25 and 27 July was a humiliating experience for Stephanie. Four warders accompanied her, never once letting go of her wrists and ankles. 'It was only the horror of the strait-jacket and the morphine injection which they threatened me with if I didn't behave, that made me give in and go quietly.'

Stephanie was not allowed to say goodbye either to her mother or to the other women inmates. She was hauled out of bed, given no opportunity to wash or do her hair, and placed on a stretcher. 'Dressed in nothing but my bloodstained nightdress, I was carried past all the men, who needless to say made coarse remarks about me.'

When she arrived in Seagoville, Stephanie had with her a large black suitcase, a travelling-bag, a handbag and $1,145 in cash. Fortunately she was well treated since, just before giving up his official post, Schofield had been to the camp and given the governor official instructions to grant special privileges to his beloved princess, such as permission to use a telephone outside the camp. He also obtained permission for Stephanie's mother to visit her outside official visiting hours. For, as soon as the baroness heard that her daughter was being moved, she left the cool east coast for the oppressive summer heat of Texas and immediately booked into the Jefferson hotel for several weeks.

In 1942 the psychoanalyst Walter C. Langer made contact with the Office of Strategic Services, the US intelligence service in the war years. This organisation had created a new department, that of the Coordinator of Information. It was headed by Colonel (later General) William J. Donovan – better known as 'Wild Bill'. One of the tasks of the new department was to organise and manage psychological warfare. Langer took an interest in this. True, he had never dealt with this problem himself, but during the First World War in Europe – in which he had served – he had been very unimpressed by the efforts at that time to wage psychological warfare.

After some departmental restructuring Langer was given the job of assembling material on Hitler as a man, which was more reliable than that put out by German propaganda and fed to foreign correspondents. The work appealed to Langer, though he had to admit that Hitler's psyche and the fascination he exerted over the German people were a complete mystery to him. Therefore Langer set off across the USA and Canada in search of people who at one time had had more than superficial contact with Hitler. He did indeed find a number of such people and talked to them at length, since he hoped that in this way he might gain important first-hand information for his study. For the most part these conversations proved interesting and revealing, yielding insights that at the time would not otherwise have been available.

It was in the summer of 1942 that Walter C. Langer arrived at Seagoville, far out on the Texas prairie, to interview Princess Stephanie in her internment camp. She seized the opportunity to deny having any sympathy with the Nazis; she also roundly condemned the FBI and all its agents both for the 'unjust' charges against her and for the humiliating treatment she had been subjected to. The truth was, she insisted, that she had done her utmost to deter Hitler from his aggressive policy, because she was always convinced that such a policy was bound to lead directly to a war.

Langer had been warned in advance that the princess was a very plausible individual, and not to be trusted. So he listened patiently to her tirades and hoped that, once she had got all this off her chest, they would get to the actual purpose of his visit. It is worth mentioning that, as there was a guard present, the interview was conducted in German.

It turned out that Langer had been excessively optimistic and had underestimated his informant's abilities. Stephanie demanded a price for her information: she was only willing to cooperate and to tell Langer everything she knew about Hitler, provided he promised to help her get out of the internment camp. Her plan was as follows: she had influential connections in Europe, she said, with whose help she could get directly in touch with Hitler. If Langer's boss, General Donovan, were to arrange her release and take her on to the staff of the OSS, she would then act as a go-between in secret negotiations aimed at bringing the war to an end. She was also prepared to tell all she knew about the Nazi hierarchy, the way they worked and so on, and also to obtain any secret information that Langer wanted.

Langer assured Stephanie that he had absolutely no personal influence with Donovan, and that in matters like this he was used to doing things his own way. In the end the two reached a compromise. The princess declared her willingness to cooperate on condition that Langer submitted her plan in detail to General Donovan. Langer agreed and so the interview could proceed.

However, Langer was not only after political information. He was also interested in intimate details about Hitler's personal life. When he asked Stephanie about Hitler's relationship with Eva Braun, his hidden mistress, Stephanie was able to pass on what her friend Wiedemann had told her, that 'Eva quite often spent the whole night in Hitler's bedroom in Berlin'.

On his return to Washington Langer kept his promise. General Donovan was very amused but made no further comment. However, the episode did not end there. When about a month had passed and still nothing had happened about her release, Stephanie apparently came to the conclusion that Langer had taken her for a ride. She said of him: 'He's certainly no gentleman. But in Seagoville I would have talked to the Devil incarnate.' She tried to get her revenge by telling the FBI that Langer had admitted her detention was unjustified, the charges against her were false and that she had been badly treated.

The FBI did in fact immediately give Langer a severe talking-to, and angrily demanded an explanation as to the basis of his assertions, and what he was trying to achieve. All Langer could do was explain the purpose of his mission and emphasise that their entire conversation had taken place in the presence of a guard who could testify that he had heard Princess Hohenlohe complaining about the alleged injustices done to her. However, it emerged that the guard knew no German.

Within the camp Stephanie von Hohenlohe was moved to a building known as the German House. 'It is quieter and cleaner. But the Germans living here have already let me know, frankly and unambiguously, that they don't want to have me in their midst. Even before I moved in, they were already protesting against my presence, and since then there has been no change in their attitude. This situation would alone be enough to make my life here intolerable, since in effect it condemns me to solitary confinement.'

Suddenly she heard nothing from Schofield for quite some time. So Stephanie now went to the lengths of trying to win the favour of J. Edgar Hoover himself. Several times she offered to provide him with revelations about Schofield, but there was no reaction from Hoover.

It was very depressing for Stephanie to find that she had to wait until autumn 1943 before a hearing by the review committee was allowed. In fact it did not take place until 1 March 1944. Stephanie acted as her own defence counsel. Large parts of her biographical statement had more than a hint of the fairy-tale about them. Yet at the end of the hearing the three-man committee unanimously recommended that the princess be released:

> We are convinced that her position is one of determined and unqualified opposition to Hitler and that she earnestly supports the Allied cause. It is our view that, once she is at liberty again, she will do everything in her power to further our war effort. She has explained her friendship with Wiedemann to our satisfaction and it is obvious to us that the friendship with this man and his wife was a long-standing one; it was essentially a social connection, based on friendship.

Stephanie's son Franzi was released on parole from his internment camp at the end of February 1944. In the summer of that year he volunteered for the US armed forces, was drafted on 7 September and, after his basic training, served as an ordinary GI 'somewhere in the Pacific'.

In April 1945 Stephanie's mother received a letter from the Attorney-General, Francis Biddle, in which he agreed 'to reconsider the case of your daughter in the near future and decide whether at this juncture in the war any change in her internment status is justified'.

This 'near future' eventually turned out to be VE Day (Victory in Europe). Stephanie von Hohenlohe was the last detainee allowed to leave Seagoville on 9 May 1945. She had been kept locked up until the very last moment. And that was done on the orders of President Roosevelt, who had been constantly irritated by the princess. To make matters worse, the princess had complained to the president's wife, Eleanor, about the graft and corruption in the 'Washington bureaucracy'.

By the day of the German surrender, 8 May 1945, the Third Reich lay in ashes and rubble, Hitler had committed suicide, and the woman who was allegedly such a great threat to the United States as a Nazi spy was free once more after four years of internment.

At the end of her long incarceration, she drove with her mother to California, where the temperate climate was a pleasant contrast to the terrible Texas heat. However, she was still under the supervision of the Alien Control Commission and was being watched by the immigration authorities. As an enemy alien she was placed under the guardianship of a wealthy Beverly Hills real-estate agent named Harry H. Bennett.

Among the few friends she still had was the man who was as deeply in love with her as ever – Major Lemuel Schofield. She now needed him again urgently, as the immigration authorities had given notice that she was to be deported on 9 April 1946. Schofield visited her frequently in California and asked her to move to New York, to be near him. He was once again back in a successful law practice in New York and wanted to have Stephanie close to him, as he had started proceedings to divorce his wife. He also hoped that, as just one among millions of New Yorkers, Stephanie could live in complete freedom from the unwelcome attentions of the press. The princess agreed to come to New York, though not to give up her little house in Beverly Hills.

Yet it was not long before the press had its claws in her again. The columnist Robert Ruark, writing in his 'Society Notes' of 26 March 1947, gave free rein to his caustic pen:

Princess Stephanie Hohenlohe Waldenburg-Schillingsfürst plays a not insignificant role in New York society today. This is no less interesting than if I were to report that Joachim von Ribbentrop had been seen dancing at the Stork Club, or that Eva Braun was staying as a guest at the Long Island home of Mr and Mrs Bigname. Compared to this Hohenlohe hustler, Mata Hari was definitely bottom of the range, and Edda Mussolini a raw beginner, a tool of the fascists, who couldn't say 'no'. In her field, the Hohenlohe girl was absolutely top-notch; she was so good that only a short time ago she was released from one of our top-security prisons for spies.

And now here she is, dolled up like a duchess, popping up under the aegis of one of society's most venerable names, at all the lorgnette-and-liqueur evenings. Unless she has moved since I last saw her, the princess is holed up in the Gotham hotel.

Before the war, la Hohenlohe was a close friend of Adolf Hitler and his most trusted female spy. Wherever there were dark dealings afoot, you could be sure to find the princess, described by insiders as 'Hitler's Madame de Steel' [sic]. It was Hohenlohe who arranged the famous meeting between Hitler and Lord Rothermere. She set up the Sudetenland talks between Viscount Runciman and Konrad Henlein, the German *Gauleiter* in Czechoslovakia. The outcome of those talks, as I recall, was the glowing fuse before the world blew up.

This gaudy butterfly of New York society is the same girl who persuaded Hitler to send Fritz Weidemann [sic] to London as his special envoy, and who maintained an intimate relationship with Fritz, when he continued his espionage activities over here.

I am not suggesting that this charming creature should be stood up against the nearest wall and shot, because I am not basically vindictive by nature. But in Nuremberg we have strung up a number of her old buddies for similar misdeeds, and, judged on her connections with high-ranking Nazis, Hohenlohe is a legitimate candidate for anyone's noose.

I also know that no less than 42 countries refused to accept her, when we tried to deport her at the beginning of the war. That's why we had to lock her up in a concentration-camp until the shooting was over. But surely we should be able to do something better than pay court to her at Park Avenue parties.

Maybe we could offer her to the Russians, for whom she would doubtless be extremely effective as a sharp-eared international party-girl. But I doubt whether the Russians would take her, even if we were to throw in a top-class basketball-player and their highly controversial claim on Greece. Stephanie has far too noxious a reputation as a Nazi, and she makes trouble wherever she goes. At 50, she may already be too old to switch ideologies, no matter how basically similar they may be.

But what I simply cannot understand is how New York society, which is normally so impervious to titled tramps, can nurture a one-time member of the Nazi hierarchy in its bosom. For the strongest of stomachs, there is a point where it gets too much, even when a name is listed in the Almanach de Gotha.

To be honest, if Hitler had not committed suicide, it would come as no surprise in my present distraught condition, if he were suddenly to turn up in Carnegie Hall on the arm of some beauty. . .

On 23 June 1947 the princess appeared with Schofield before the immigration authorities in New York. Under oath she stated that her son Franzi, as a member of the US armed forces, had been granted American citizenship in Tokyo on 16 July 1946. She also asked the board to take into consideration the fact that the small income Franz earned as a translator at the United Nations would be insufficient to maintain both himself and his grandmother, if Stephanie were forced to leave America. Stephanie told the authorities that she could not return to Hungary because, after an absence of ten years, her Hungarian citizenship had lapsed. Nor could His Majesty's Government allow her to return to the United Kingdom.

The new head of the immigration authority was himself at a loss as to what to do. Then in May 1950 the Attorney-General's office ordered another hearing, this time in Philadelphia. After studying all the papers in the case of Stephanie von Hohenlohe, the view was reached that since her entry to the USA in 1939 she had not engaged in hostile activities of any kind. Her internment as an enemy alien had, it was stated, been dictated by the exceptional circumstances of war, and for ten years she had been pursued on false grounds as a 'Nazi spy'.

By now the princess had been living for some time at Schofield's farm, Anderson Place, near Phoenixville, Pennsylvania. She had convinced Schofield that a life in the country would be healthier for him too. Stephanie put the rather run-down farmhouse back into shape, and there now began a tranquil period of her life, at least for the next three years, until the death of her mother. The baroness was walking down the road one evening to go to the mailbox when she was hit by a car and severely injured; she died soon afterwards.

In 1953 Stephanie took part in the Easter Fashion parade, and was delighted to find that her name featured in the New York Dress Institute's list of 'best-dressed women'. At last there were gratifying press reports about her: 'Austrian-born Princess Stephanie Hohenlohe, who divides her time between Salzburg, Paris, and her apartment on Philadelphia's Rittenhouse Square, definitely belongs in the list of best-dressed women. Before she came to the United States in 1941 [sic, in fact 1939], her name was constantly among the Paris fashion trend-setters. At the Easter Parade the princess will be wearing an original Paris model, a black-and-white chequered woollen dress by Chanel, and with it a white straw-hat from Mr John.'

After an absence of eleven years, Stephanie returned to Europe to show 'Brad', as she called Schofield, her Austrian homeland. The following year the couple travelled to Europe again, this time with Schofield's two daughters. They had a chauffeur who drove them through France, Germany, Austria and Italy. Schofield's daughter Helen later married the internationally respected Hungarian historian, John Lukacs, and Stephanie was a witness at the ceremony.

On the second trip Stephanie could not resist revisiting her beloved Schloss Leopoldskron. It brought back many memories. But her home was now Anderson Place, Schofield's beautiful farm. Sadly, this happiness only lasted until 1954, when Schofield suffered a heart attack and died. He was only sixty-two.

The death of the celebrated attorney had major consequences. The *Philadelphia Reporter* published a lengthy story which created an uproar in the city, with its revelation that the late Lemuel B. Schofield had been evading taxes for the past six years and that the sum owed to the Internal Revenue Service, including interest, was in the region of one million dollars. The tax inspectors went to work and checked out other 'prominent citizens' who had known the attorney: his family, his business partners and, of course, the woman in his life. In the course of their investigations the IRS established that since her arrival in the USA, Stephanie had earned no money at all, but that for the years 1951, 1952 and 1953 she had made no tax declaration. An initial inspection revealed unpaid taxes of $250,000.

The princess now had the guile to make a voluntary declaration, and in fact managed to show she did not have a single dollar of back taxes to pay. She claimed that her famously luxurious lifestyle was 'financed by the sale of jewellery, works of art and antiques,' which had been in safe keeping during her internment, some in Britain and some with her mother. In this way she had made 'a few hundred dollars a month'. This could well be true. And in any case, during the years which the IRS were scrutinising, she had been living with a wealthy lawyer.

In mourning after Schofield's death, the princess left that part of her life behind her, and moved to another beautiful farm, Cobble Close, near Red Bank, New Jersey. The property had originally belonged to Herbert N. Straus, owner of Macy's, the world's largest department store. Living nearby was another multimillionaire, Albert Monroe Greenfield, the richest man in Philadelphia. With him as an agreeable new lover, Stephanie would spend the next three years at Cobble Close. Then her life took a completely new direction.

CHAPTER FIFTEEN

The International Journalist

In the autumn of 1955 the princess, now sixty-four, began earning money again. She was given a job as special correspondent for the *Washington Diplomat*, an 'international society magazine'. Now and again she was described *sotto voce* as a 'super-spy', or as 'Hitler's mistress', but that no longer annoyed her. Her work involved a lot of travelling, both to Europe and to the American west coast. Someone who became a close friend was Lady Lawford, wife of an English general, Sir Sidney Lawford, and mother of the actor Peter Lawford who, in 1954, had married Pat Kennedy, the sister of Jack and Bobby. The Women's Press Club of New York was proud to welcome Stephanie as a member.

The new admirer in her life was 'Del' Wilson, a US Air Force general. A good-looking giant of a man, he had been married several times and had just divorced again. He was several years younger than the princess, and she turned down his proposal of marriage.

She eventually left her farm in New Jersey and moved to an apartment on East 72nd Street, in a fashionable area of Manhattan.

At the age of sixty-eight, the princess returned permanently to Europe and settled in Geneva, where her son Franz was working for a Swiss bank. To begin with, mother and son shared a small apartment in the rue du Bourg-de-Four. She then moved to a larger flat in the rue Alfred-Vincent, in a building wedged between the Hôtel d'Angleterre and the Hôtel Beau Rivage. The address that Stephanie gave herself was, however, grander: 15 quai de Mont-

Blanc, since from her large terrace she could see both the mountain peak and Lake Geneva.

By this time, Fritz Wiedemann had reappeared, having survived the war and de-Nazification.[1] She had often met him on trips to Europe and he had told her of his plan to write his memoirs. The two got together on this and the result was Wiedemann's book, *Der Mann, der Feldherr werden wollte* ('The Man who Wanted to Command') – a work which makes no reference whatever to their relationship and the years they spent together.

Since the princess, despite being nearly seventy, was still extremely agile, she now decided to build a new career in Europe. She had heard on the grapevine that the editor-in-chief of *Quick*, the popular German illustrated magazine, was looking for journalistic contacts in the USA. She offered her services and in September 1962 was given a very well-paid contract as 'consultant' to the Th. Martens company, publishers of *Quick*. Her job would consist of setting up contacts with important and newsworthy people, and coming up with ideas for interviews and lead stories. With her unique network of acquaintances, she was to open as many doors as possible for reporters and photographers. Her remuneration was set at $1,000 per month, plus expenses. And she would be entitled to a special bonus if she arranged something really spectacular.

In New York she met for the second time a man whom she knew from her Vienna days and who gave a new direction to her life. This was Drew Pearson, mentioned in Chapter 1 as the son-in-law of Count Gisycki. He was now the highest-paid and most famous columnist in America. On Pearson's 65th birthday in December 1962 Stephanie sent him a bouquet of carnations. She then met him for tea and told him that she too was now working as a journalist. Drew Pearson quickly noticed what a remarkable memory the princess possessed – and anyway he knew all about her life history – so he considered some form of collaboration with her in the future. His political column, *The Washington Merry-Go-Round*, was syndicated in 600 newspapers and played an important role in forming American opinion.

In July 1963 Pearson had interviewed King Paul of Greece for *Quick* and punctually delivered his copy to Stephanie for the German magazine. Unfortunately the royal Greek court did not immediately give approval for publication, and then in March 1964 the king died suddenly. The princess now had to take up the matter. However, it was Drew Pearson who wrote on 20 April 1964 to Queen Frederika of Greece, in order to pave the way for Stephanie:

> Your Majesty, I was heartsick over the tragic news of the death of His Majesty . . . I know that these have been most trying days for you and that there is little your friends can do to help. I quite understand how the interview I did last summer has been held up by red tape; needless to say, it cannot now be published. I am sorry about this, because I felt I had drawn a really excellent portrait of His Majesty, of his problems and of the courage with which he faced them.
>
> The bearer of this note, Princess Stephanie Hohenlohe, is associated with *Quick* magazine in Munich, for which I wrote the interview of last summer. She has been commissioned by her editor to talk with you about a signed article outlining some of the problems that His Majesty and you discussed last year in Corfu, or any other subject.
>
> The editor of *Quick*, who is a friend of mine, believes that the time might be appropriate for such an article. Naturally we would want you to be fully satisfied with it and approve it down to the last comma and semi-colon. Princess Hohenlohe will of course be able to discuss the details.
>
> I hope that this is not an intrusion at this time. Please call on me if I can ever be of service. I continue to be, as always, at your command.

Stephanie von Hohenlohe travelled to Greece, and the widowed queen gave her permission for Drew Pearson's interview with her late husband to be printed.

After this success, Stephanie's contract was renewed for another year, and her basic fee was increased by 50 per cent. The editor of *Quick*, Karl-Heinz Hagen, wrote to her: 'I am convinced that in this second year we will work just as well and successfully together, and continue the work which reached its culmination with the Kennedy interview that you set up for us.' The Pearson–Hohenlohe partnership had indeed managed to arrange an interview for Hagen with President John F. Kennedy. Assistance was given by his press secretary, Pierre Salinger, who was told by Stephanie that Pearson had received a sum of $5,000 simply for acting as an intermediary.

Even after the assassination of President Kennedy, Stephanie remained in touch with Pierre Salinger. He was now employed by Continental Airlines, and his memoirs, entitled *With Kennedy*, were about to be published. Through Stephanie he offered *Quick* exclusive pre-publication rights for extracts specifically covering the following topics: the relationship between Kennedy and Khrushchev and the two days that Kennedy spent with the Soviet leader in Russia; the links between the world's press and the US government; the Cuban Missile Crisis as seen through the eyes of an insider; glimpses of life in the White House and personal details about the president, Jacqueline Kennedy and their children. He would also write about the role of the USA in South-East Asia as it appeared to American diplomats.

Quick was not only the first German publication to run an interview with President Kennedy, it was also the first to interview his successor, Lyndon B. Johnson. Hagen was received by Johnson in April 1964 and again in the following year. In a manner of speaking, the door of the White House was open to Stephanie, since Pearson had been a friend of L.B.J. for many years.

Quick gave the princess another substantial pay increase, awarded her an additional success-related bonus of $2,500, and renewed her contract for a further three years.

It gave Stephanie belated satisfaction to be invited to President Johnson's inauguration on 20 January 1964. After all, there had been a time when the country called her a 'Nazi spy' and wanted to deport her, and now she was honoured in this way.

While preparing for the second interview with President Johnson, Pearson had supplied her with a mass of important material. But at that precise moment *Quick* was sold by its publishers, and Hagen parted company with the magazine. This led to some complications for Pearson, as Stephanie's best informant. He wrote to her on 29 April 1966:

Dear Stephanie,

It's been good talking to you over the phone! What a pity it is that Hagen has picked this time to leave *Quick*, when for once I had gotten the desired appointment in Texas without postponement or hitch of any kind, which has now ironically gone to waste.

As for the new interview *Quick* wants, I must first get all the details concerning the new person they want to send: a curriculum vitae, name, age, background etc., before I can take the responsibility for asking for one. Because I must be able to vouch for the person they will send. But please tell them, with the war in Vietnam and the political situation as it is, it will not be an easy job for me to get the desired interview. However, I will endeavour my very best to get it.

I rely on your friendship to tell me truthfully if this new situation with *Quick* protects my best interests.

I took it upon myself to introduce Hagen to the most important people in Washington DC on the three occasions he came here. I arranged one interview for him with Kennedy and two with Johnson. He met Rusk and MacNamara, Senator Fulbright, Johnson when Vice-President, Hubert Humphrey as Senator and later Vice-President, to name only a few. I have given *Quick* and Hagen a terrific build-up, and will now have to explain the sudden change. I naturally trust you and rely on your judgement, as I did with Hagen. I hope you will remind the editorial office of *Quick* that it is after all the President of the US, and not just anybody.

I believe it would be advantageous if you could come here for a few days. I would arrange a dinner-party and you could explain the newly developed situation. It would be more plausible and effective coming from you. I'm thinking particularly of Bill Moyers [President Johnson's press secretary], whom you can handle much better than I.

Take care of yourself – with best wishes

Sincerely yours
Drew

PS: The Secret Service is very demanding these days about who is admitted to the White House. For this reason alone I have to have the new man's credentials.

Even after Karl-Heinz Hagen's resignation, Stephanie stayed in close touch with him and he wrote her a particularly nice 'farewell letter': 'It was only through your efforts that I was able to obtain an interview with the late President Kennedy; it was through your mediation that I have been able to talk to Vice-President Johnson, Messrs MacNamara and Dean Rusk and a great many American senators. Thanks to your intervention, in 1964 *Quick* achieved that sensational interview with President Johnson, in which he spoke of the Soviet Union's fear of Federal Germany and made a plea to the Germans to strive for a better understanding with the Russians. This interview had enormous resonance all over the world and brought great prestige to *Quick*.' Unfortunately, as it turned out, Stephanie did not hit it off with the new owner of *Quick*. This was also noticed by *Quick*'s chief competitor, *Stern*, who had been courting her for a long time.

At that time Stephanie often used to stay in Munich. She attempted to sell her collection of letters and documents to the Institute for Contemporary History in that city, but was unsuccessful. The then director of the institute, Prof. Helmut Krausnick, was very attracted by the 75-year-old princess, who really did not look her age. What is more, she acted 'a good dozen years younger', looking like an American woman with a lot of make-up and her hair in a ponytail. In Munich she looked for a ghost-writer for her memoirs. In this connection she thought of the Austro-Hungarian author, Hans Habe, but he was 'booked up' for the next three years. Another of her contacts living in Munich was the Hungarian Josef von Ferenczy, today a big entrepreneur in the media. But she was unable to do a deal with him either.

At the beginning of July 1966 Stephanie officially signed up with *Stern* magazine. The publisher at that time, Dr Gerd Bucerius,[2] invited the princess to a meeting at his Hamburg headquarters. On 1 August Stephanie was introduced to the editor of *Stern*, Henri Nannen.[3]

Within a few days she was receiving interim payments totalling $2,000 in respect of her first month's salary. In the middle of August the Gruner & Jahr company, publishers of *Stern*, sent her a contract, with a covering letter from Dr Bucerius.

Dear Princess,

You have been employed by us since 10 July 1966; your task is to develop story opportunities for *Stern*; in particular you have said you are willing to use your connection with figures in public life, or of public interest, in order to give our reporters and photographers the opportunity to produce stories about these personalities for *Stern*.

You have agreed to remain continuously in touch with us in order to make such proposals and to receive proposals from us, and if these proposals are accepted, to lend your support in despatching reporters and photographers.

For this work you will receive the monthly sum of $2,000.

Travel and other expenses arising from editorial assignments will be reimbursed by us.

You will work exclusively for *Stern*.

This contract terminates on 30 September 1967, unless renewed before that date.

I am sure we will enjoy a pleasant and successful collaboration.

Yours sincerely,

Gerd Bucerius

For the interview with President Johnson, she and Pearson together were paid $20,000 by *Stern*. During the preparations in Washington, Bucerius told Stephanie that Henri Nannen would be bringing with him the political editor of *Die Zeit*, Theo Sommer. The two men were invited to lunch by the president, were driven round his ranch, and were able to discuss German problems and many other topics. (The second interview between Henri Nannen and President Johnson took place in the summer of 1967. Drew Pearson took part in the five-hour conversation, which was also held at LBJ's Texas ranch.) In general, working with Pearson became difficult, since his attitude towards the Kennedy clan, and especially towards the president's widow, was rather hostile. This meant that his articles, or the material he offered to *Stern*, were not free from prejudice, though they were accepted nonetheless.

The next people Nannen wanted to interview for his magazine were Vice-President Hubert Humphrey and the Supreme Court judge, Earl Warren, who had headed the commission investigating the circumstances surrounding Kennedy's assassination. The commission had concluded in effect that this had been a senseless act committed by a lone individual, and that there was no political conspiracy behind it. The findings of the investigation were revealed to the readers of *Stern* in a series of three articles.

The year 1966 would end with particular difficulties for Princess Stephanie. She was furious that the British consul in Geneva had refused her a visa to visit Britain. She was still regarded there as a Nazi spy. Her son, Prince Franz, was now working in the London branch of the Swiss bank that employed him. Franz telephoned the Home Secretary, Roy Jenkins,[4] then went to call on him in person and explained his mother's wish for a visa to enter the United Kingdom. Stephanie herself wrote to the Home Secretary:

Dear Mr Jenkins,
Please accept my heartfelt thanks for being kind enough to receive my son when he called on you, I believe rather unceremoniously, two weeks ago in London.

I understand you told him you knew nothing of my case, but that you would order a personal investigation. I am immensely relieved to know that you are taking this matter into your own hands. However, since you know nothing about me, I am wondering if you may not think that my son exaggerated when he said that my case could be of great importance to you. Especially at the present time. Believe me, he was not exaggerating!

None of this is contained in my Home Office file, made up for the major part of newspaper stories, gossip, hearsay and a great deal of deliberate distortion.

I beg of you not to turn over my file to a subordinate but to deal with it yourself, your time permitting. [. . .]

She ended the letter with a PS:

After the outbreak of war on 20 December 1939, my mother, Baroness Szepessy, and I left London for the United States. In other words, we lived in wartime London for a full three months with the British authorities' knowledge and consent, unlike so many other foreigners who were immediately interned.

Stephanie wanted to be allowed to speak personally to Roy Jenkins, but to do so she needed an entry permit, even if it was only for 24 hours. She suggested as an alternative that Jenkins should choose someone trustworthy to meet her outside England. She added emphatically that she had no intention of coming to England with a view to settling there. Two weeks later, Roy Jenkins' private secretary informed the princess that she could immediately apply for a British visa.

One of Stephanie's most successful interviews was with Princess Grace of Monaco, the former Hollywood actress, Grace Kelly. Stephanie had a meeting with Prince Rainier's press secretary in the fashionable Neuilly district of Paris. The ruler of Monaco agreed to the interview since *Stern*'s circulation of 1.4 million would guarantee huge publicity for his tiny principality.

Stephanie's next coup was with another monarchy: she interviewed the wife of the Shah of Iran, Queen Farah Dibah. Drew Pearson then worked assiduously to set up an interview with Lady Bird Johnson, the wife of the US President. On 9 October 1967 he sent these precise instructions from the States:

Dear Stephanie,

I was sorry to miss your telephone call, but I have been on an ungodly rat-race through the Middle West on a speaking tour.

Here are the points the White House would like to make regarding an interview with Lady Bird:

(1) They would like to have questions prepared. These do not have to be submitted in advance but on the day of the interview.

(2) Mrs Johnson will speak into a tape-recorder. She finds this is a little easier for her and perhaps for the interviewer.

(3) It is suggested that I do the interviewing. However, I don't believe this is any more necessary than it was with the President. In other words, a representative of *Stern* can be present and ask some or most of the questions. Mrs Johnson said she would feel a little more comfortable if I were there, in effect conducting the interview (my name does not have to appear in the matter at all).

(4) It is suggested that a *Stern* photographer could go with her on some of her trips any time in the near future. The White House has a lot of unused photos which are available, but they recognize that Stern would like to take some originals. This is agreeable.

. . . I have put in a request for a ticket to the Lynda Bird wedding [the Johnsons' daughter] but I'm afraid it's about hopeless. Space in the East Room is very limited and most of the correspondents are working through a 'pool' arrangement . . . I suggest that the interview be held early and saved for the week when Lynda is getting married.

The interview with Lady Bird Johnson was conducted in Washington by Anneliese Friedmann, who wrote under the name 'Sybille'. The reporter thanked Stephanie von Hohenlohe – 'Her Royal Highness' – and added that Mr Pearson had looked after her 'like an angel'.

However, Henri Nannen noticed that the princess had suddenly become less active than hitherto and was often not seen for weeks on end. He concluded that she was no longer interested in renewing her contract when it expired. And that was indeed the case.

Karl-Heinz Hagen, her former boss at *Quick*, was now working for Axel Springer.[5] Hagen warmly recommended Stephanie as the 'cosmopolitan princess' with contacts in important political circles. According to one journalist, Springer was 'the final Caesar to her Cleopatra, on the stage of her life'. What the German publishing tycoon found so fascinating was that Stephanie worked with the popular but much-feared American columnist Drew Pearson.

The first person to research and painstakingly document the Springer–Hohenlohe relationship was a Czech-born historian, Boris Celovsky: 'On 4 June 1967 one of the Springer companies drew up a one-year contract with Stephanie, securing her exclusive services in establishing contacts in Germany and other countries. The contract provided for a monthly salary of $2,000, plus $190 for office costs and, of course, an expense account. In the spring of the following year the Axel Springer Verlag AG renewed the contract for a further three years. In 1971 Stephanie, now all of eighty years old, signed a new contract with Springer. This time her monthly salary was $2,500 plus expenses. The contract ran until 31 December 1975.'

When Stephanie began working for the Springer Group, Drew Pearson was still on hand in the early stages. In May 1968 he wrote to Springer: 'I was very pleased to get the papers about your endowment at Brandeis University. I have taken a look at the campus and it is really very interesting. It was also a pleasure for me to write something about you and about the attempts by Berlin students to attack you on account of your honest behaviour. However, in my opinion, only part of the whole story has been told so far. I have uncovered a conspiratorial link between left-wing students, which runs from Berlin, via Paris, to New York. I am in the process of writing some articles on this really important subject.'

Brandeis University is in Waltham, Massachusetts, not far from Boston. The endowment of a professorship there was Axel Springer's personal contribution to making recompense, at least in a small way, for the appalling wrongs done to the Jews in the Second World War.

When Pearson finished one of the articles mentioned, he sent a copy to Springer with a covering letter: 'Princess Hohenlohe has been very helpful to me by obtaining information. I am sure you were unaware that when the students stormed your building, this was intended to be the start of an almost worldwide student revolt. If you like, you are free to publish this article. I will quickly send the rest to Princess Hohenlohe, or direct to you, as I finish them.'

On 16 July 1968 Springer wrote a long and detailed letter to Drew Pearson. He had heard via the princess about an article Pearson had written in the *Washington Post* on the left-wing academic and author, Herbert Marcuse. Springer had decided that this article should be published in Germany at a later date. Springer also gave an answer in this letter to Pearson's enquiry about how it could be that a photo existed of him in Nazi uniform. Springer put him right on this point. Shortly after the Nazis seized power in 1933, he wrote, they began making things more and more difficult for the local newspaper in Hamburg's Altona district, owned by his father, a staunch democrat. No member of the Springer family belonged to the National Socialist Party.

> Then – I was 21 at the time – it was suggested to me that, as I was a member of the German Automobile Club, I should also become a 'paying member' of the National Socialist Corps of Drivers (the NSKK). I applied – in the face of strong resistance from my mother – and was accepted, was given a uniform and had my picture taken in it. Being a paying member did not involve any duties of any kind. In the autumn of 1933 this changed. I was now asked to become a full member and to take part in paramilitary exercises. I refused to do so and the predictable result was that my membership was cancelled.

Springer went on to say that thanks to his membership of the NSKK his father was able to go on publishing his newspaper for a while longer without hindrance.

In the same letter Springer warmly invited Drew Pearson to Berlin. 'I would be delighted to show you Berlin. There is no better place from which to study the city's problems than my publishing house, right beside the Wall, and not far from Checkpoint Charlie. So please come sometime this autumn, if you can. Princess Hohenlohe has already agreed to join us.' The Berlin visit took place on 2 September and was a great success for all concerned.

Once back in Washington, Pearson shared his opinion of Axel Springer with the readers of the *Washington Merry-Go-Round*; he is an anti-fascist, anti-communist, a champion of the free market economy and a generous friend of the state of Israel. 'Springer is a remarkable man. As the son of a small newspaper publisher he had already begun his career before the war. Today he is the mightiest press magnate in West Germany, perhaps in the whole of Europe.'

Princess Stephanie was grief-stricken when, a few weeks later, she heard that her friend Drew Pearson had died of a heart attack. She continued working with Jack Anderson, Pearson's erstwhile associate and now his successor. The new man was also invited by Springer to Berlin without delay.

Stephanie's obvious weakness for powerful newspaper owners, first Rothermere, now Springer, cannot be ignored. It soon became apparent that the relationship between Axel Springer and the princess went far beyond the purely commercial. Stephanie was very attracted by Springer's good looks and his resolute demeanour even in difficult situations. As Stephanie's son Franz confirms, 'Springer and Steph liked each other from their very first meeting. They agreed about politics. He liked her as a career woman who had lost none of her femininity, she admired his elegance, his attractive looks and the fact that he had the courage of his convictions. Quite apart from the employer–employee relationship, a warm personal friendship quickly developed between the two of them.'

Whereas forty years earlier Lord Rothermere had presented her with a Rolls-Royce, Axel Springer now gave her a second-hand Bentley S2 from his fleet of cars.

In March 1969 Springer visited Israel to attend the inauguration in Jerusalem of the library that he had endowed at the Museum of Israel. Stephanie was pleased to get a telegram from him: 'What a shame that you cannot be with me on this solemn and important occasion.'

Late in 1970 Springer wrote to his soul-mate: 'Dear Stephanie . . . I must thank you for the handsome clock, which only counts the good hours. As the year comes to an end I must also thank you for your many kind words, to me and to other people about me. The future is a black thunder-cloud. America is our destiny! The East–West shuttle diplomacy of Brandt, with his whole corrupt entourage, will nonetheless earn him plaudits as the Prince of Peace . . . Grace, mercy and peace to you and your son. Yours Axel S.'

Another publisher, Robert Letts Jones, chairman of Copley Newspapers, got in touch with Stephanie and Springer, and from this developed a personal friendship. One of his vice-presidents, Ray McHugh, wrote a letter to Stephanie:

Dear Princess,
Mr [Robert L.] Jones just phoned on his return from California.
  You, Mr Springer and Ernst [Cramer]⁶ made a conquest!
  He had a wonderful time in Berlin and was completely impressed by the Springer operation and viewpoint. I knew he would be.
  . . . Our congressional elections are keeping me busy . . . but I have been paying attention to European trends. If [Chancellor Willy] Brandt tumbles soon, isn't there a danger that the Christian Democrats will have to bear the full burden of the inflation problem? I wonder if it wouldn't be better if Brandt were left in office long enough to prove his incapacity . . .
  I am delighted to hear that you plan a US visit in December.
  We have much to discuss. Ernst Cramer was here briefly . . . Ernst and I are agreed that we must act to improve cooperation between our two organisations . . . I suggested a weekly exchange of six to eight articles and editorials, selected for impact in Europe or the US.
  This exchange could be created without monetary consideration to either party . . . If Herr Springer and my superiors agree, we could start such an exchange in January . . .
  I believe we also can do quite a bit through our contacts with the Nixon Administration and with Congress, and via reprints in the Congressional Record, to encourage more awareness of German realities.
  We must discuss these ideas when you come to America. I will meet you in New York or in Washington, whichever you wish.
Warm good wishes
Sincerely, Ray

At the end of 1970 Stephanie was particularly active once more. A meeting with McHugh at the Mayfair hotel in New York led to an important assignment for her:

Dear Stephanie,

So you have it in writing – when Donald Kendall, president of PepsiCo Inc, reached Henry Kissinger in California yesterday and explained your interest in arranging a meeting for Axel Springer with Kissinger and possibly President Nixon, Kissinger responded very favourably.

'I know Axel very well,' Kissinger told Kendall.

He added that 'The Germans know that I agree with him on most issues.'

Kissinger said he would be happy to meet with Axel, should he come to the United States. Any decision on a meeting with President Nixon would be made at that time.

Kissinger emphasized that any meeting must be private and that Axel should have some public reason for visiting the US.

'If the meeting were publicized', Kissinger said, 'the Brandt government would immediately complain that I was trying to run Germany through Axel's office.'

Kissinger plans to be in California for about two weeks. He said he can meet Axel any time after January 15, but urges that he have some advance notice since his schedule is always at the mercy of the President.

You can tell Axel that I would be happy to make our Washington office available to him, should he wish to confer with Kissinger somewhere other than in the White House.

Should you wish to telephone Kissinger in California, the best way to handle it will be through the White House switchboard in Washington. . . Ask for Dr Kissinger's office. Introduce yourself to his secretary and tell her it is urgent that you speak to Kissinger. The secretary will then locate him and he will return the call promptly. Explain that Axel Springer is the subject to be discussed.

This procedure is necessary because of the White House security precautions. They are very reluctant to release personal phone numbers for presidential advisers, but the White House phone operators are very efficient and they are always able to reach Kissinger within minutes.

I hope you have a wonderful visit in Washington.
Warm best wishes for the new year.

> Sincerely,
> Ray

Springer did not travel to America, because he went down with a stubborn flu virus that was to keep him in bed for several weeks. But his visit was only postponed to a later date and Stephanie worked hard on preparations for the following autumn.

It was Stephanie who arranged Springer's link with the Roman Catholic Temple University in Philadelphia. Here the princess exploited her old contacts with a scrap-metal dealer named Irving H. Kutcher, once a close friend of Lemuel Schofield. Kutcher, who had set up the introduction to the university's president, Paul R. Anderson, came to Berlin, where he met Springer's associate, Ernst Cramer. He then went on to Geneva to see the princess. Finally, on 28 October 1971 – in the company of Hollywood director Frank Capra and New York radio chief Robert H. McGanon – Springer was awarded an honorary doctorate by Temple University – piquantly for Stephanie, in its Albert Monroe Greenfield Conference Centre.

In Geneva Stephanie waited expectantly for a word from across the Atlantic. Then a telegram arrived from Axel Springer: 'Greetings and lots of kisses from your excellent Barclay hotel, which I have just left as your "Doctor". Axel.'

In 1971 Stephanie von Hohenlohe was also building her hopes on contacts with the *Readers' Digest* empire. She had met several times with the company's founder DeWitt Wallace, who was co-chairman with his wife Leila, in their home town of Pleasantville in upstate New York. At that time, admittedly, Wallace was not prepared to publish an article about Springer, still less to do so as a 'favour' to the princess. Rather annoyed, Stephanie pointed out to her friend 'Wally' that he ought to know 'what a newsworthy figure Springer is on today's international scene'. Furthermore, among the 36 million subscribers to *Readers' Digest*, the Jewish element at least would be interested to read about him.

Springer wrote to Wallace: 'I believe there can be no substitute for the impressions that can be gained from a personal visit here at the bridgehead of the East–West confrontation – no background material that we could send you, and not even Stephanie's eloquent descriptions, even though she is certainly the most charming and persuasive "ambassadress" I have. Please make your visit here possible!'

In 1972 there was a new assignment for the 'ambassadress'. She was to arrange a meeting between Springer and the editor of the French newspaper, *Le Figaro*, Jean-François Brisson. Springer was also to be introduced to another editor from France, Philippe Bernet of *L'Aurore*. Both meetings were scheduled to take place in Berlin, but they had to be cancelled. Stephanie, who was staying briefly in England, went straight to Paris to explain to the two editors that their visit did not have to be cancelled completely, but only postponed. At that time, Axel Springer had been warned that there might be demonstrations and riots, some of which would target him personally.

In Paris Stephanie met Jean-François Brisson and attended a lunch arranged by Philippe Bernet. She also gave a small dinner-party for the Duc and Duchesse de Doudeauville.

As she was not feeling very well, she returned to Geneva. From then on, she seldom left her apartment in the rue Alfred-Vincent; she was suffering from Paget's Disease, a progressive affliction of the bones, and had to take strong painkillers. Added to this was the irritating fact that the apartment block in which she was the sole remaining tenant was to be sold. The other apartments were temporarily occupied by noisy Italian immigrant workers. Axel Springer had said he would be willing to buy the whole rather run-down property for her, but that came to nothing. Stephanie lived a very lonely existence in her apartment, with only her elderly Italian servant Lina, and her beloved dachshund Puck, for company.

On 12 June 1972, the princess had invited her neighbour Gisela Tornay to dinner. Lina had the evening off, though she would have much preferred to stay at home. When her friend arrived, Stephanie complained of a severe, stabbing pain in her chest. A doctor was summoned, and he suggested she should go into hospital for an x-ray.

In a private clinic, La Colline, the duty doctor found that Stephanie had a stomach ulcer that was threatening to burst. Since there was no anaesthetist on hand, her operation was delayed. But it came too late. She did not survive the surgical intervention. Stephanie's son was then in London. Thus only Mme Tornay was with her when she died. It was 13 June 1972. Stephanie von Hohenlohe died three months before her eighty-first birthday. But since she had told the hospital her date of birth was 1905, she was thought to be fourteen years younger than she really was.

The last resting-place of Princess Stephanie von Hohenlohe-Waldenburg-Schillingsfürst is in the village cemetery of Meinier, in the mountains above Geneva. The burial took place on 16 July. An announcement of her death was not sent out until later. The Abbé Bernard Ricardi, priest of the neighbouring parish of Corsier, conducted the funeral. It was attended by Stephanie's son Franz and her nephew Herbert Bach, the Austrian Consul-General Herr Maier-Thurnwald, the German Consul-General Baroness von Kotzebue, as well as the wife of the American ambassador to Switzerland, and Stephanie's loyal friend of many years, Count Benedikt Esterházy.

An oak cross was erected at the grave, bearing a small plaque with the words: 'S.A.S. Princess Stéphanie Hohenlohe. 1905–1972.' So even here the date of her birth is wrong.

On 28 July the *Frankfurter Allgemeine Zeitung* published a short item on the princess's death. It said that the death of Princess Stephanie von Hohenlohe had gone unnoticed by the public. The piece, which contained no less than eight factual errors, drew an angry letter from Prince Franz. The public certainly *did* take notice of his mother's death, he said. 'No fewer than twelve ambassadors came to her funeral. No less than 300 syndicated American newspapers reported it. So far, over a thousand letters of condolence have been received.' Franz went on to say that his mother did not come originally from Hungary, but from Austria, that her maiden name was not Fischer but Richter; furthermore, neither she nor Captain Wiedemann had ever tried to persuade the British government to surrender. Lastly, she had not been interned as an 'allegedly dangerous alien', but because her visa had expired.

Baroness Dr Erika von Kotzebue, then German Consul-General in Switzerland, had got to know Stephanie while serving in that post, and had made friends with her. Looking back today, Erika von Kotzebue says: 'She was very much alive, from the first day to the last. She was always frank, but was one of those rare people who go through life totally without prejudice.'

Axel Springer was not among the mourners. He sent her son his condolences in a telegram: 'Dear Prince Hohenlohe. I was in Jerusalem when I heard the sad news of your dear mother's passing. In deepest sympathy, I remain yours, Axel Springer.'

Ray McHugh, vice-president of Copley Newspapers and head of their Washington office, wrote to Axel Springer on 15 June 1972: 'The news of Steph's death was a personal blow to me . . . At a moment like this a newspaper-man doesn't send flowers. He tries to tell the world about a really extraordinary human being.'

Stephanie's friend McHugh wrote a two-page tribute to this exceptional woman:

> If we are to believe the history-books, then Stephanie Hohenlohe's world ended on 11 November 1918. But Stephanie did not believe in history-books . . . With her unmistakable style and the flair of her 19th century ancestors . . . she chatted and flirted and spun like a top for sixty long years through the drawing-rooms of Europe and America . . . The old Europe will mourn her death; the young Europe is the poorer, because it no longer has the chance to know her.

After his mother's death, Prince Franz kept her beautiful apartment in Geneva for a while, but then chose the USA as his home. As an American citizen, who has never married, he lived for a long time in the exclusive resort of Palm Springs in the Californian desert, not far from Los Angeles. The prince, an extremely likeable cosmopolitan, today lives in one of Europe's major capitals. As well as a biography of his mother, he has written a book about his time in the US Army.

When one talks to him about his mother, it is clear that he holds her in great affection and admiration. 'Think of all she lived through, the poor thing', says Prince Franz, now in his late eighties. To this day he still worships her as 'the Lady with Connections'.

Appendices

I: STEPHANIE VON HOHENLOHE: 'PREFATORY MORNING MONOLOGUE'

This document is held in the Hoover Institution Archives, Stanford, USA, and appears to be intended by Stephanie as an introduction to her memoirs, which were never published. Written in her own English, with its breathless punctuation preserved, it probably dates from 1940, soon after she emigrated from Britain to the United States. Tr.

Ah . . . oh . . . ah . . . What is it, Anna? . . . Ah . . . the mail . . . What's the time? . . . Nine, already? . . . Really? . . . Well, I suppose, another day . . . Ah, what a heap of letters . . . ! And probably not a letter in it . . . not what I call a letter . . . No . . . no . . . no . . . just some orange-juice and coffee . . . Printed Matter, Printed Matter, Printed Matter . . . Four-fifths of my so-called mail . . . What a waste! . . . Does anyone ever read this rubbish? . . . Well, I suppose the post-office and the printers must live . . . Ah, a letter . . . ! No . . . bills, bills, bills . . . I'm not in a paying mood . . . alas. I shall have to, some day . . . *noblesse oblige* . . . What does the world want of me, day after day . . . ? They want me to buy, or they want me to pay . . . to buy, to pay . . . Another business letter . . . Well, at least something different . . . A literary agency . . . Ah . . . the story of my life . . . my memoirs? . . . 'Of great interest . . . some inquiries . . .'

They want my memoirs . . . well . . . am I so old already? What is the proper age for looking back . . . ? When I was fifteen I loved to sit at a window in the sunset, to remember . . . to remember . . . I don't know what I remembered then, but I loved those hours of sweet melancholia. I felt so deep and wise and I meditated on the vanity of all things . . . *vanitas vanitatum* . . . It's a long time since I indulged in those evening moods of looking back . . .

My memories . . . How old am I really . . . ? Without the benefit of the doubt . . . just facing the stern realities of documents . . . I was born in Vienna in September 1899 [in fact, it was 1891. *Tr.*]. But they must think me much older, if they want 'the story of my life' . . . How pompous, anyhow . . . Of course, I have a grown-up son . . . an Oxford graduate . . . That dates me, definitely . . . But still – my memoirs . . . 'As a political woman . . .' A political woman . . . a political woman . . . how *heavy*! A political woman . . . ! Am I a political woman? What is a political woman??

Let's begin at the beginning . . . the Bible . . . well, there was Potiphar [she presumably means Potiphar's *wife*, who tried to seduce Joseph. *Tr.*] . . . a woman in her dangerous age . . . that's all . . . The Queen of Sheeba [*sic*] . . . Judith, cutting off the head of Holofernes . . . patriotic, by all means . . . but more characteristic of an angry woman than of a political woman . . . Queen Esther intervened . . . intervened gloriously, on behalf of her persecuted nation, but she is more like a lovely phantom out of 'A Thousand and One Nights' than a political schemer . . . And as to all others out of both Testaments . . . well, they are just lovers, mothers, sisters, daughters . . . They are all so feminine, because the Bible is so masculine . . . Written by men, of course . . .

Aspasia[1] . . . was she a political woman? What was she anyhow? The Greeks had a word for it . . . [Stephanie adds the word *hetaira*, meaning 'female companion' or 'courtesan', but has crossed it out.] . . . The friend or the mistress of statesmen, philosophers, poets and rich men . . . Was she a bluestocking, because she allowed poets to lie at her feet, or was she a political woman, because she let statesmen do likewise? . . . Who can tell? . . . Then there was Lysistrata . . . Was she a real person, or just a character in a comedy?[2] Anyhow, she was a practical pacifist . . . Her idea to get the boys out of the trenches by bedtime, was eminently more political than Henry Ford's idea to get them out by Christmas . . . It was political all right . . . And what about the Amazons?[3] Mythological or real – it was politics to organize a state of women . . . I wonder if they really existed . . . ?

The empress Theodora [of Byzantium] was certainly a political woman . . . Lucrezia Borgia . . . ? She was for the Borgias, that was all. Did she really use poison . . . ? Was it politics, or was it murder for profit? . . . No, she was *not* a political woman . . . Catherine de Medici[4] . . . Yes! . . . All the French ladies of the French Louis? Decidedly, no! . . . They were interested in Kings, but not in political ideas or systems . . . Court intrigues – yes; politics, no! . . . Joséphine Beauharnais [Napoleon's first wife] . . . a courtesan amongst politicians, but was not a 'political woman' . . . the Empress Eugénie [wife of Napoleon III] . . . perhaps . . . ?

The Empress Maria-Theresa [of Austria] . . . She preserved an embattled empire . . . She fought several wars . . . She withstood Frederick the Great [of Prussia] . . . But was she a political woman? No, she was a mother, a mother of her family, a mother of her country, always the mother . . . If she had inherited a laundry instead of an empire, she might have been Madame Sans-Gêne,[5] if she had inherited a restaurant, she might have been Frau Sacher,[6] smoking a cigar . . . How amazingly like her was Queen Victoria! The same motherly virtues, the same amorous devotion to the husband, the same jealousy of her power and divine rights, the same puritanism and the same vast progeny . . . Surrounded by statesmen for more than sixty years, she still remained the woman Victoria . . . Both used the best political minds of their age, but both remained almost naively apolitical . . .

But Queen Elizabeth, the Virgin Queen . . . Yes, a thousand times, yes! . . . The political woman, *par excellence* . . . Obviously I cannot formulate a definition . . . Yet, I feel somehow the meaning of the phrase . . . Elizabeth was political! In instinct, in desire, in thought, in action . . . Perhaps because she was childless . . . perhaps because she was a virgin . . . even if she wasn't one . . .

And the suffragettes . . . ? I'm probably wrong, but they seem to me more hysterical than political . . . Isn't it telling that they achieved the vote, but not the power . . . ? How strange that hardly one of the militant suffragettes ever received the votes they secured! Wherever the women's suffrage movement succeeded, the suffrage leaders disappeared. Where are the Pankhursts *e tutti quanti* . . . ? Gone with the votes . . .

Is Margot Asquith, Lady Oxford, a political woman? . . . No, she was merely devoted to her husband[7] . . . Is Lady Astor[8] a political woman . . . ? No, she is simply annoyed by tobacco and alcohol . . . Are Lady Snowden[9] and Mrs Sidney Webb[10] political women? Was Mrs Woodrow Wilson[11] a political woman? Perhaps, although . . . no offence meant . . . I suspect she only wanted to be cheered in the Champs Elysées . . . what about Miss Perkins, Mrs Roosevelt, Dorothy Thompson?[12] . . . I wonder . . . And the Duchess of Atholl, Lady Londonderry, Mrs Greville[13] . . . I don't know . . . Political hostesses are not necessarily political women, nor are wives concerned with the political careers of their husbands, nor trade union leaders or officials of similar pseudo-political [sentence unfinished] . . .

Damn that letter . . . Who wrote it anyhow? . . . How like a businessman . . . utterly illegible signature . . . Ah . . . I beg your pardon, sir . . . the name is typed as well as written . . . My mistake, Mr Thompson . . . Who are you, Mr Thompson? . . . What are you like? . . . Apart from being a Vice-President of a literary agency . . . And why in heaven's name do you consider me a political woman?!? . . . Am I? . . .

Well, I am at a loss . . . When might I first have felt or thought politically? . . . certainly not as a 'flapper' . . . As a war nurse, perhaps? . . . I was only seventeen . . . There was no time for thinking . . . I am sure my disposition was not cerebral . . . Cursing the war was not exactly thinking . . . I was a Red Cross nurse . . . My soul, my heart, my mind were just Red Cross . . . nothing else . . . I wanted to help and I did help . . . It hardly mattered on which side I nursed . . .

Did political passion surge up in me at the fall of Austria-Hungary? Did I thirst for revenge? . . . Did I think about ways and means of reconstructing the stricken monarchy? . . . Did I think at all? . . . No, I didn't . . . My mind was fully occupied with the day-to-day problems of any individual in a defeated and starving country . . . First I had to get back from the Isonzo front to Vienna . . . That was not as simple then as it sounds . . . Thereafter came the hourly problems of lighting, heating, feeding . . . of money and a thousand other necessities in the dying, decomposing capital of a state that had suddenly vanished . . . Like millions of others I was just a stunned human being . . . a stunned human being, yes . . . but not a 'political animal' . . .

Then came love . . . marriage . . . childbirth . . . No time for politics . . . The horizon seemed to be clouded by nasty monsters called the succession states[14] . . . but that was all . . . Names like Versailles, St Germain, Trianon[15], filled the air . . . but when did I find myself first directly concerned with a political problem? I suppose it must have been much, much later . . . probably in London . . . probably in the late Twenties . . . at the time when the propaganda for the resurrection of Hungary first started . . . the reunion of the lands of the crown of St Stephan [sic] . . .

Strange . . . I was born in Vienna . . . I grew up in Vienna . . . I loved Vienna . . . I was a Vienna girl . . . And like all the others I sang: 'Wien, Wien, nur Du allein . . .' at my most sentimental . . . Yet it never occurred to me to dream or to think of a reborn Austria-Hungary . . . An almost pleasant nostalgia for the past filled our hearts and eyes . . . but the future never reached our imagination . . . My family and my friends certainly desired the return of the Hapsburgs [sic, the correct spelling is 'Habsburgs', something an Austrian 'princess' should surely have known] . . . but it was more the proper façon de parler than the expression of political thoughts or emotions . . .

There was no backbone to it . . . The renaissance of a Danubian empire or, at least, an economic federation of the Danubian countries was a frequent conversational topic . . . but hardly more than that . . .

I had married a Hungarian prince . . . that is to say my husband belonged to the Hungarian branch of a mediatized[16] German dynastic family . . . Thus I became a Hungarian citizen, which I still am . . . But when I found myself agitated by the bleeding frontiers of Hungary, when I began myself to agitate for the healing of 'the wounded land' . . . why, at that time I had already been divorced from my husband for several years . . . Would I have acted for Tschecho-Slovakia [sic] if I had married a Prince Lobkowitz instead of a Prince Hohenlohe? . . . It might have happened . . . No, no . . . my language was Viennese, my sentiments were Austrian, my tastes were cosmopolitan and my reactions were humanitarian . . . The political intermezzi in my life, such as they were, must have been due to circumstances, but not to political impulses . . . No, no, I don't think I am a political woman, Mr Thompson . . . You probably think so because my name has been linked with Lord Rothermere and other such celebrities or notorieties as Adolf Hitler, Admiral Horthy, Gömbös[17] . . . Isn't that a little superficial? . . . I believe that I have a friendly and helpful disposition . . . I like human beings . . . I enjoy helping others . . . and, God knows, this is a time when help is needed . . . but . . .

What, Anna? . . . It's eleven?! . . . I hate you, illegible Mr Thompson . . . Your letter set me day-dreaming . . . I missed my manicure and my massage . . . memories . . . I shall have to forego a good deal of my present, if I am to start remembering . . . What indulgence! . . . Do you want me to? Even if I am not really a political woman?

I must admit that there is much to remember . . . My years of maturity fell into a most turbulent period . . . I happened to be near the whirlpool . . . and I escaped . . . But there are many things I wish I could forget . . . You want me to remember them particularly? . . . I'll try.

II: LETTER FROM ADOLF HITLER TO LORD ROTHERMERE, 7 DECEMBER 1933

It should be noted that Hitler wrote this letter only a few weeks after taking Germany out of the League of Nations and the Disarmament Conference in October 1933. There is evidence that Hitler feared sanctions by the League of Nations, in the form of physical invasion of Germany by France, Poland and

Czechoslovakia. Had this taken place, Germany would not have been strong enough at that time to repel it.

This helps to explain Hitler's uncertain tone, a mixture of injured innocence and veiled threats.

It was Hitler's custom to dictate or draft a letter in German and then have it translated by one of his staff, often his interpreter, Paul Schmidt. The English is far from perfect. Tr.

Dear Lord Rothermere,

You have been good enough to communicate to me through Princess von Hohenlohe a number of suggestions for which I wish to express to you my most sincere thanks. I would furthermore like to give expression to the feelings of numberless Germans who consider me as their spokesman, for the journalist support, both wise and happy, of the policy of which we all hope that it will contribute to the final liberation of Europe. Princess von Hohenlohe gave me a translation of the great article written to which I took the liberty of referring already some time ago. I particularly welcomed the reference contained in this article with regard to the usefulness of an Anglo-French defensive alliance. I am convinced that an Anglo-French friendship for the maintenance of a real peace can be very useful. Germany herself has no aggressive intentions against France; however fanatically we may be resolved to defend ourselves against an attack we are against any idea of provoking, ourselves, a war. As old soldiers of the world war – I was myself in the front line for four and a half years facing British and French soldiers – we have all of us a very personal experience of the terrors of a European war. Refusing any community with cowards and deserters we freely accept the idea of duty before God and our own nation to prevent with all possible means the recurrence of such a disaster. This cannot be definitely achieved for Europe unless the treatment of the critical problem, whose existence cannot be denied, is transferred from the atmosphere of hatred in which victors and vanquished face each other, to a basis on which nations and countries deal with each other on a footing of equality. This equality for Germany does not involve any danger for *French* security, for:

In the first place this equality of rights is at the same time connected with a solemn recognition of the territorial situation as created between Germany and France by the world war subject to the return of the Saar Territory.[1]

In the second place I am moved by the idea to attempt thereby to put an end, once and forever, to the fruitless struggle of the two nations against each other. Nobody can deny that the importance of the objects and the greatness of the results which might in all cases be achieved, would be in no proportion to the consequences of a war between the two nations, which might only too easily degenerate also in future into a new world war. Even if the parts were equally distributed, any possible gain would not be justified if compared with the unspeakable sacrifices. A reconciliation of these two nations however would take a burden from everybody except perhaps a small international clique, who wants fighting and disagreement among the nations because it may require these for political and other transactions.[2] In particular however I want to express my conviction that no soldier who served during the Great War at the front, of whatever nationality he may be, desires another war.

Such reconciliation would however presuppose the removal of the defamatory provisions of the peace treaties. Material differences can be discussed objectively but dishonourable defamations and insults cannot.

In the third place: From the military point of view, France would not be menaced either by such a development. France has surrounded herself with a system of fortification[3] which can even resist the material means of attack used in a world war. The fact is that without the most enormous sacrifices and without the heaviest offensive arms any attack against this system would be absolute madness. Germany has not the slightest intention of attacking. This is also the reason why we are ready in principle to renounce the possession of such aggressive arms, which might perhaps appear dangerous to France. But even if France is anxious to strengthen her security when Germany is no less anxious, we are therefore not inclined to renounce the possession of defensive arms. Germany would have more reason to feel herself menaced by France's offensive armaments than France has to fear Germany's defensive arms. France has a common frontier with Germany of hardly 400 kilometres [240 miles].[4] Behind that front there is the greatest instrument of war of all times. Germany has a frontier of over 3,000 kilometres [1,800 miles], and what is there behind it? We are not inclined to recognise the situation as permanent, nay even as one corresponding to the laws of nature. We are ready to disarm to the last, but only subject to the condition that the other nations will do the same. If they don't, we are not prepared to allow ourselves to be permanently treated as a second-rate nation. Nor can we admit this in the interest of the guarantee of peace. *A country like Germany which has economically such an important element constitutes, if it is completely defenceless, by the mere fact of its existence in disturbed times, a certain incentive to become the object of an attack!*

In the fourth place: The demand for an army of 300,000 men, particularly when it is put forward together with a renunciation of heavy aggressive arms, and if account is taken of Germany's situation in regard to her military defence, constitutes a menace to nobody. Across her frontier, Germany has France with over 600,000 men, Poland with 370,000 men, Czechoslovakia with 250,000 men.

All these nations possess offensive arms of the *heaviest kind*. Apart from the wholly inadequate fortress of Königsberg,[5] Germany does not even possess defensive works at her frontiers. To speak of a menace means deliberately mis-stating the truth.

In the fifth place: Germany has no more ardent desire than to achieve with the other European nations a situation excluding the use of force in Europe for the future, possibly by a system of non-aggression pacts, in order thereby to relieve the economic life which is suffering from depression in all countries from the nightmare of warlike complications.

The objection according to which we would thereby separate France from her allies is not intelligible. Germany has no reason to oppose alliances which, in so far as they are defensive, only constitute an increased guarantee of peace. In the same way it is wrong to object that, by an anticipated settlement of the Saar problem, we would be depriving France of one of her rights. For, in the first place, this solution can only be found by agreement among the two countries, and in the second place it is not a right which France holds in respect of the Saar Territory, but Germany was given a concession in so far as the population of the Saar territory would be placed in a position in 1935 to decide upon their future. This decision will be almost 100 per cent in favour of Germany.[6] Now I believe that in these circumstances a settlement of this problem before 1935 would already mark a beginning of détente in Europe and above all [would] be liable to influence most favourably the relations between France and Germany. If I wished for triumph, then I could only want the plebiscite because it will involve a heavy defeat for France. I could therefore quietly wait another 18 months. But I want understanding and conciliation and therefore I believe that precisely this problem should already be dealt with in the spirit of this new development. The allegation, however, that I need this or a similar success for reasons of internal policy can only be made in complete ignorance of the situation in Germany.

I can assure your Lordship that I and the present German regime do not need such cheap successes of popularity. Our regime cannot be destroyed in

Germany, not because we are holding the power, but because the hearts of the whole nation belong to us. The nation cannot give me in future more confidence than it has given me on 12 November.[7] If I favour the settlement of Franco-German relations I do so merely because I desire to substitute a real peace of conciliation for a situation overladen with hatred. *Finally it must also be borne in mind that I am offering the friendship of a nation of 66 million and which is not valueless in other respects.* And just as I see no reason for the war in the west, I don't see any in the east. The endeavour to reach an understanding between Germany and Poland springs from the same desire to exclude force and to approach soberly and dispassionately the various tasks set to us. In how far however, the re-establishment of equality of rights for Germany should affect Great Britain in her relations to France I am all the more unable to understand. I believe on the contrary that equality of rights to Germany could only enhance the value of an Anglo-French friendship or alliance.

If I have thus submitted quite frankly these ideas to your Lordship, I have done so in order to give proof of my appreciation of the high value of the journalistic attitude adopted by your Lordship in the British press.

Thanking you again most sincerely for the support which you are giving to a truly European policy of peace, I am

Yours faithfully
Adolf Hitler

III: LETTER FROM CROWN PRINCE WILHELM OF GERMANY TO LORD ROTHERMERE, 20 JUNE 1934

Prince Wilhelm (1882–1951) was the eldest son of Kaiser Wilhelm II, who abdicated in 1918. This document is written in English, from Unter den Linden, Berlin W8. Its unidiomatic language suggests that it was written by the crown prince in his own English. There is no royal crest on the copy document, it is not hand signed, and it comes from a central Berlin address, not from his Cecilienhof palace in Potsdam. All this suggests that the crown prince typed it himself as secretly and anonymously as possible, in case the letter was intercepted. Following the abdication and exile of his father, the crown prince had no royal or even official status, still less after Adolf Hitler came to power in 1933. For Prince Wilhelm to write a letter like this was risky. Only days after this letter was written, Hitler had hundreds of his political opponents and rivals, including conservatives like ex-Chancellor Schleicher, murdered in cold blood. Tr.

Dear Lord Rothermere,

Princess Hohenlohe's visit gives me the opportunity to send you a letter safely, a letter which might possibly interest you. It is hardly necessary to accentuate, that the contents of this letter are meant only for you personally.

In my life until now I have always held to it, to try at certain periods of time to render account to myself about my own existence, but also, and perhaps particularly so, about the great issues of the age and the problems concerning my fatherland. I was trying to do the same thing, as it were, that a business man does, who, at certain periods, is determining the balance, or, what we army leaders during the world war did, when we prepared reports on the general situation at certain moments. At such stops I have always found it very valuable to discuss my findings with some person, who seemed certain to possess enough knowledge and experience of his own, to make an exchange of one's views with his, helpful to both. For some time I have also felt the desire to express to you frankly my thoughts about the situation here in Germany, and to beg you then to communicate to me just as frankly – applying your great experience in political matters and your deep knowledge of human beings and of social interdependencies – your own reaction to my views.

How things in Germany appear to me today, I shall try to set forth as follows:

Hitler came into power at the right psychological moment. A lost war with its tremendous sacrifices, the revolution following it, all the humiliations of the Peace Treaty of Versailles, the senseless destruction of our entire war material, the degrading reparation payments, which burdened our people with insane debts, the consecutive inflation, which ruined the most valuable parts of the nation, the middle classes, the incredible confusion and corruption amongst the bosses of the Red regime, the inwardly utterly decayed democratic parliamentarism under the perilous leadership of the Social Democrats and the Zentrum [centre parties] – all this had created an atmosphere enveloping the whole German people, within which all faith had disappeared, all authority of the State had been undermined, and where only the individual as such was still trying, in crassest egotism though, to provide for its existence somehow. Such was the mood, when Adolf Hitler, whose genius had understood [how] to hammer into the broad masses of the workers the faith in a new National Socialist Germany, began his ascent. Hitler found his followers not

only among labourers; every decent German, who had hated and despised
the black-red-gold [Weimar] republic from the innermost of his soul, saw in
him the saviour of our people. The more so as even men like General von
Seeckt, Stresemann, Brüning and also General von Schleicher,[1] to all of
whom I cannot deny the recognition of their great abilities and best
intentions, had never shown the will and the energy, required for really
thoroughgoing action. Thus I also joined Adolf Hitler, already at a time,
when wide circles of the Stahlhelm[2] and particularly of the German
nationalists refused to recognise him. May I remind you of our last
conversation at Cecilienhof and of the things I had to say in favour of
Hitler? May I summarise it once more shortly:

I had tried repeatedly to induce already Chancellor Brüning to retire
voluntarily, and to recommend Hitler as his successor, to the Field-Marshal
[President Hindenburg]. I continued these attempts under the
Chancellorship of General von Schleicher. At the Presidential elections I
stated publicly that I would vote for Adolf Hitler and against the Field-
Marshal. I believe to have thus secured for Adolf Hitler about two million
votes[3] from my Stahlhelm comrades and from the German nationalists. I
also intervened personally to obtain the cancellation of the interdict against
the National Socialist formations. – At last the old Field-Marshal, after the
negotiations of Franz von Papen, entrusted Adolf Hitler with the leadership
of the Reich, as its Chancellor. All I can say is that on that day
indescribable jubilation went through the whole German nation. Then
came the day at Potsdam (Church of the Garrison), a speech deeper and
more moving than any I had ever heard from a German statesman. Only
one who has been present on that occasion can realise the sublime mood of
the Germans in those hours. Large parts of the nation expected already
then that Adolf Hitler would express on that day the reunion with the
monarchy in some form.[4]

The first actions of the new government were highly satisfying; they
showed the determination to penetrate all spheres without any inhibition.
They launched their program of work, magnificently and brilliantly. The
corruption of the Red bosses was thoroughly exterminated. Social
Democrats, Communists and the Zentrum were liquidated. The
rearmament of the nation was recognised as a necessity. The withdrawal
from the League of Nations and from the Disarmament Conference
announced to the world at large the determination of the new German
government, behind which, for the first time, the whole nation was

concentrated, not to tolerate any longer [being] treated as a second-class people. At the same time everything was done to re-start [the] German economy. The motor-car industry experienced an unparalleled expansion. Monumental road-building was begun; the 'labour service' undertook the profitable task of cultivating unused and, until then, uninhabitable land. And German aviation was revived under a new impulse.

All these things filled every sincere German with pride and joy. And thus the respect for, and the confidence in the personality of the Führer Adolf Hitler grew from month to month. That was also the time when my personal relations with Adolf Hitler were friendly and enjoyable.

Slowly, and hardly noticeably at first, shadows began to fall upon this scene so full of light. To understand why it was possible at all that such clouds should invade the sky of the Third Reich, one must realise that it was not Hitler alone who determined the policy of the National Socialist Party. His pure intentions and his occasional greatness of thought cannot be disputed. But the National Socialist Party consists, as you know, of the most variegated elements. In their ranks you can find the formerly German nationalist land owner, as well as the formerly Communist mechanic; naturally, the best friends and advisers of the Führer, who have been at his side since the time of their earliest struggle for power, are of equally different coinage. The names of Hess, Röhm, Göring, Goebbels, Darré, Baldur von Schirach[5] and others represent – although they are all National Socialists, and although they are certainly faithful followers of the Führer – just as many programmes. Each of them according to his inclination and to his predisposition. And thus one can distinguish clearly two different trends within the movement; the one which accentuates the word 'National' and the other which accentuates the word 'Socialist' in their party's name. One of the representatives of the second trend, or rather its spiritual leader, is the Minister of the Reich, Dr Goebbels, an exceptionally intelligent man, a former pupil of the Jesuits, who is a master of all the arts of demagogy. Everything in the Germany of today that we can only contemplate with grave concern, such as the ever growing radicalisation of the movement, the continual catering to the masses, the fight against Judaism, against the Catholic Church, against the intellectuals, against the 'Reaction' (which comprises all the parts of the nation, which are today still monarchistic) – is the work of the Minister of Propaganda and of the men of his spiritual orientation.

Conditions are now such that the entourage of the Führer is isolating him more and more, and that men of independent opinion are rarely or never admitted to his presence. On the other hand, the influence of the Minister of the Reich, Dr Goebbels, who spends his days and nights with the Führer, appears ever-increasing. The greatest part of the German people have today only one desire: tranquillity. To pursue one's trade or occupation undisturbedly, to earn one's living in a way securing a fairly decent existence – that is the general hope of all sober Germans. This mentality does not suit at all the men who think as the Minister of Propaganda does. They thrive on conflict and unrest. The people must be whipped up again and again, must never settle down to start thinking. And that's why we have to witness these everlasting parades and mass meetings, why we have to listen to all the demagogic speeches against the Jews, against the Churches, against foreign countries and against the past. Therein lies the danger: the young generation is being more and more brought up in the radical spirit of the Left. Within the 'Hitler Youth' the authority of the parental home is being undermined systematically. Children, who have learned yet nothing, are told continually that they represent the most valuable part of the population. All men over thirty are represented as oldsters, already senile, who have no longer any right to exist. This tendency, crystallised in the person of the Minister of Propaganda, disquiets deeply all of us, who are sincerely concerned with the welfare of the fatherland, and who are today still standing solidly behind our Führer, Adolf Hitler. Recently I have discussed frequently the present situation and my anxieties with various men, whose judgement means a great deal to me. The result of all these conversations was always the same: it will be possible to overcome the great difficulties of the immediate future only if one should succeed in opening the eyes of the Führer to the development of the 'movement' in Germany – a development certainly much against his intentions – and to growing discontent. He must be told the truth about the doings of the so-called Nazi bosses, and be convinced that the zero hour has arrived for him to intervene drastically – particularly in matters of the personnel – and to remove all the crowd unfit for their positions and of direct menace.

In my personal view the Führer would strengthen and fortify his own position in the German nation to a quite extraordinary extent, if he could bring about a union with the monarchy in some form or other. How this is to be done is a question of staging. But for the time being it does not seem as if the Führer has arrived already at the recognition of such a necessity. In view of your great experience and of the respect which you enjoy in Germany, it might be of great profit to our fatherland, but also to the whole world, I think, if you, dear Lord Rothermere, would acquaint the Führer with some of these observations and thoughts, provided that you also consider them as true, and that an opportunity for doing so should arise. Only quite independent men like you, Lord Rothermere, who are also elements of power in themselves, can afford to tell the Führer the truth frankly.

That's how I see the situation as a whole. It would interest me more than I can say, to hear how our affairs appear to you, an observer under no influence.

I have always regretted it that until now all contacts between our family and the English Royal Family have remained entirely disrupted. The happier I was, therefore, when I heard that my son Hubertus has had the opportunity of seeing the Prince of Wales and the Duke of York. He related to me enthusiastically his impressions of the cordial and comrade-like manner of the Prince of Wales. During the present year my son Fritz is to accept the invitation of Lord Jellicoe, and to participate at the regatta in Cowes. Personally, I would consider it a great joy if I too could pay an *unofficial* visit to England at some time or other. My sympathies for your people have always been very great, so great that before the World War I had proposed to the Kaiser and his Government a restriction of our naval construction, and an alliance with England. Should such a visit become feasible, I would have to know, of course, what my attitude towards the Royal Family of England is expected to be. On the one hand I would not like to visit your country without paying my dutiful respects to the Royal Family; on the other hand I do not know if the King and Queen[6] would feel inclined to receive me. Perhaps the situation has become more favourable – as the Duke of Braunschweig [Brunswick] and my little sister have been seen recently by your King and Queen. Incidentally I believe it would make a good impression everywhere if the old hostilities of the war were buried by such a meeting, and if the solidarity of the royal houses were thus proved anew.

Hoping to be able to welcome you soon again as a guest in my house, I remain,

In old friendship
Your
Wilhelm

IV: LETTER FROM ADOLF HITLER TO LORD ROTHERMERE, 3 MAY 1935

Before being sent, this letter was, like other letters from Hitler to Rothermere, translated into English by one of Hitler's staff, whose first language was clearly not English. The translator's original punctuation and spelling have been reproduced here. Hitler's German text has been lost, which is unfortunate, since the translation contains some very obscure passages, which might have been clearer in the original German. Tr.

Dear Lord Rothermere,

May I thank you most sincerely for the letter which you were kind enough to send me through Princess von Hohenlohe.

For me to know that I have met you, Lord Rothermere, a sincere friend of an English-German understanding, is all the more propitious and meaningfull [*sic*] because therein lies the duty for which I have often fought relentlessly, long before my official political activity and my chancelorship [*sic*]. The rightness of these trains of thought will find no better proof than the course of the great world war, its victims and its results.

I believe that a day will come when, upon reviewing the European History of the last 300 years methodically and scientifically, it will become apparent that $\frac{9}{10}$ of all the blood shed on the battlefields, was shed completely in vain. In vain that is compared with the naturalistic interests of the participating peoples.

I do not exclude Germany from that, on the contrary: Our country has lost at least 20–25 million people in the course of these 300 years; but probably more, through wars which, on the whole were without benefit to the nation, if one wishes to see success not in the light of dubious fame, but in that of practical utility. On occasions Europe squandered its strenght [*sic*] thoughlessly [*sic*]. The only state which had enough sense to obtain from these proceedings, at least for long intervals and which derived certain benefits from so doing, was England. Thanks to the cleverness of the English people and of many of its governments it has built the world's biggest empire with a fiction of such victims. I do not think a cool check of the English participation in the world war, will attribute the same useful meaning to this happening, for the strengthening of the British Empire, as was indubitably accomplished by means of many actions with an infinitely better effort. Germany has lost everything through its battle with its great Germanic neighbour. England has – I dare say this in all modesty – at least not gained anything, but probably contributed towards creating expectations of a world development which does not lie within the interests of the British Empire. I do not say this in order to give sentence in the question of guilt. I believe that knowing the extend [sic] and consequences of this happening, no responsible statesman would have wished the war, just as it is certainly sure to say that no one entered upon this war, from either side, with eyes wide open, but only due to faulty failures and unfortuante [sic] prejudices combined with an incomplete knowledge of the true European interests. For 500 years the two Germanic peoples have lived close together without having become involved in any serious military difference. England opened a great part of the world to the white race. An immortal and never-ceasing service! Germany was a coloniser in Europe, whose aggregate cultural and, also, economic activities for the welfare and the greatness of this old Continent are difficult to estimate. This 4½ years' war swept away the pick of the manhood of both nations; severely hit Germany's influence in Europe; and by no means strengtened [sic], if it did not actually weaken, England's importance in the world. Worst of all, however, there was left behind a legacy of prejudice and passion, which affords appropriate soil to those who aim at the sabotaging of the consolidation of Europe and to those who are inwardly hostile to the strengthening of White supremacy in the world. I believe that clever German statesmanship, and a no less calm British, in the years from 1900 to 1914 would have found ways and means not only to assure peace to the two Germanic peoples but also to bring them high advantages. The picture that the world today offers is at any rate, from the point of view of both peoples, less satisfactory than it might otherwise have been. Bolshevism tears away a mighty slice of European-Asiatic breathing-space (*Lebensraum*) from the structure of what is, in our conception, the only possible international world economy. The safety of the British Empire, which is to the interest of the whole White race, is weakened rather than strengtened [sic] by the lining up of, in part, new international power factors. The tendencies of a declaration of independence of former colonial territories grew in the same way as the attempts to destroy by means of an unnatural industrialisation – because it is crutifical [sic, does he mean 'crucial', or 'artificial'?] – of given territories for raw materials, the order between production and consumer territories, which was built up in the course of many centuries. When will reason set in at last, and when will the white race obtain from a development which perforce would mean its end?

I believe, dear Lord Rothermere, that if it does not emanate from England or Germany, one might as well bring [does he mean 'abandon'?] any hope for the future, at least for the duration of our own life expectancy.

Of course, one cannot behold these problems with the eyes of day-by-day politicians, whose horizon is frequently limited by the smallest types of interests. In any event, I have attempted not to look for compromises in certain things, but instead to consider the fundamentals as real and determining. Consequently I have been ridiculed for 15 years by day-to-day politicians, who had no understanding for the fundamental handling of the problems and I have been lamborsted [sic] as a dreamer. But right continued on my side, and these small opponents recognised that their concepts were wrong and mine right. In the end they could no longer dispute my success. But this experience of the last 15 years gives me hope that it will be the culmination of the next 15 or 20 years, provided the work is equally fundamental, right and solid in principle, to help the natural interests to break through in a larger framework, and to get the small naggers to keep silent.

As already stated, Lord Rothermere, if today I stand for an Anglo-German understanding, this does not date from yesterday or the day before. During the last 16 years I have spoken in Germany at least 4,000 to 5,000 times before small, large and immense mess [sic] audiences. There does not, however, exist a single speech of mine, nor a single line ever written by me, in which I have expressed myself, contrary to this opinion, against an Anglo-German understanding. On the contrary, I have during all this time fought for it by word and in writing. Before the war, I had this conception of the necessity of the collaboration of the Germanic peoples against the rest of the awakening world, and was profoundly unhappy when the events of August 4th 1914 led to Anglo-German hostilities. I never saw in this war anything but a desperate, Niebelung-like war of annihilation, rising to frenzy, between the Germanic peoples. Since the War, as an active politician, I have preached unswervingly the necessity of both nations burying the hatchet for ever. Anyhow, I am convinced that such an understanding can only take place between honourable nations. I hold that there is no possibility of concluding agreements with a people without honour, and I regard such agreements as entirely worthless. I have derived from Fate the heavy task of giving back again to a great people and State by every means its natural honour. I see in this one of the most essential preparations for a real and lasting understanding, and I beg you, Lord Rothermere, never to regard my work from any other point of view.

The world may, however, for what I care, reproach me with what it will. One reproach they certainly cannot level at me: that I have been vacillating in my views and unreliable in my work. If an unknown man with such weaknesses set out to win over a nation in 15 years he would meet with no success. Herein resides perhaps the faith – exaggerated, as many believe – in my own personality. I believe, my dear Lord Rothermere, that in the end my unchanging standpoint, undeviating staunchness and my unalterable determination to render a historically great contribution to the restoration of a good and enduring understanding between both great Germanic peoples, will be crowned with success. And believe me, Lord Rothermere, that this is the most decisive contribution to the pacification of the world. All the so-called mutual-assistance pacts which are being hatched today will subserve [*sic*] discord rather than peace. An Anglo-German understanding would form in Europe a force for peace and reason of 120 million people of the highest type. The historically unique colonial ability and sea-power of England would be united to one of the greatest soldier-races of the world. Were this understanding extended by the joining-up of the American nation, then it would indeed be hard to see who in the world could disturb peace without wilfully and consciously neglecting the interests of the White race. There is in Germany a fine saying: that the Gods love and bless him who seems to demand the impossible.

I want to believe in this Divinity!

I have just read the manuscript of Viscount Snowden under the title 'Europe drifts towards war', which Princess Hohenlohe has brought me.

While I understand the difficulty of speaking such a language, I am strengtened [*sic*] in my conviction that in the end both recognition and truth still find their courageous champions, even today.

In approximately 10 days, I shall hold a big comprehensive and detailed survey of my understanding and the understanding of the political problems which are presently engrossing all of us. I believe that this speech will be mailed [*sic*, does he mean published?] by these Englishmen whom you have invited, my dear Lord Rothermere, in the *Daily Mail*, to take an official stand.

To you yourself, dear Lord Rothermere, I should like to express my thanks once again with all my heart, for the attempts which, should these things come to pass, will be looked upon as one of the most felicitous developments which the people could aspire to thanks to their leadership of State.

With sincere friendship
Adolf Hitler

V: LETTER FROM ADOLF HITLER TO LORD ROTHERMERE, 19 DECEMBER 1935

This document is marked as being the draft translation of Hitler's German text, made by his interpreter, Paul Schmidt. It is certainly rough, with many crossings-out. It would not have been sent to Rothermere in this form. Tr.

Dear Lord Rothermere,
You were good enough to communicate to me [deleted] Princess Hohenlohe a letter in which you expressed the desire to be informed of my views on some of the burning questions of the day. Owing to the great pressure of work which has steadily increased towards the end of the year, I have been quite unable, in spite of every good will, to reply at once to your letter. In replying to you now I ask you, dear Lord Rothermere, not to make any public use of my reply because it contains opinions which I would otherwise express in a different wording or probably not express at all. This letter contains only opinions and I have not the slightest doubt that they are entirely unsuited to influence public opinion or to make it change its own views in a world and at a time in which public opinion is not always identical with the innermost insight and wisdom.

You ask me, dear Lord Rothermere, whether in my opinion oil sanctions against Italy will put an end to the Italo-Abessynian [sic] war.[1]

It is impossible to reply to this question apodictically.[2] But I would like to seize this opportunity to explain to you, as fully as is possible in a short letter, my views on the principles underlying this problem:

(1) Governments very often err as regards the percentage of raw materials which a nation requires for military purposes. The percentage is very low compared to the total requirements of a population for non-military purposes – 15 per cent [rather] than 95 per cent of all necessary raw materials. I admit that in the case of oil this percentage may not be quite exact in a war. However, a restriction placed on the non-military

uses will certainly enable [i.e. not prevent] an army for a long time to cover its own requirements.

(2) Sanctions naturally lead to restrictions and in consequence to certain tensions. Weak systems of government may perhaps be defeated by such tensions. But a strong regime will hardly be exposed to that danger. It is even possible that a powerful regime will, on the contrary, receive fresh and increased strength as a consequence of such tensions. At any rate, time and perseverance play a decisive part on both sides.

(3) Sanctions are not only a burden upon those against whom they are directed, but also upon the powers applying the sanctions. And here again, time and perseverance have a decisive influence.

(4) In the Great War Germany was not defeated by the sanctions but exclusively by the internal process of revolutionising. If I had been in Bethmann-Hollweg's place in 1919 as Chancellor of the German Reich, no revolution would ever have occurred. The collapse in 1918 would have been avoided. I presume that the Great War would ultimately have reached its end without victors or vanquished.[3] I know, dear Lord Rothermere, that you as an Englishman, will have a different opinion but I am merely explaining my own conviction. Today an oil sanction against Germany would be of no avail, as our own oil-fields can produce an annual quantity several times as much as we needed in 1914–1918 during the Great War.

I do not know the conditions in Japan. For it is obvious that the question of existing stocks is also in all these cases of decisive importance.

(5) In my opinion the decisive factor is only a question of systems of government and thus of personalities. Who governs in the sanctionised countries [i.e. countries on which sanctions are imposed] and who governs in Italy? I would like to say here that the man who is today Italy's leader will be one of the rarest and most important personalities of world history, whatever may happen. Much that may appear bad in English eyes in this man finds its simple explanation in the different mentality of the two nations. And a great man will almost always be the most characteristic representative of the innermost character of his own nation.

In making these sober statements I ask you, dear Lord Rothermere, not to forget that I as a German cannot take any real interest in this conflict. You know that we are the nation concerning which a more than stupid treaty said that it did not belong to the 'progressive' nations, which had a right to administer colonial territories.[4] In addition I can say that from the human point of view there is much that attracts us to the English, while on the other hand, from the political point of view, we have a good deal in common with present-day Italy. Obviously the German nation will not today be able to give noisy expression to its enthusiasm for a nation which, only a year ago, referred in its press to Germany very unfavourably, not to say rudely. On the other hand, we cannot forget that, years before that, Italy and Signor Mussolini in particular have given us many proofs of a reasonable and often more than decent sympathy with our fate. We cannot be ungrateful. There are people in Europe [who] believe that we [have] every reason as Germans to welcome this conflict. They say that it provides for us the best opportunity to rearm. My dear Lord Rothermere, these people know neither me nor the Germany of today. Since the outbreak of this conflict I have taken a single step which cannot be planned long before and which I [would] not have taken otherwise. The decision to restore the German position was taken, initiated and carried through at a time when nobody could have the slightest inkling of this sad conflict. There is nobody in Germany with any political insight who welcomes this conflict, except perhaps some enemies of the State who may cherish the hope that it might constitute an international example which could one day also be applied to Germany. But these elements must not be confused with the German people. The only thing which fills us with certain satisfaction, I must admit, is the revelation of the true value of all so-called collective agreements. For here we are concerned with two collective agreements which have ultimately both failed: the Covenant of the League of Nations and the Stresa Alliance,[5] and it is the only pleasure we have in this matter to know that we are outside the agreements and that we have no longer anything to do with the League of Nations.

For believe me, dear Lord Rothermere, the problem is not whether this and that sanction will today bring down Italy on her knees, the real problem is whether one is [in] a position to remove the causes underlying the tensions from which the world suffers at present. For a hundred million years this earth has been moving around the sun, and during this long period it has always been filled with the struggle of living beings for nourishment and later for dwellings and clothing etc. It is certain that beings who we can call men have existed on it for many millions of years. Innumerable influences produced constant changes in the distribution of property. Just as in each nation. The economic structure is constantly changing, changes occur outside the national limits. Climatic changes, discoveries of raw materials, [produce] more or less strong increases of the nations on the one hand, while other nations become sterile, continually produce tensions which urgently require solutions. And now in a certain year after millions of years have moved around, an American professor[6] proclaims the formation of a league of partly heterogeneous nations with completely opposed interests, with a view to excluding any future change in this world. That means from the year 1919 of our Christian era, or say from the 997 million 365 thousandth revolution around the sun, the whole earthly development must come to a standstill. Only one thing was forgotten: this league can perhaps prevent the *adjustment* of the tensions, but it can by no means prevent the tensions themselves from *arising*. The only consequence will be that while formerly the tensions arising out of the national laws of development were currently adjusted, at least partially, the safety valve is now abolished, which means that the tensions must accumulate. If that, however, is the ultimate result of the so-called 'collective policy' the end can only be disaster of the first magnitude.

I deeply regret Sir Samuel Hoare's resignation[7] because I feel that a great British patriot and an excellent man has fallen victim to public opinion and that he was one of the first to have recognised this weakness in the League of Nations system. For it is clear that the League of Nations is not governed today by the influence of wisdom but by the influence of the street, that is today by the so-called public opinion which, as history shows, hardly ever has Reason as its godmother. I would be very glad, dear Lord Rothermere, if, beyond all present misgivings, people in England were ready to study the problems from the point of view of the underlying principles and perhaps to discuss them in a small committee. I think that the English can do this better than the other nations because they are broad-minded and realistic to a greater extent than other peoples. I believe that our Anglo-German Naval Agreement[8] was a striking proof of this. You will understand, however, dear Lord Rothermere, that these problems more than others are wholly unsuited to be handled in front of the masses, but that ultimately they can only be discussed in a small and select group. If you come again to Germany I would be very glad if you would see me and if I could discuss these problems with you or other Englishmen.

Whatever may happen, I want to assure you at the conclusion of this letter that I firmly believe that a time will come in which England and Germany will be the solid pillars in a worried and unstable world.

You ask me, dear Lord Rothermere, whether I do not think that the moment has now come to put forward the German colonial wishes. May I ask you, dear Lord Rothermere, not to raise this point now because, looking forward to closer collaboration with Great Britain, I do not want to give the impression as if I wanted to avail myself of the present situation of your Government and its many difficulties and of the British Empire to exercise a certain pressure.

In conclusion I send you, dear Lord Rothermere, my best wishes for Christmas and for a happy New Year.

Yours truly
(signed) Adolf Hitler

VI: STEPHANIE VON HOHENLOHE: ANNIVERSARY OF DISASTER

Thoughts on the Hungarian Uprising, 1956

In October 1956, Hungary attempted to throw off the yoke of Soviet communism. In Budapest students and workers toppled a giant statue of Stalin. The government briefly lost control and within hours, on 24 October, Soviet tanks were rumbling into the streets of the capital. They were attacked by civilians with Molotov cocktails. The freedom fighters called on the west for help, but none was offered. By 30 October it was all over and a new, hardline premier, Janos Kadar, had been installed.

Stephanie von Hohenlohe, nominally a Hungarian citizen, used this occasion to recall her own visit in 1938 to the Hungarian head of state, Admiral Horthy. She tries to draw a parallel by claiming that Horthy wanted to retain his independence from Hitler's Germany. There is an element of truth in this. Nonetheless, Hungary hoped that by riding on Germany's coat-tails it might regain some of the territory lost under the Treaty of Versailles, which transferred parts of the old Hungarian kingdom to the new states of Czechoslovakia, Yugoslavia and Rumania.

This document, written in her own English, when Stephanie was still living in the USA, appears to have been sent to her literary agent, Curtis Brown, in New York, with a view to publication in the press. Tr.

Budapest, 1956
RUSSIAN GANGSTERS HAVE BETRAYED US; THEY ARE OPENING FIRE ON ALL BUDAPEST. PLEASE INFORM EUROPE.

In the dead of night a solitary teletypist chattered a desperate cry for help.

A FEW HUNDRED TANKS ATTACKED BUDAPEST . . . A THOUSAND . . . THERE IS HEAVY FIGHTING . . . WE SHALL INFORM THE WORLD OF EVERYTHING.

And then a few hours later:

ANY NEWS ABOUT HELP . . . QUICKLY . . . WE HAVE NO TIME TO LOSE . . . NO TIME TO LOSE . . . WHAT IS THE UNITED STATES DOING . . . GIVE US A LITTLE ENCOURAGEMENT.

Heartbreaking words, but still no help came.

Finally:

GOODBYE FRIENDS.

GOD SAVE OUR SOULS

THE RUSSIANS ARE TOO NEAR.

Yes, the Russians were too near, and for the second time in only a few years, a gallant and courageous people have had to face the awful fact of dying alone . . . terribly alone.

It is a chilling thing to see history repeat itself twice in one lifetime. I cannot pretend to understand, but I cannot help wondering, and being a little afraid as I remember . . .

Budapest, 1938

After the First World War the peacemakers and treaty-signers obliterated empires and acted as midwives at the birth of some awkward and unruly children. Nations had been truncated and carved apart like so many Christmas puddings to meet the idea of a new Europe. Millions smouldered under the pressure of unnatural boundaries, but none more so than the fiercely proud Hungarians.

The patch on the map that marked Hungary was certainly the most curious jigsaw on the continent. Countless families suddenly found themselves as citizens of a foreign nation whose language they did not speak, whose customs they did not share. Divorced from their homeland and their birthright, those people had only one thought – to become Hungarians once again. They turned eagerly and impulsively to any promising corner, without thought of immediate consequence or eventual outcome.

But in 1938 the political balance of Europe was so delicate that no nation could afford to hold out a helping hand. Of all countries, only Nazi Germany offered hope. Join our orbit, become our ally, the propagandists of

Berlin said, and we will give you back your land, make you a nation once more.

This siren song from the Rhine was not entirely a gesture of goodwill and friendly interest. Germany knew that France and Britain were firm allies, and that France, in turn, was committed to the support of the Little Entente – a group of three nations, Rumania, Czechoslovakia and Yugoslavia – that bitterly opposed any Hungarian expansion.

At the time, sympathy in England was strongly for the Hungarian people, and yet England certainly could not risk offending the avowed policies of France, its strongest friend on the continent. This tangle was artfully exploited by the Nazis to drive a wedge between the western democracies. They strummed on the strings of Hungarian patriotism with a heavy-handed but effective Teutonic touch – by sending thousands of smiling 'tourists' into the country each summer, by planting agents and spies in many key positions, by creating ever-closer economic ties with Hungarian industry, and most important of all, by masquerading as the saviour of the Hungarian nation.

This then was the situation when I visited Budapest in 1938 on a short trip. As always, I made it a point to pay my respects to the sprawling 100-year-old palace that brooded over the troubled city. At the time, Hungary was a kingdom without a king, governed by a Regent, His Highness Admiral Nicholas Horthy, a vigorous patriot who had given many years of selfless devotion to the cause of his country.

I had planned to leave Budapest the day after calling on the Regent, and I was making preparations for my departure when a telephone call interrupted me. It was a Captain Scholz,[1] who was Admiral Horthy's personal adjutant. He was calling, he said, upon the instructions of the Regent, who requested me to come to the palace at once.

It was impossible to refuse such a summons, and as I drove to keep my appointment, I speculated as to what he could want with me. I knew von Horthy could not tolerate Hitler. He realised that friendship with the Nazis meant death to his nation, but I also knew that popular pressure was slowly pushing him into an impossible situation, for he was but a single voice against national sentiment.[2]

When I arrived, I was immediately ushered up the magnificent stairway, past gorgeously uniformed guards into the Regent's office.

He came forward and took my hand warmly, apologising for the urgent telephone call that had brought me to him. He wasted little time.

'Princess Hohenlohe', he said, 'I want you to write me a letter.'

'A letter?' I echoed.

'Yes. Several years ago Sir Austen Chamberlain,[3] half-brother to the present prime minister of England, Mr Neville Chamberlain, paid me a visit. One day, before Sir Austen left, he told me how he had come to admire and deeply respect this country, this city, and our people. We discussed the melancholy situation of Hungary, and he assured me that we would eventually find friends in the west, and particularly in England. He told me that the time was not yet ripe for action, but that when the day came, I would only have to appeal to the conscience of his country, and aid would be sent.'

Admiral Horthy held up his hand. 'I know, I know, Sir Austen is dead. But I would like to remind his brother of his promise.'

At this point, Captain Scholz entered the room to announce the arrival of a caller. I saw a look of anger pass over the Regent's face.

'Princess Hohenlohe', he said, 'our situation is becoming more intolerable every day. Only last week I was informed – unofficially, of course – that certain circles felt I was having too much social contact with Jews, that I must be careful to avoid the displeasure of the Germans.' We smiled bitterly. 'Yes, is that not difficult to believe? However, I immediately sent out an invitation to Mr and Mrs Manfred Weiss to attend a luncheon here at the palace. Do you know Manfred Weiss?'

Of course I knew the man. He was a Jew, an extremely wealthy manufacturer, and probably Hungary's leading industrialist. Such a gesture on Admiral Horthy's part was typical of his spirit.

'And now,' he continued, 'do you know who this latest caller is?'

He did not wait for my answer. 'He is the head of the Mercedes-Benz company. He has come to give me a personal gift from Hitler – an expensive automobile, which I do not want, do not need and will never use.'

With a gesture of distaste, he paced across the carpet. 'I will now have to return this compliment by sending the Führer an equally lavish gift. I shall send him a set of Heren china, and he will be pleased. However, I shall not be pleased, but I will not be under Hitler's obligation.'

He walked quickly to where I was seated.

'Princess Hohenlohe', he said earnestly, 'I want you to write me a letter, and I want you to take that letter to the British prime minister. I do not want to send it through official channels because the Germans have too many spies in too many places and I do not want my message to be relayed to the Reichstag. I am asking you this because your English is more fluent than mine. I want you to ask Mr Chamberlain for help. Help in the name of the Hungarian people, in the name of humanity, in the name of the solemn promise given to me by his dead brother. I expect no miracles, Princess Hohenlohe, but I must reach out to someone.'

Naturally I accepted the assignment. I returned to my hotel and wrote the following letter:

Dear Mr Chamberlain,

It is not in my official capacity as the Regent of Hungary that I am writing this letter to you, but as Admiral Horthy, a Hungarian who loves this country above all.

Three years ago I had the pleasure to see your brother Sir Austen Chamberlain here as my guest.[4] He showed great interest in all the questions concerning my country. He asked me to explain to him the case of my country – the wrongs and injustices done to her. Sir Austen understood that Hungary's claims are just and fair and told me when I asked him to give me his help and advice: 'keep quiet now. I promise you when the right moment comes, I will help you.' The past three years are proof that I carried out Sir Austen's advice loyally. I waited for 'the right moment' to come and therefore I am appealing to you – the man who has shown so much wisdom and courage lately – asking you to accept your brother's promise to help us, as a legacy to you and to all in your own and in your great country's power, to assist us now in this eventful hour. German insistence is mounting. I am under constant pressure from without and within. I will be unable to justify my insistence much longer without your help.

I pledge my word that you will never have to regret it and assure you of the undying gratitude of the entire Hungarian nation.

Sincerely yours,
Nicholas v. Horthy.

Later that afternoon I travelled once more to the palace. Once more I was announced immediately and ushered in to the Regent. He read over my letter carefully and gratefully took my hand in his.

'Thank you, Princess Hohenlohe', he said sincerely, 'This is exactly what I wanted.'

He sat down behind his enormous desk and laboriously copied the unfamiliar English in his own hand, sealed it himself and gave it to me.

As he took me to the door of his office, he put his hand on my arm. 'Tell Chamberlain that the Germans are too near. They must listen, for if one country goes under, all are threatened.'

That was the last time I saw Admiral Horthy.

I drove to the airport, took my plane, and the same day was back in London. A good friend, Sir Thomas Moore MP, agreed to deliver my note to the prime minister. A few hours later it was in his hands.

The rest, of course, is history. Admiral Horthy was right. The Germans were too near and absorbed his country. Within a year Britain was fighting for her life. Within two years the entire free world was engaged in that struggle.

And then again, twenty years later, I saw the messages that came from Budapest.

GOD SAVE OUR SOULS.

THE RUSSIANS ARE TOO NEAR.

Once again the world listened helplessly, unable to act because of the tangle of international conditions. It may be a fateful and prophetic message, because, except for a single word, it was the same message a very brave man had tried once before to deliver.

* * *

Notes

1: The Girl from Vienna

1 All quotations in this chapter, unless otherwise indicated, are taken from the Hoover Institution Archives, Stanford, *Outline for the Memoirs of Princess Hohenlohe Waldenburg*, Box 5.

2 Hoover Institution Archives, Hohenlohe Box 3 – *Prefatory Morning Monologue*.

3 Gina Kaus was born in 1893 in Vienna, the daughter of Max and Ida Wiener. Not until her father died did she discover that she had a half-sister, Stephanie. Gina married and became a successful novelist in the 1930s, but then her books were publicly burned, along with those of many leading Jewish and anti-Nazi writers, and she emigrated to California in 1938. In postwar Germany, two of her later novels, *The Devil Next Door* and *The Devil in Silk*, became bestsellers; in 1956 the latter was made into a film starring Curt Jürgens and Lilli Palmer.

4 See Stoiber/Celovsky, *Stephanie von Hohenlohe*, p. 51.

5 See Charles-Roux, *Coco Chanel*.

2: A Mission for Lord Rothermere

1 An alliance between France and Czechoslovakia, Yugoslavia and Rumania, which was designed to contain a resurgent Hungary.

2 From 1928 Bella Fromm, who came from a prosperous Jewish family, wrote for the *Berliner Zeitung* and other liberal newspapers. She had access to influential political circles in Berlin and knew everyone who mattered. Until the Nazi marginalisation of Jews began, she was extremely popular. Even when excluded from her profession, she refused for a long time to leave Germany. On advice from friends she finally emigrated to the USA, where she continued to work as a

journalist. Some of her diaries were published in English in 1943.

3   Otto Abetz (1903–1958) was a schoolmaster who in 1930 co-founded the Sohlberg Club for the furtherance of understanding between the youth of Germany and France. He made frequent visits to France but in July 1939 he was expelled in connection with the trial of a secret fascist organisation known as the *Cagoulards*. After working in the German Foreign Ministry he was appointed in August 1940 as ambassador to the collaborationist French government in Vichy.

4   Brook-Shepherd, G. *Zita, the Last Empress*, London, HarperCollins, 1991, p. 229. Brook-Shepherd writes about two women being sent to see the empress: one was Steffi Richter 'who was well known in high society . . . as the *amie attirée* of Lord Rothermere'. The other was a member of the Austrian nobility, Princess Stephanie. But these were, of course, one and the same person.

5   Brook-Shepherd, *op. cit.*

6   Brook-Shepherd, *op. cit.* From an interview given to the author by Otto von Habsburg in 1990.

3: Hitler's 'Dear Princess'

1   Fromm, *When Hitler Kissed my Hand.*

2   Fromm, *op. cit.*

3   Picker, *Hitler's Table Talk.*

4   Jochmann (Ed.), *Monologues at the Führer's Headquarters 1941–44.*

5   Sharply censured by the League of Nations, Italy was becoming dangerously isolated. Hitler exploited this by establishing closer ties with Mussolini. Germany shipped coal and steel to Italian industry. However, at the same time Hitler secretly prolonged the war by supplying war materials to Abyssinia, in order to increase further Mussolini's dependence on him.

6   Two weeks previously, on 25 December, Hitler had changed his personal doctor and put himself in the hands of Dr Theodor Morell. The latter treated his stomach pains with a medication containing strychnine.

7   Dodd, Martha, *My Years in Germany*, London, Gollancz, 1939.

8   Dodd, *op. cit.*

9   In December 1941 FBI agents found and photographed this badge with its swastika, as they searched her house in Alexandria, Virginia. It was in a jewel-case in her bedroom.

10   Dirksen later succeeded Ribbentrop as Germany's ambassador in London, a post he held until the outbreak of war.

4: Stephanie's Adversary: Joachim von Ribbentrop

1   Schwarz, *This Man Ribbentrop*.
2   Kershaw, *Hitler Vol II, 1936–1945: Nemesis*, 2000.
3   Kershaw, *op. cit.*
4   Speer, A., *Inside the Third Reich*, p. 108.

5: Lady Astor and the Cliveden Set

1   2nd Viscount Elibank (1877–1951) was a career civil servant in the Colonial Office, with many senior overseas postings. On retirement he became chairman of several large companies.
2   19th Baron Sempill (1893–1965). A pioneer aviator, he joined the Royal Flying Corps (1914–19) and later headed a mission to organise the Imperial Japanese naval air service. In 1925 and 1928 he lectured to the German Aeronautical Society in Berlin. He competed in the King's Cup round-Britain air race every year from 1924 to 1930, and was president of the Royal Aeronautical Society (1926–30).
3   At the beginning of the war, one of Astor's sons, David (d. 2001) took over as editor of the *Observer*, and always took a strongly *anti*-Nazi position, aided by German emigrés such as Sebastian Haffner.
4   The Astors originally came from Spain, from the town of Astorga in Galicia. In the eighteenth century they moved to Germany, adopted the name Astor and went into business as butchers. The three sons born in Germany emigrated to the USA and Britain where they made huge fortunes.
5   In the early 1960s Cliveden again hit the headlines, when the house was the scene of events that became known as 'The Profumo Affair'. At Cliveden house-parties, John Profumo, a senior member of the Conservative government, met and began a relationship with Christine Keeler, whose 'services' were concurrently being enjoyed by the military attaché at the Soviet Embassy. Cliveden is now a luxury hotel.
6   Margaret ('Margot') Tennant (1862–1945) married H.H. Asquith in 1894. She had no public career, but was highly influential behind the scenes. She published an autobiography in 1922.
7   Herbert Henry Asquith (1852–1928) was Chancellor of the Exchequer in the Liberal government (1905–8) and prime minister of

a Liberal-Conservative coalition (1908–16). On his retirement in 1926 he was created 1st Earl of Oxford and Asquith.

6: Stephanie, Wiedemann and the Windsors

1   Wallis Warfield was born in Pennsylvania in 1896. In 1916 she married a naval officer, Earl W. Spencer. She divorced him in 1927, and the following year married Ernest A. Simpson, an American who worked in London and had taken British nationality. In October 1936 she divorced Simpson, in order to be free to marry King Edward VIII, with whom she had already had a relationship for several years.

2   See Kershaw, Ian, *Hitler* Vol II, p. 24.

3   Goebbels, J. *Diaries*, 7 January 1937.

4   Stanley Baldwin, statement to the House of Commons on the Abdication of Edward VIII, 10 December 1936.

5   Unity Mitford (d. 1948) was one of the daughters of Lord Redesdale and sister of Diana (d. 2003), wife of Sir Oswald Mosley, leader of the British Union of Fascists. Unity spent much of her time in Germany and was on close terms with Hitler. When war between Britain and Germany broke out, she tried to shoot herself in Munich, and eventually died of her injuries.

7: Trips to the USA and their Political Background

1   The Polish Corridor was the term given to the strip of territory linking the Polish interior with the Baltic coast at Danzig (today Gdansk). The corridor, comprising most of what was West Prussia, was ceded to Poland in 1919 and separated the German province of East Prussia from the rest of the Reich.

2   In 1936 Thomsen had been appointed First Secretary at the Washington embassy, and then in November 1938, Chargé d'Affaires. From 1943 to 1945 he was Nazi Germany's ambassador to Sweden.

8: Rivals for Hitler's Favour: Stephanie and Unity

1   The eldest sister, Nancy, became a famous author, whose books, such as *The Pursuit of Love*, *The Sun King*, and *Madame de Pompadour* are still read. Her sister Jessica ran off at the age of eighteen with Esmond Romilly, a nephew of Winston Churchill. Romilly, who was then flirting with communism, fought in the Spanish Civil War and died in

action in 1941. Jessica then made a career as a writer in the USA. The beautiful Diana first married and divorced Brian Guinness, the brewery heir, then had a long affair with Sir Oswald Mosley, the leader of the British Union of Fascists. On the death of Mosley's wife, he and Diana married. At the outbreak of war they were both imprisoned for treason, and after the war settled in France. Lady Mosley died in 2003. Pamela Mitford married an academic and spent most of her life in a castle in Ireland. The youngest sister, Deborah, married the Duke of Devonshire, with whom she runs one of Britain's great stately homes, Chatsworth, in Derbyshire.

2   Pryce-Jones, Alan, *Unity Mitford*.

9: Wiedemann's Peace Mission

1   In December 1934 Hitler had secretly appointed Göring as his successor. He was promoted to *Generalfeldmarschall* in February 1938, and in July 1940 was given the title *Reichsmarschall* of the Greater German Reich.

2   At that time the western border regions of Czechoslovakia, known as Sudetenland, were largely populated by ethnic Germans. After 1918, they claimed they were being disadvantaged by the Czech government and civil unrest developed under the pro-Nazi Sudeten leader, Henlein. Hitler saw this as the perfect pretext to invade Sudetenland and later the whole of Czechoslovakia.

3   This is not correct; she was Austrian by birth, but took Hungarian citizenship when she married.

10: Mistress of Schloss Leopoldskron

1   Stoiber, *Des Führers Prinzessin* (The Führer's Princess).

11: Wiedemann's Dismissal: Stephanie Flees Germany

1   Dr Hjalmar Schacht (1877–1970). President of the Reichsbank 1923–9, he was appointed Reich Minister of Economics by Hitler in 1933 but, never a committed Nazi, he resigned his office in 1937. Suspected of implication in the July 1944 plot to assassinate Hitler, he was imprisoned and narrowly escaped execution.

2   Kershaw, Ian, *Hitler 1936–1945: Nemesis*, London, 2000.

3   Wilhelm Canaris (1887–1945) fought as a young officer in the

German navy at the Battle of the Falkland Islands in 1914. He was captured but escaped through Chile and Argentina. From 1916 onward he worked in intelligence and was appointed head of the Abwehr in January 1935. However, as early as 1938 he was in contact with anti-Hitler resistance groups, and was able to play a complex double game. Not until the attempt on Hitler's life in July 1944 did he come under suspicion. He was tried and executed for treason in April 1945.

4   Hans Oster (1888–1945) was chief assistant to Admiral Canaris in the Abwehr. Ever since the purges of 1934, Oster had been strongly anti-Nazi but was protected by Canaris, who used him to make contact with Britain during the Czech crisis. Oster also tried to warn Denmark, Norway, Belgium and the Netherlands of impending invasion. He was arrested after the July 1944 Bomb Plot and executed with Canaris in the last days of the war.

5   Ulrich von Hassell (1881–1944), an aristocratic diplomat, was ambassador to Rome from 1932 to 1938. When dismissed by Hitler for disagreeing with his policies, Hassell joined senior generals and civil servants in a plot to arrest Hitler and put him on trial in the summer of 1938. After the July 1944 Bomb Plot Hassell was arrested and hanged.

12: The Lawsuit against Lord Rothermere

1   Once Hitler was in power, he was anxious to remove senior political and military figures who were not in sympathy with his ambitions. Field-Marshal Werner von Blomberg, Minister of Defence from 1933 to 1938, was opposed to Hitler's re-occupation of the Rhineland in 1935 and his invasion of Czechoslovakia in 1938. In that year Blomberg married a new young wife, and Göring, as chief of police, managed to find evidence that she had once appeared in a pornographic photograph. Blomberg was forced to resign. At the same time, the Commander-in-Chief of the army, General von Fritsch, was framed in a homosexual scandal and also made to resign. Hitler then took over both posts himself.

13: The Spy Princess as a 'Peacemaker' in the USA

1   Rudolf Kommer, like Stephanie, came from Vienna's Jewish community. He died in 1943 and since he had no living relatives, his

property went to the US government. The manuscript on which he worked with Stephanie disappeared.

2   Hermann Rauschning (1887–1982) was appointed president of the Danzig senate in 1933 under the Nazi regime, but resigned a year later. In 1936 he emigrated to Switzerland and wrote a number of books attacking Hitler, including *Germany's Revolution of Destruction*, Zürich/London, 1939. In 1940 he emigrated to the USA and took up farming.

3   Fritz Thyssen, the German industrialist, was an early promoter of Hitler. However, in 1936 he denounced Nazi ideology and from 1940 to 1945 was held in the concentration camps of Oranienburg, Buchenwald and Dachau. Afterwards he wrote a book entitled *I Paid Hitler*.

4   Kommer's thoughts are not easy to interpret here. The bombing of cities by German aircraft had certainly begun by this date, for example the destruction of Warsaw and Rotterdam by the Luftwaffe, but the London blitz did not begin until the autumn of 1940, and the saturation bombing of Hamburg, Cologne, Berlin, etc. later still. Kommer must have been extraordinarily far-sighted to predict, in May 1940, an Allied alliance even being formed, let alone Germany's destruction and dismemberment.

5   Dr Heinrich Bruening (1885–1970), a centre-party politician, was Reich Chancellor under the late Weimar republic, from 1930 to 1932. In 1934, when Hitler began eliminating his opponents, he fled to Holland and then the USA. There, in 1939, he became Professor of Government at Harvard. He taught at Cologne University 1952–5 but died in the USA.

6   Count Wolf Heinrich von Helldorf (1896–1944) was a member of the Nazi Party and was elected to the Reichstag in 1933. He was appointed chief of police in 1935, but in 1938 joined the military anti-Hitler group. He was executed in 1944 for complicity in the July Bomb Plot.

7   Franz Halder (1884–1972), a career army officer, was appointed army chief-of-staff in 1938 and was instrumental in planning the invasions of Poland, western Europe and Russia. Yet he made cautious approaches to the anti-Hitler resistance without openly defying Hitler. In the Russian campaign Hitler increasingly took charge of operations and Halder was dismissed in September 1942. In 1944 he was

arrested in connection with the Bomb Plot and imprisoned in Dachau for the rest of the war.

15: *The International Journalist*

1   Wiedemann was called to give evidence at the Nuremberg War Crimes Tribunal (7 October 1945). He was in detention until 3 May 1948. He published his memoirs in 1964, and died at the age of 78 in Fuchsgrub on 24 January 1970.

2   Gerd Bucerius (1906–95) was an influential figure in the postwar German media. In 1946 he was co-founder of the weekly newspaper *Die Zeit*, and from 1951 onward was the majority shareholder of *Stern* magazine.

3   Henri Nannen (1913–96), another key figure in the German media scene, was for many years editor-in-chief and then publisher of *Stern*, which grew to be Europe's top-selling magazine.

4   Roy Jenkins (1920–2003), later Lord Jenkins of Hillhead, was Home Secretary, then Chancellor of the Exchequer in the Labour government of 1964–70. In 1981 he was one of the 'Gang of Four' who formed the breakaway Social Democratic Party; this later merged with the Liberals. Later Jenkins was appointed President of the European Commission.

5   Axel Springer (1912–85) was a major publisher who, in the 1960s, became the figurehead of German conservatism. He owned, among other things, the tabloid *Bild* and the broadsheet *Die Welt*.

6   Ernst Cramer was one of Axel Springer's closest associates and is still active in the Springer publishing concern.

Appendix I

1   Aspasía of Miletus, beautiful and intelligent, was only 20 when Pericles, the ruler of Athens, fell in love with her in 445 BC. Pericles was already 50 at the time, and had divorced his wife a few years earlier.

2   In Aristophanes' comedy of the same name, Lysistrata persuades the women of Athens to withhold their sexual favours until their menfolk renounce war.

3   According to the ancient Greek historian, Herodotus, the Amazons did exist and lived in the Caucasus region. They got their name, meaning 'without breasts', from the fact or legend that they cut off their breasts in order to fire their longbows more effectively.

4   Powerful Italian wife of the French king, Henri II, in the early sixteenth century.

5   *Madame Sans-Gêne* was a comedy by Sardou about intrigue at Napoleon's court, first performed in 1893. Its chief character is Madame Lefebvre, wife of one of Napoleon's marshals. Originally a laundress, she was nicknamed 'Madame Sans-Gêne', meaning 'thick-skinned' or 'inconsiderate'.

6   Owner of the most famous hotel and restaurant in Vienna.

7   She was married to H.H. Asquith (1852–1928), British prime minister 1908–16.

8   Nancy, Viscountess Astor, was the first woman to take a seat in the House of Commons, in December 1919.

9   Wife of Philip Snowden (1864–1937), who was Chancellor of the Exchequer in the Labour governments of 1924 and 1929–31. Created 1st Viscount Snowden.

10   Beatrice Webb (1858–1943) and her husband Sidney (1859–1947) were joint authors of influential books on left-wing politics, such as *The History of Trade Unionism*, 1894. Sidney Webb held various cabinet posts in the Labour governments of 1924 and 1929–31.

11   Wife of US President Woodrow Wilson (in office 1913–21), the architect of the 1918 peace settlement in Europe.

12   Three American women whom Stephanie had met: Miss Perkins was probably a society figure, Mrs (Eleanor) Roosevelt, wife of President F.D. Roosevelt, and Dorothy Thompson, a journalist who interviewed Hitler in 1931.

13   Influential society hostesses in London in the 1930s.

14   The republics and kingdoms established by the Treaty of Versailles to replace the Austro-Hungarian Empire: Czechoslovakia, Yugoslavia, Hungary, Rumania, etc.

15   The Treaties of St Germain (1919) and Trianon (1920) were subsidiary to the Treaty of Versailles, and signed by the Allies and Austria and Hungary respectively.

16   Historically, under the (German) Holy Roman Empire, a 'mediatised' prince or state was one reduced from being an immediate vassal of the Empire to one owing allegiance to a monarch (in this case, the King of Hungary) who in turn was subordinate to the Emperor.

17   Admiral Horthy was the Regent of Hungary after 1918, and Gömbös the prime minister.

Appendix II

1 The Saar is a German-speaking territory to which France laid claim unsuccessfully in the nineteenth century. It was ceded to France under the Treaty of Versailles in 1918, and was thus under French rule when this letter was written. However, a plebiscite in 1935 resulted in the return of the Saar to the German Reich. After the Second World War, the Saar came under the French zone of occupation, but following the creation of the German Federal Republic, the Saarlanders voted once again to be part of Germany.

2 This is Hitler's indirect way of blaming the Jews for promoting war for financial ends – a frequent theme in his speeches and writings.

3 The Maginot Line was a series of massive underground defences built along France's northern frontier in the 1920s. Ironically, in 1940, the German army simply bypassed this obstacle by invading France through the supposedly impassable forests and mountains of the Ardennes.

4 About half of this is represented by the river Rhine.

5 Formerly in East Prussia, Königsberg was captured by the Russians in 1945 and is now Kaliningrad, in the Russian enclave on the Baltic between Poland and Lithuania.

6 In the Saar plebiscite held on 13 January 1935, 91% of the votes cast were in favour of rejoining Germany.

7 Hitler is referring to the 'general election' held on 12 November 1933 to vote for an all-Nazi list of candidates for the Reichstag. The list received 92% of the poll. Simultaneously Hitler asked the electorate to ratify his decision, of 14 October, to withdraw Germany from the League of Nations and the Disarmament Conference. Of the 96% who voted, 95% supported the withdrawal.

Appendix III

1 General von Seeckt was in charge of the Reichswehr (regular army) during the Weimar years. He secretly and illegally built up its strength and weaponry. Gustav Stresemann, Heinrich Bruening and Kurt von Schleicher all briefly served as Chancellor during the Weimar Republic, 1918–33.

2 The *Stahlhelm* (steel helmet) was a militant, right-wing, but non-Nazi ex-servicemen's organisation founded in 1918 and dissolved in 1933.

3   Paul von Hindenburg was aged 85 in 1932, when he stood for re-election as President of Germany. Hitler stood against him and in the second round of voting polled 13.4 million votes against Hindenburg's 19.4 million. Hitler had increased his poll by 2.1 million compared with the first round. Within a few months Hindenburg reluctantly appointed Hitler as his Chancellor. When Hindenburg died in 1934, the presidency was abolished.

4   Hitler, of course, had no intention of reviving the monarchy. His Potsdam speech was simply intended to win over the predominantly Prussian senior officers in the army.

5   Rudolf Hess, Hitler's deputy, who flew to Britain in 1941, apparently on a self-appointed peace mission, and was disowned by Hitler; Ernst Röhm, Hitler's longest-serving colleague, head of the SA storm-troopers, murdered on Hitler's orders in 1934; Hermann Göring, the pleasure-loving chief of the Luftwaffe, who tried to replace Hitler in the last days of the war; Joseph Goebbels, Nazi propaganda chief, who committed suicide with his wife and children, beside Hitler in April 1945; Walter Darré, agrarian ideologue, who ran the wartime food programme, but was dismissed for black-marketeering; Baldur von Schirach, upper-class student of partly American parentage, who built up the Hitler Youth movement, but later fell from Hitler's favour.

6   King George V and Queen Mary.

Appendix V

1   On 3 October 1935, in defiance of the League of Nations covenant, Mussolini's Italy invaded the ancient African kingdom of Abyssinia (modern Ethiopia). The League imposed partial economic sanctions on Italy, but they were timidly enforced. They did not cause Italy to halt the invasion, but had the effect of driving Mussolini into the arms of Hitler. The Germans were delighted with this turn of events. If Italy got bogged down in Africa, it would be less able to oppose Germany's annexation of Austria (hitherto protected by Italy), and if Italy triumphed it would weaken the position of France and Britain. Either way, Germany would benefit.

2   This unusual word is probably a direct translation of the German 'apodiktisch', used in philosophy to denote a necessary and hence absolute truth.

3 Hitler's version of history is typically distorted. The blockade of German ports was highly effective and in 1918 Germany was close to starvation. The German army was conclusively defeated for a combination of reasons: the increased effectiveness of American troops, the use of tanks by the British, but most of all by the German army's lack of food and supplies. This caused the last German offensive to stall, when German troops started looting well-stocked French shops. Furthermore, there was no 'revolution' as such in Germany, though there were strikes in some cities, and a naval mutiny in Kiel, in the last weeks of the war. Political reform was urged on the Kaiser and his government by parliamentary parties of the centre and left joining forces in the Reichstag. Chancellor Bethmann-Hollweg was forced to resign in July 1917, over a year before Germany finally sued for peace.

4 The Treaty of Versailles, among other things, deprived Germany of its shortlived colonies in Africa and the Pacific.

5 Earlier in 1935, Hitler had blatantly flouted the military restrictions imposed on Germany under the Treaty of Versailles, among other things by introducing compulsory military service. This provoked the British, French and Italians to meet at Stresa on 11 April. They issued a statement condemning Germany's action and reiterating their support of Austria's independence and of the Treaty of Locarno (1925) under which Weimar Germany undertook to respect existing European frontiers.

6 Hitler is referring to US President Woodrow Wilson (in office 1913–21), who was instrumental in the creation of the League of Nations. He had indeed been a professor at Princeton University.

7 Sir Samuel Hoare was appointed Foreign Secretary in Baldwin's National Government that was elected in June 1935. In September he made a powerful speech at the League of Nations, warning Italy against any invasion of Abyssinia, an independent country and member of the League. However, there was nervousness about splitting the Stresa Front, linking Italy, France and Britain. The Hoare–Laval Pact, negotiated shortly afterwards with France, effectively gave Italy *carte blanche* in Abyssinia. There was a public outcry in Britain and Hoare resigned early in December.

8 This bilateral treaty, signed in June 1935, allowed Germany to increase the size of its navy to 35% of that of the British navy, with

submarines to at least 45% of the British strength, or to parity in the event of a threat from the Soviet Union.

Appendix VI

1 Herbert Scholz was a German, and an ambitious Nazi careerist. He had doubtless been placed in that post in order to keep an eye on Horthy. We do not know the date of Stephanie's 1938 visit to Hungary, but we do know that on 23 November 1938, she asked Fritz Wiedemann to write to Scholz and send him a gift, because she wanted her son Franz to get a job in I.G. Farben, the company whose Finance Director was Scholz's father-in-law (see Chapter 10).

2 Horthy did his best to maintain civilised government in Hungary, and was relatively benign towards the Jewish population, but during the war he was progressively undermined by the Nazis. Hungary had its own Nazi-type organisation, the Arrow Cross. By 1944, Horthy was trapped between a pro-Nazi prime minister, Sztójay, and a German 'plenipotentiary', Veesenmayer. As if this was not enough, the Nazis kidnapped his son in order to blackmail Horthy into doing their bidding, including the mass deportation of Jews to Auschwitz. Horthy chose to resign and spent the rest of the war under German 'protection' in Bavaria.

3 Austen Chamberlain (1863–1937) was leader of the Conservative Party 1921–2 and Foreign Secretary 1925–9. He won the Nobel Peace Prize for his prominence in negotiating the Treaty of Locarno in 1925.

4 Chamberlain would have been 72 years old then and no longer in office as Britain's Foreign Secretary.

Index of Names

Note: Stephanie von Hohenlohe is abbreviated to SH.